CORE HARDWARE/OPERATING SYSTEM EXAMS

Test Yourself

A+® CERTIFICATION

Fourth Edition

Michael Pastore

McGraw-Hill/Osborne
New York Chicago San Francisco
Lisbon London Madrid Mexico City
Milan New Delhi San Juan
Seoul Singapore Sydney Toronto

McGraw-Hill/Osborne
2100 Powell Street, 10th Floor
Emeryville, California 94608
U.S.A.

To arrange bulk purchase discounts for sales promotions, premiums, or fund-raisers, please contact **McGraw-Hill**/Osborne at the above address. For information on translations or book distributors outside the U.S.A., please see the International Contact Information page immediately following the index of this book.

Test Yourself A+® Certification, Fourth Edition

1234567890 CUS CUS 019876544

ISBN 0-07-222775-3

Publisher	**Acquisitions Coordinator**	**Compositor**
Brandon A. Nordin	Jessica Wilson	Jeffrey Wilson,
		Happenstance Type-O-Rama
Vice President and Associate	**Technical Editor**	
Publisher	Jane Holcombe	**Series Design**
Scott Rogers		Maureen Forys,
	Copy Editor	Happenstance Type-O-Rama
Acquisitions Editor	Kim Wimpsett	
Timothy Green		**Series Cover Design**
	Proofreader	Greg Scott
Project Editor	Andrea Fox	
Laurie Stewart,		**Cover Image**
Happenstance Type-O-Rama		imagebank

This book was composed with QuarkXPress 4.11 on a Macintosh G4.

Information has been obtained by **McGraw-Hill**/Osborne from sources believed to be reliable. However, because of the possibility of human or mechanical error by our sources, **McGraw-Hill**/Osborne, or others, **McGraw-Hill**/Osborne does not guarantee the accuracy, adequacy, or completeness of any information and is not responsible for any errors or omissions or the results obtained from the use of such information.

To my daughter, Erin, who never ceases to amaze me.

ACKNOWLEDGMENTS

I'd like to thank all the incredibly hardworking folks at McGraw-Hill/Osborne: Brandon Nordin, Scott Rogers, Timothy Green, Gareth Hancock, Jenn Tust, and Jessica Wilson.

ABOUT THE CONTRIBUTORS

Author

Michael Pastore, MA (A+, Net+, Security+, MCP), is a 30-year veteran of the IT field. During his career he has been involved in support, programming, and administration of numerous networks. Michael has been involved in CompTIA certifications since 1996. He was part of the Network+ design committee and has published several books about Microsoft and CompTIA certifications.

Michael teaches for the University of Phoenix and DeVry and is currently pursuing his doctor's degree in clinical psychology.

Technical Editor

Jane Holcombe (MCSE, A+, CTT+, Network+, CNA) is an instructor and writer with 20 years of experience that began with a 1983 installation of a PC LAN. She developed numerous training courses, including one of the earliest for PC support. She cofounded a company that delivered support-level training nationally. After selling her interest in the company, she spent several years working with Windows NT and Windows 2000 servers and delivering MCSE training as an MCT. In recent years, Jane and her husband, Chuck, have worked as a writing and editing team. They've written several books and are now working on the second edition of their *Survey of Operating Systems*, published by McGraw-Hill/Osborne. Since the spring of 2003, they've been living and traveling full-time in their motor home, keeping in touch with editors, family, and technology through the use of a mobile satellite dish.

CONTENTS

v

INTRODUCTION

This book's primary objective is to help you prepare for and pass the required A+ exam so you can begin to reap the career benefits of certification. I believe the only way to do this is to help you increase your knowledge and build your skills. After completing this book, you should be confident that you've thoroughly reviewed all of the objectives that CompTIA has established for the exam.

In This Book

This book is organized around the actual structure of the A+ exam administered at Prometric and VUE testing centers. CompTIA has published the test information and all the topics you need to cover for the exam on their web site at www.comptia.org. I've followed their list carefully, so you can be assured you're not missing anything.

Test Yourself Objectives

Every chapter begins with a list of Test Yourself objectives—what you need to know to pass the section on the exam dealing with the chapter topic. Each objective has one or more practice questions associated with it. These practice questions are similar in type and content to the actual exam. You'll know you're ready to take the exam when you satisfactorily complete each chapter with at least an 80 percent pass rate! Should you find you need further review on any particular objective, you'll find that the objective headings correspond to the chapters of McGraw-Hill/Osborne's *A+ Certification Study Guide, Fifth Edition.*

Practice Questions and Answers

In each chapter you'll find detailed practice questions for the exam, followed by a " Quick Answer Key" section where you can quickly check your answers. The "In-Depth Answers" section contains full explanations of both the correct and incorrect choices.

Practice Exams

If you've had your fill of explanations, review questions, and answers, the time has come to test your knowledge. Turn toward the end of this book to the Test Yourself practice exams in Chapters 11 and 12 where you'll find simulation exams. Lock yourself in your office or clear the kitchen table, set a timer, and jump in.

A+ Certification

This book is designed to help you pass the A+ Certification exam. At the time this book was written, the exam objectives for the exam were posted on the CompTIA web site, www.comptia.org. I wrote this book to give you a complete and incisive review of all the important topics targeted by the exam. The information contained in the book will provide you with the required foundation of knowledge that'll not only allow you to succeed in passing the A+ Certification exam but will also make you a better A+ Certified Technician.

How to Take an A+ Certification Exam

This introduction covers the importance of your A+ Certification as well as prepares you for taking the actual examinations. It gives you a few pointers on methods of preparing for the exam, including how to study and register, what to expect, and what to do on exam day.

Importance of A+ Certification

The Computing Technology Industry Association (CompTIA) created the A+ Certification to provide technicians with an industry-recognized and valued credential. Because of its acceptance as an industry-wide credential, it offers technicians an edge in a highly competitive computer job market. Additionally, it lets others know your achievement level and that you have the ability to do the job right. Prospective employers may use the A+ Certification as a condition of employment or as a means of a bonus or job promotion.

Earning A+ Certification means that you have the knowledge and the technical skills necessary to be a successful computer service technician. Computer experts in the industry establish the standards of certification. Although the test covers a broad range of computer software and hardware, it isn't vendor-specific. In fact, more than 45 organizations contributed and budgeted the resources to develop the A+ examinations.

To become A+ Certified, you must pass two examinations: the Core Hardware exam and the OS Technologies exam. The Core Hardware exam measures essential competencies for a break/fix microcomputer hardware service technician with six months of experience. The exam covers basic knowledge of desktop and portable systems, basic networking concepts, and printers. Also included on the exam are safety and common preventive maintenance procedures.

The 2003 revision of the A+ Certification includes the OS Technologies exam, which covers basic knowledge of the Windows 9*x*, Windows NT 4, Windows 2000, and Windows XP operating systems. You'll be tested on the procedures for installing, upgrading, troubleshooting, and repairing microcomputer systems running these operating systems.

Computerized Testing

As with Microsoft, Novell, Lotus, and various other companies, the most practical way to administer tests on a global level is through Thomson Prometric or Pearson VUE testing centers, which provide proctored testing services for Microsoft, Oracle, Novell, Lotus, and the A+ computer technician certification. In addition to administering the tests, Prometric and VUE also score the exam and provide statistical feedback on each section of the exam to the companies and organizations that use their services.

Typically, several hundred questions are developed for a new exam. The questions are reviewed for technical accuracy by subject matter experts and are then presented in the form of a beta test. The beta test consists of many more questions than the actual test and provides for statistical feedback to CompTIA to check the performance of each question.

Based on the performance of the beta examination, questions are discarded based on how good or bad the examinees perform. If a question is answered correctly by most of the test takers, it's discarded as too easy. The same goes for questions that are too difficult. After analyzing the data from the beta test, CompTIA has a good idea of which questions to include in the question pool for the actual exam.

Test Structure

Currently the A+ exam consists of a *form*-type test (also called *linear* or *conventional*). This type of test draws from a question pool of some set value and randomly selects questions to generate the exam you'll take. I'll discuss the various question types in greater detail later in this introduction.

Some certifications use *adaptive* type tests. This interactive test weights all of the questions based on their level of difficulty. For example, the questions in the form might be divided into levels one through five, with level-one questions being the easiest and level five being the hardest. Every time you answer a question correctly, you're asked a question of a higher level of difficulty, and vice versa when you answer incorrectly. After answering about 15–20 questions in this manner, the scoring algorithm is able to determine whether you'd pass or fail the exam if all the questions were answered. The scoring method is pass or fail.

The exam questions for the A+ exams are all equally weighted. This means they all count the same when the test is scored. An interesting and useful characteristic of the form test is that you can mark questions and return to them later. This helps you manage your time while taking the test so that you don't spend too much time on any one question. Remember, unanswered questions count against you. Assuming you have time left when you finish the questions, you can return to the marked questions for further evaluation.

The form test also marks the questions that are incomplete with a letter "I" once you've finished all the questions. You'll see the whole list of questions after you finish the last question. The screen allows you to go back and finish incomplete items, finish unmarked items, and go to particular question numbers that you may want to look at again.

Question Types

The computerized test questions you'll see on the examination can be presented in a number of ways. The A+ exams are composed entirely of one-answer multiple-choice questions.

True or false   We're all familiar with true/false questions, but because of the inherent 50 percent chance of guessing the right answer, you won't see any of these on the A+ exam. Sample questions on CompTIA's web site and on the beta exam don't include any true/false questions.

Mulitple choice   A+ exam questions are of the multiple-choice variety. Below each question is a list of four or five possible answers. Use the available radio buttons to select one item from the given choices.

Graphical questions   Some questions incorporate a graphical element in the form of an exhibit either to aid the examinee in a visual representation of the problem or to present the question itself. These questions are easy to identify because they refer to the exhibit in the question, and there's also an Exhibit button on the bottom of the question window. An example of a graphical question might be to identify a component on a drawing of a motherboard.

Test questions known as "hotspots" actually incorporate graphics as part of the answer. These types of questions ask the examinee to click a location or graphical element to answer the question. As a variation of the previous exhibit example, instead of selecting A, B, C, or D as your answer, you'd simply click the portion ofthe motherboard drawing where the component exists.

Free-response questions   Another type of question that can be presented on the form test requires a *free-response* or type-in answer. This is basically a fill-in-the-blank question where a list of possible choices isn't given. You won't see this type of question on the A+ exams.

Study Strategies

There are appropriate ways to study for the different types of questions you'll see on an A+ Certification exam. The amount of study time needed to pass the exam will vary with the candidate's level of experience as a computer technician. Someone with several years of experience might only need a quick review of materials and terms when preparing for the exam.

For others, several hours may be needed to identify weaknesses in knowledge and skill level and to work on those areas to bring them up to par. If you know you're weak in an area, work on it until you feel comfortable talking about it. You don't want to be surprised with a question when you knew it was your weak area.

Knowledge-Based Questions

Knowledge-based questions require that you memorize facts. The questions may not cover knowledge material you use on a daily basis, but they do cover material that CompTIA thinks a computer technician should be able to answer. The following are some keys to memorizing facts:

Repetition   The more times you expose your brain to a fact, the more it "sinks in" and increases your ability to remember it.

Association   Connecting facts within a logical framework makes them easier to remember.

Motor association   It's easier to remember something if you write it down or perform another physical act, such as clicking the practice test answer.

Performance-Based Questions

Although the majority of the questions on the A+ exam are knowledge-based, some questions may be performance-based scenario questions. In other words, the performance-based questions on the exam actually measure the candidate's ability to apply one's knowledge in a given scenario.

The first step in preparing for these scenario-type questions is to absorb as many facts relating to the exam content areas as you can. Of course, actual hands-on experience will greatly help you in this area. For example, knowing how to install a video adapter is greatly enhanced by having actually performed the procedure at least once. Some of the questions will place you in a scenario and ask for the best solution to the problem at hand. It's in these scenarios that having a good knowledge level and some experience will help you.

The second step is to familiarize yourself with the format of the questions you're likely to see on the exam. The questions in this study guide are a good step in that direction. The more you're familiar with the types of questions that can be asked, the better prepared you'll be on the day of the test.

The Exam Makeup

To receive the A+ Certification, you must pass both the Core Hardware and the OS Technologies exams. For up-to-date information about the number of questions on each exam and the passing scores, check the CompTIA site at www.comptia.org or call the CompTIA Certification Area at (630) 678-8700.

The Core Hardware Exam

The 2003 Core Hardware exam comprises six domains (categories). CompTIA lists the percentages as follows:

> Installation, configuration, upgrading: 35 percent
>
> Diagnosing and troubleshooting: 21 percent
>
> Preventive maintenance: 5 percent
>
> Motherboard, processors, memory: 11 percent
>
> Printers: 9 percent
>
> Basic networking: 19 percent

The Operating System Technologies Exam

The 2003 Operating System Technologies exam comprises four domains (categories). CompTIA lists the percentages as the following:

> Operating system fundamentals: 28 percent
>
> Installation, configuration, and upgrading: 31 percent
>
> Diagnosing and troubleshooting: 25 percent
>
> Networks: 16 percent

Signing Up

After all the hard work preparing for the exam, signing up is an easy process. Sylvan operators in each country can schedule tests at any authorized Thomson Prometric or Pearson VUE testing center. To talk to a Thomson Prometric registrar, call (800) 77-MICRO, which is (800) 776-4276. Pearson VUE's phone number is (877) 551-PLUS, or (877) 551-7587. Many test takers have found the web registration process to be convenient; the two web sites are www.2test.com (Prometric) and www.vue.com (VUE).

There are a few things to keep in mind when you call:

1. If you call during a busy period, you might be in for a bit of a wait. Their busiest days tend to be Mondays, so avoid scheduling a test on Monday if possible.

2. Make sure you have your Social Security number handy. Sylvan needs this number as a unique identifier for their records.

3. Payment can be made by credit card, which is usually the easiest payment method. If your employer is a member of CompTIA, you may be able to get a discount or even obtain a voucher from your employer that'll pay for the exam. Check with your employer before you dish out the money. The fee for one exam is $93 for members and $145 for nonmembers. This price is subject to change, and you should check the CompTIA web site to verify that this price is still accurate before you register for the exam.

4. You may take one or both of the exams on the same day. However, if you only take one exam, you only have 90 calendar days to complete the second exam. If more than 90 days elapse between tests, you must retake the first exam.

Taking the Test

The best method of preparing for the exam is to create a study schedule and stick to it. Although teachers have told you time and time again not to cram for tests, there just may be some information that doesn't quite stick in your memory. It's this type of information that you want to look at right before you take the exam so it remains fresh in your mind. Most testing centers provide you with a writing utensil and some scratch paper that you can utilize after the exam starts. You can brush up on good study techniques from any quality study book from the library, but the following are some things to keep in mind when preparing for and taking the test:

1. Get a good night's sleep. Don't stay up all night cramming for this one. If you don't know the material by the time you go to sleep, your head won't be clear enough to remember it in the morning.

2. The test center needs two forms of identification, one of which must have your picture on it (in other words, a driver's license). Social Security cards and credit cards are also acceptable forms of identification.

3. Arrive at the test center a few minutes early. There's no reason to feel rushed right before taking an exam.

4. Don't spend too much time on one question. If you think you're spending too much time on it, just mark it and go back to it later if you have time. Unanswered questions are counted wrong even if you knew the answer to them.

5. If you don't know the answer to a question, think about it logically. Look at the answers and eliminate the ones you know can't possibly be the answer. This may leave with you with only two possible answers. Give it your best guess if you have to, but you can resolve most of the answers by using a process of elimination.

6. Books, calculators, laptop computers, or any other reference materials aren't allowed inside the testing center. The tests are computer-based and don't require pens, pencils, or paper; however, as mentioned, some test centers provide scratch paper to aid you while taking the exam.

After the Test

As soon as you complete the test, your results will show up in the form of a bar graph on the screen. As long as your score is greater than or equal to the required score, you pass! Also, a hard copy of the report is printed and embossed by the testing center to indicate that it's an official report. Don't lose this copy; it's the only hard copy of the report that's made. The results are sent electronically to CompTIA.

The printed report will also indicate how well you did in each section. You'll be able to see the percentage of questions you got right in each section, but you won't be able to tell which questions you got wrong.

After you pass the Core Hardware exam and the OS Technologies exam, an A+ certificate will be mailed to you within a few weeks. You'll also receive a lapel pin and a credit card–sized credential that shows your new status: A+ Certified Technician. You're also authorized to use the A+ logo on your business cards as long as you stay within the guidelines specified by CompTIA. If you don't pass the exam, don't fret. Take a look at the areas where you didn't do so well, and work on those areas for the next time you register.

Once you pass the exam and earn the title of A+ Certified Technician, your value and status in the IT industry increases. A+ Certification carries along an important proof of skills and knowledge level that's valued by customers, employers, and professionals in the computer industry.

CORE HARDWARE/OPERATING SYSTEM EXAMS

Part I

A+ Core Hardware

CHAPTERS

CORE HARDWARE/OPERATING SYSTEM EXAMS

Installing, Adding, and Removing System Components

Becoming a CompTIA A+ technician requires that you have a good grounding in the components and types of devices found in a PC system. The two most common PC systems are desktops and portables. Desktop computers are relatively easy to work on, but portables frequently require special training and tools. Most modern PC systems allow for expansion and upgrades, and you need to be able to identify, remove, replace, and troubleshoot components in the system.

QUESTIONS

1. You've been asked to upgrade the processor in a relatively new PC system. The socket for the processor looks similar to the socket for an adapter card. What type of processor socket are you dealing with?

   A. ZIF

   B. DIP

   C. SEC

   D. PGA

2. Which of the following statements correctly describes the function of direct memory access?

   A. It's used by the processor to communicate directly with devices.

   B. It's used by devices to communicate directly with memory.

   C. It's used by devices to interrupt the processor.

   D. It's used by the processor to directly access the RAM.

3. What's another name for a CRT?

   A. Video adapter

   B. Monitor

   C. Television

   D. Phone

4. Which type of video card is found in modern PC systems?

   A. ISA

   B. PCI

    C. VESA

    D. MCA

5. A type of expansion device that depends partially on the processing power of the CPU to operate is referred to as what?

    A. Riser card

    B. Sound card

    C. Network adapter

    D. Communications card

6. Which of the following types of video card is the best choice for a new system?

    A. AGP

    B. PCI

    C. MCA

    D. VESA

7. Which statement correctly describes the actions you must perform while taking out a Pentium 4 processor?

    A. Release the lever of the socket, and pull out the processor carefully.

    B. Push the retaining clips on each side; the processor will become free in the slot.

    C. Push the retaining clips outward on each side, and pull the processor safely out of the socket.

    D. Release the lever of the socket, and use the chip puller to take out the processor.

8. If you were asked to install an ATAPI CD-ROM drive on a PC, which of the following actions would make it a primary slave drive?

    A. Use the central connector of the primary hard drive cable, and set the configuration jumper to Slave.

    B. Use the central connector of the primary hard drive cable, and leave the default configuration jumper setting.

    C. Use the end connector of the primary hard drive cable, and set the configuration jumper to Slave.

    D. None of above. The CD-ROM drive can't be connected to the hard drive controller.

9. You want to upgrade the memory of a Pentium 4 processor. Of the following memory cards, which type is the most commonly used in these systems?

    A. SIMM

    B. RIMM

    C. SECC

    D. DDR

10. One of your friends has sought your advice on how to replace the keyboard of his laptop computer. Which of the following would be your best suggestion to him?

    A. Get a compatible keyboard from a computer store.

    B. Get any laptop keyboard because all laptops use similar keyboards.

    C. Get a replacement keyboard from the manufacturer.

    D. Send the laptop to the manufacturer to replace the keyboard.

11. You want to add networking capability to your laptop. Which of the following options isn't viable for most laptop systems?

    A. Installing a PCI NIC card in your laptop

    B. Installing a USB network adapter

    C. Installing a PC Card network adapter

    D. Adding a wireless adapter to the laptop

12. You're traveling to Europe for an extended business trip. You need access to a laptop PC during this trip. Your laptop is a relatively new system. Which of the following is the best method for accomplishing this?

    A. Purchase a new laptop that offers compatibility with European power standards.

    B. Purchase a new power supply for your laptop that's designed for European power.

    C. Purchase a DC-to-AC power converter.

    D. Purchase a new power cable with the appropriate connectors for European power connections.

13. You've just purchased an old sound card that requires setting the jumpers for configuring the IRQ setting. What IRQ settings are usually required by a non–Plug and Play ISA card by default?

A. IRQ 5

B. IRQ 4

C. IRQ 13

D. IRQ 15

14. Which IRQ is always available for PCI card usage?

A. IRQ 9

B. IRQ 1

C. IRQ 13

D. IRQ 15

15. You want to add a PCI board to your PC. How do you normally configure the IRQ address for a PCI device?

A Use Device Manager.

B. Plug and Play will normally configure PCI devices automatically.

C. Run the setup program.

D. Run the Add/Remove Hardware program to configure a PCI device.

16. How many DMA controllers are included on a Pentium-class processor?

A. 1

B. 2

C. 3

D. 4

17. Your friend has purchased a new printer with a parallel interface that he wants to attach to his PC. Unfortunately, he lost the cable for connecting the PC to the printer. He has asked you to buy a new cable for him. Which of the following types of connectors would you look for on the cable for this purpose?

A. DB-25 male connectors on both ends

B. DB-25 male on one end and Centronics 36-pin male on the other

C. Centronics 36-pin connectors: female on one end and male on the other

D. DB-25 female on one end and Centronics 26-pin female on the other

18. Fiber-optic cables are immune to which of the following type of interference?

    A. Electrical

    B. Magnetic

    C. Electromagnetic

    D. All of above

19. Which of the following types of cables can't be connected in the reverse direction?

    A. A cable connecting the network adapter to the wall jack

    B. A cable connecting the modem to the telephone jack

    C. A cable connecting the monitor to the computer

    D. A cable connecting the cable modem to the wall socket

20. You open your PC to install a second hard drive with a capacity of 80GB. You find by looking at the motherboard that there are only two connectors for hard drives, as shown in the following illustration. Each of these connectors has a ribbon cable with two black connectors. You disconnect the ribbon cables from the motherboard.

Which of the following is the type of hard drive you're going to install?

A. EIDE

B. IDE

C. SCSI

D. ESDI

21. You want to add disk capacity to your computer system. When you open the case, you discover that your computer has IDE controllers and that the following devices are connected to it: two hard disks, a CD-ROM player, and a DVD player. Which option is the best method to add disk space to this computer?

A. Replace the hard drive with a larger hard drive.

B. Add the additional hard drive to the existing controller.

C. Purchase an additional ISA hard drive controller, and add the drive to this.

D. You can't expand the capacity of this system.

22. You want to add an additional CD-ROM to your computer system. When you open the case, you discover that there's a hard drive installed to the primary master connector and a CD-ROM installed on the secondary master. Which configuration would yield the best performance?

A. Move the existing CD-ROM to the primary slave, and add the new CD-ROM to the secondary master.

B. Add the new CD-ROM to the primary slave position.

C. Add the new CD-ROM to the secondary slave position.

D. Add the new CD-ROM to the primary master position, and move the hard drive to the primary slave position.

23. Which of the following statements is correct regarding the difference between Enhanced IDE and SCSI devices?

A. EIDE controllers are much faster than SCSI devices because they have to handle a maximum of four devices.

B. The number of EIDE devices is limited to four, but there can be up to 31 SCSI devices in a system.

C. EIDE devices are connected in a daisy-chain fashion, but the SCSI devices have to be configured as the master and slave.

D. EIDE devices require a separate IRQ and I/O address for each device, and SCSI devices require only an ID.

24. You want to add hard disks to your computer to increase the storage capacity. The computer has a SCSI 2 controller card. If there are two SCSI hard disks and a SCSI scanner attached to the system, how many SCSI IDs are free to allow you to add new hard disks?

A. 2

B. 4

C. 8

D. 10

25. Your computer has two SCSI adapters, one of which is connected to three internal SCSI hard drives and the other of which is meant for external SCSI devices such as a scanner and CD burner. Which of the following will be the most likely problem if the terminator is missing in the external SCSI chain?

A. The last device connected to the internal SCSI chain won't work.

B. The last device connected to the external SCSI chain won't work.

C. All SCSI devices in the computer will stop working.

D. None of the external SCSI devices will work.

26. You want to install a new device to your SCSI chain. Currently you have addresses 3, 4, 5, and 6 available for use by this device. Which of the following addresses will give this new device the highest priority?

A. 3

B. 4

C. 5

D. 6

27. You've just installed a new SCSI device to an existing SCSI chain that has operated reliably for some time. You notice that the SCSI devices intermittently malfunction. There doesn't seem to be any pattern that you can ascertain in the malfunctions. Which of the following is the most likely problem with the SCSI chain?

A. The terminator has malfunctioned and needs to be replaced.

B. You most likely have a passive terminator and should switch to an active terminator.

C. The new device is malfunctioning.

D. The cable to the new device is defective.

28. You've experienced intermittent problems over the past two months with your PC. The system reboots for no apparent reason, it also locks up, and it displays unusual information on the monitor. You haven't made any configuration changes since these problems started. Which of the following is the most likely solution to fix this problem?

A. Replace the power supply in your computer.

B. Install a UPS and suppressors to the power line of your computer.

C. Install a safety ground for your electrical power distribution.

D. Replace the motherboard on your computer.

29. You've just purchased a new digital camera and want to transfer pictures from it to your PC. Which choice will require the least expense to accomplish this? Your computer is relatively new.

A. Install an Apple FireWire controller because most digital cameras support this interface.

B. Use a bidirectional printer cable to connect your camera to the computer.

C. Purchase a memory card reader for your computer.

D. Connect the camera using the USB connection.

30. Your computer has an integrated modem connection on the motherboard. The modem isn't working properly. Which of the following is the least expensive method of correcting this problem?

A. Replace the motherboard.

B. Install a modem using an existing PCI slot.

C. Install a modem using your existing parallel port.

D. Purchase a USB modem.

31. What is the command to hang up a modem using the Hayes modem command set?

A. ATH

B. ATZ

C. +++

D. ATDT

32. You want to upgrade an existing CRT monitor with an FPD monitor. What will be required to accomplish this?

A. Replace the video adapter with one that's compatible with FPD monitors.

B. Replace the CRT monitor with the FPD monitor; no additional hardware is required.

C. Systems designed for CRT monitors can't accept FPD monitors.

D. Purchase a converter cable for the FPD monitor.

33. You want to expand the storage capacity of your computer system significantly. You've determined that four EIDE channels are being used. Which option is the most viable?

A. Remove the EIDE devices and replace them with SCSI devices.

B. Add a SCSI controller and devices, and keep the EIDE devices.

C. Add additional devices to the EIDE controller.

D. Add an additional EIDE controller, and use that for expansion.

34. Which of the following RAID configurations doesn't offer fault tolerance?

A. RAID 0

B. RAID 1

C. RAID 3

D. RAID 5

35. Which of the following expansion slots is the best choice for a network adapter?

A. ISA

B. PCI

C. AGP

D. EIDE

36. You have a PC with 128MB of RAM in the four available memory slots on the motherboard. You want to upgrade to a minimum of 256MB of RAM on this PC. Each of the memory cards has 32MB of RAM. Which option is probably the least expensive?

    A. Replace the four 32MB RAM cards with one 256MB memory card.

    B. Replace the four 32MB RAM cards with four 64MB RAM cards.

    C. Replace the four 32MB RAM cards with two 128MB RAM cards.

    D. Replace two of the 32MB RAM cards with two 96MB RAM cards.

37. You've upgraded your system to include a CD-R drive and a hard disk. The system intermittently shuts down. Which of the following is the most likely problem?

    A. The power supply can't handle the load and should be upgraded.

    B. The hard disk has malfunctioned and should be replaced.

    C. The BIOS can't handle the new CD-R device.

    D. You can't have a CD-R and a hard disk on the same system.

38. You want to change your system from a Pentium III to a Pentium 4. What will you have to do to accomplish this?

    A. Replace the power supply and the motherboard.

    B. Replace the motherboard.

    C. Install a new processor into the existing slot on the motherboard.

    D. You can't upgrade in this situation.

39. You want to upgrade a Pentium 4 1.2 GHz CPU to a Pentium 4 1.8 GHz CPU. What steps will you need to do to accomplish this?

    A. You'll need to replace the motherboard because these speeds aren't compatible.

    B. You'll need to upgrade the BIOS to handle the newer processor.

    C. You can merely replace the chip with no changes to the configuration.

    D. You can't upgrade in this situation.

40. You have a new Pentium 4 new computer system, and the video controller has malfunctioned. Upon inspection you notice that the video card is a PCI card. Which of the following options is the best choice to repair this problem?

    A. Replace the card with a similar PCI video card.

    B. Replace the card with an AGP video card.

    C. Install a USB video controller.

    D. Install an MCA video card.

41. Which of the following best describes level 1 cache?

    A. Small amount of memory integrated in the processor for performance purposes

    B. Large amount of memory integrated in the processor for performance purposes

    C. Large amount of memory on the motherboard for performance purposes

    D. None of the above is a valid definition for level 1 cache.

42. Which of the following best describes level 3 cache?

    A. Small amount of memory integrated in the processor for performance purposes

    B. Small amount of memory on the motherboard for performance purposes

    C. Large block of memory in system memory for performance purposes

    D. Large block of memory on the motherboard for performance purposes

43. You've just installed a new hard drive on your system. At startup the drive isn't recognized by the system. You've verified all jumpers and connections and that they're proper. Which of the following is the likely cause of the problem?

    A. The BIOS doesn't support the disk; the motherboard will need to be replaced.

    B. The BIOS doesn't support the disk; it needs to be flashed to accept the new drive.

    C. The drive has an internal controller malfunction and is defective.

    D. The drive hasn't been formatted; startup won't recognize it until it has been.

44. You've just moved a new USB device from a new system to an older system. The new device worked properly on the new system but doesn't install properly on the older system. All other USB devices work properly on the older system. What is the most likely problem?

    A. The USB device has malfunctioned.

    B. The new USB device isn't backward compatible with USB 1.0 standards.

    C. The old system's BIOS is out-of-date and needs to be upgraded.

    D. The USB hub has malfunctioned.

QUICK ANSWER KEY

1.	C		23.	B
2.	B		24.	B
3.	B		25.	D
4.	B		26.	D
5.	A		27.	B
6.	A		28.	B
7.	A		29.	D
8.	A		30.	B
9.	D		31.	A
10.	D		32.	B
11.	A		33.	B
12.	D		34.	A
13.	A		35.	B
14.	A		36.	B
15.	B		37.	A
16.	B		38.	A
17.	B		39.	C
18.	D		40.	B
19.	C		41.	A
20.	A		42.	D
21.	A		43.	B
22.	C		44.	B

IN-DEPTH ANSWERS

1. ☑ **C.** Because the socket for the processor on the motherboard looks like the socket for an adapter card, it's the Single Edge Contact (SEC) processor socket. Only certain Pentium and Pentium-class processors use the SEC socket and can be mounted in these sockets on the motherboard. Currently, SEC processor packages are only used in the Pentium II and Pentium III processors, as well as some Celeron processors.

    ☒ **A** is incorrect because a zero insertion force (ZIF) socket uses a pin grid array (PGA) connection and generally lays flat on the motherboard. **B** is incorrect because dual inline package (DIP) hasn't been used for large-scale processors except in very special applications. **D** is incorrect because these processors use pin grid array (PGA) sockets that are horizontal and square in shape.

2. ☑ **B.** DMA channels allow devices to communicate with memory without involving the processor. DMA channels allow devices to write to the RAM without having to ask the processor for any action. Any device that requires this data can read it directly from the RAM.

    ☒ **A** is incorrect because the processor uses I/O addresses to communicate with different devices. **C** is incorrect because interrupting the processor is handled by interrupt requests (IRQs). **D** is incorrect because the processor doesn't need DMA to read data from or write data to RAM.

3. ☑ **B.** The terms *monitor* and *CRT* are used interchangeably in computer systems. A CRT originally referred to a specific type of monitor that uses a cathode-ray tube (CRT). Monitors today are constructed using several different technologies such as liquid plasma, liquid crystal, and CRT.

    ☒ **A** is incorrect because a video adapter is what a CRT is connected to. The most common video adapters used in modern PC systems are AGP and PCI based. **C** is incorrect because in the computer field a television wouldn't normally be referred to as a *monitor*. **D** is incorrect because a phone isn't a monitor although some new phones have monitors or displays associated with them.

4. ☑ **B.** The most modern of the video adapter choices offered is the PCI card. The PCI video card has been replaced by the AGP card as the preferred adapter in the newest generations of PC systems. You'll still find PCI video adapters in systems for several years to come.

☒ **A** is incorrect because ISA hasn't been used for many years as a video standard. ISA would be too slow for modern applications. **C** is incorrect because VESA cards were briefly popular for a short time as an alternative to the ISA card. VESA cards are rare today, and it's doubtful you'll encounter one. **D** is incorrect because MCA is a standard that was developed by IBM several years ago and was never widely accepted in the industry. PCI became the more popular choice because of its compatibility and speed.

5. ☑ **A.** A riser card attaches to the motherboard and utilizes part of the processing power of the CPU to operate. Riser cards are available for multimedia, communications, and network applications. Riser cards allow hardware manufacturers to minimize the number of components on the system, thus lowering costs.

☒ **B**, **C**, and **D** are incorrect because sound, networks, and communications cards usually contain onboard dedicated processors to free up CPU resources. Many newer systems are being manufactured with riser cards rather than with dedicated expansion cards added to the system.

6. ☑ **A.** AGP cards have become the standard video cards used in new systems. AGP offers advanced processing power and higher speeds than are available in PCI video adapter cards.

☒ **B** is incorrect because PCI is still commonly used but has largely been replaced by AGP as the video card of choice. **C** and **D** are incorrect because these two standards are very old and not commonly found in PC systems.

7. ☑ **A.** Pull the release lever and move upward, and pull the processor out of the socket. Pentium 4 processors use a PGA-type pin configuration. You want to first remove the heat sink and cooling fan before performing this operation. When you reinstall the processor, you'll want to apply thermal compound to the center of the processor to assist in heat transfer away from the processor. Make sure the processor has cooled down before you remove it or you'll potentially acquire serious burns from the processor.

☒ **B** is incorrect because the Pentium 4 socket has a single lever to release the pins. **C** is incorrect because the chip does not come free until the release lever is pulled upward. **D** is incorrect because the Pentium 4 socket is ZIF and a chip puller isn't needed and should never be used.

8. ☑ **A.** Use the central connector of the primary hard drive cable, and set the configuration jumper to slave. To make the CD-ROM drive a slave drive on the primary hard drive controller, you must connect it to the central connector of the ribbon cable and set its configuration jumper to slave position.

    ☒ **B** is incorrect because the configuration jumper on the CD-ROM drive must be set to the slave position. **C** is incorrect because the end connector of the hard drive cable is connected to the hard disk that's set to act as a master drive. **D** is incorrect because the ATAPI CD-ROM drive is always attached to the hard drive controller.

9. ☑ **D.** Most Pentium 4 systems use DDR RAM. This type of RAM is a type of SDRAM that operates at twice the speed of conventional SDRAM.

    ☒ **A** is incorrect. SIMM is a type of memory module that's usually used only in very old PC systems and some older printers and peripherals. **B** is incorrect because RIMM is a copyright term used by Rambus for memory modules that use Rambus memory architecture. **C** is incorrect because SECC is a type of connection used for Pentium III and similar processors.

10. ☑ **D.** Send the laptop to the manufacturer to replace the keyboard. Most of the laptop components are integrated with the motherboard, and it isn't an easy process to replace them. The best option to replace the keyboard is to send it to the manufacturer.

    ☒ **A** and **B** are both incorrect because usually laptop keyboards are proprietary, and you might not be able to find a replacement in the market. **C** is incorrect because it isn't advisable to attempt to replace a laptop keyboard yourself without training on the correct procedures by the manufacturer.

11. ☑ **A.** Most laptop and portable systems don't provide a PCI slot for expansion. PC Card and USB are the two most commonly provided expansion capabilities for laptops.

    ☒ **B** and **C** are incorrect because they're both the most likely choice for connecting to a network. **D** is a good option if you already have a wireless network, but a wired network requires a physical network connection.

12. ☑ **D.** Most modern laptop power supplies are universal and will operate in all standard power circuits. You can usually buy these cables either from the

manufacturer or from vendors in most countries. Verify that the power supply you have is universal before you connect it to another voltage source.

☒   **A** is incorrect. Although it might be nice to have a new laptop, it's usually not necessary to replace the laptop because it's the power supply that's the issue, not the computer. **B** is incorrect, but if your existing power supply isn't universal, you'll need to purchase one that can operate in the environment in which you're traveling. **C** is an option, but not your best one. Power converters for this type of application would be very heavy and expensive.

13.   ☑   **A.** Older sound cards used IRQ 5 by default. If jumpers on the card can be changed, you can usually change to another IRQ if a conflict exists. IRQ 5 is also frequently used by LPT2 if a second parallel port is installed on the computer.

☒   **B** is incorrect because IRQ 4 is used by COM1 by default. **C** is incorrect because IRQ 13 is used by the math coprocessor on most systems. **D** is incorrect because IRQ 15 is usually used by the secondary hard disk controller.

14.   ☑   **A.** IRQ 9 is the address used by the IRQ on PCI by default. In actuality, IRQ addresses are managed by the controller on the PCI bus and are used primarily for compatibility purposes with older hardware. All PCI devices can share IRQ 9.

☒   **B** is incorrect because IRQ 1 is used by the keyboard and is a reserved IRQ. **C** is incorrect because IRQ 13 is used by the coprocessor and shouldn't be used for other purposes. **D** is incorrect because IRQ 15 is the IRQ address for the secondary IDE controller.

15.   ☑   **B.** IRQ addresses are automatically configured by Plug and Play and the PCI bus. You don't need to normally reconfigure PCI devices manually.

☒   **A** is incorrect because you can configure IRQ addresses manually by using Device Manager, but you wouldn't want to do that normally. **C** is incorrect because a setup program is typically used to install software on a system. **D** is incorrect because Add/Remove Hardware allows you to install devices that aren't automatically detected by Plug and Play.

16.   ☑   **B.** There are two DMA controllers included on virtually all Intel-based microprocessors since the 80286 processor. Early PC systems based on the 8088 used a single DMA controller. Each DMA controller is capable of managing four DMA channels.

☒   **A** is incorrect because only very early PC systems had a single DMA controller. These systems were extremely difficult to configure because of this limitation. Many manufacturers added a second DMA controller to allow for additional expansion. **C** and **D** are incorrect because most microprocessors only provide two DMA controllers. Interrupting the processor is handled by IRQs. **D** is incorrect because the processor doesn't need DMA to read data from or write data to RAM.

17. ☑ **B.** The standard parallel printer cable uses a DB-25 male connector for the PC side and a 36-pin Centronics connector for the printer side.

    ☒ **B, C,** and **D** are incorrect because these cables wouldn't be used for a parallel printer configuration in most situations.

18. ☑ **D.** Fiber-optic cables have the advantage of being virtually immune to all forms of electrical and magnetic interference. Fiber-optic is unfortunately the most difficult to work with and the most expensive cabling option commonly available.

    ☒ **A, B,** and **C** are incorrect because fiber-optic is immune to all three of these types of interference.

19. ☑ **C.** Monitor cables are monodirectional. This means that they'll only work in a single direction. By convention, monitors and adapter cards use different pin layouts from each other.

    ☒ **A, B,** and **D** are incorrect because each of these cables is reversible and will work equally well in either orientation.

20. ☑ **A.** Enhanced Integrated Device Electronics (EIDE) is an advanced version of Integrated Device Electronics (IDE) that allows you to have up to four hard drives in a PC. There are typically two connectors on the motherboard known as primary and secondary controllers. Each of the controllers can have two EIDE hard drives installed as master and slave drives. This gives you the ability to have a maximum of four hard drives in the PC.

    ☒ **B** is incorrect because IDE has a limit of only two hard drives. **C** is incorrect because the SCSI controller has only one cable with multiple connectors, usually more than two. With a SCSI interface, all the devices are connected in a chain with a SCSI terminator attached to the last device. **D** is incorrect because the Enhanced Small Device Interface (ESDI) hard drive controller also has a limit of two hard drives per computer.

21. ☑ **A.** Your best option of those given is to replace the drive with a larger drive to add capacity. This will give you the best performance. If you find yourself in this situation, it may be a good time to add SCSI capability to your system.

This would improve overall system performance and would allow for additional disk expansion if needed later.

☒ **B** is incorrect because the system already has four IDE devices attached and that's the limit of an integrated IDE or EIDE controller. **C** is incorrect because ISA hard drive controllers would offer unacceptably low performance and would be extremely slow. **D** is incorrect because you can expand this system.

22. ☑ **C.** You'd want to have this CD-ROM on a channel that isn't shared with the system disk if possible. The system disk in this case is on the primary master, and you wouldn't want an additional device on that channel for optimum performance if you can help it.

☒ **A** is incorrect because moving the existing CD-ROM drive to the primary would decrease performance of the primary channel. **B** is incorrect because adding the new CD-ROM drive to the primary would slow performance down when the CD is accessed. **D** is incorrect because moving the CD-ROM to the primary master position would be your worst choice and could prevent your system from booting from the hard drive.

23. ☑ **B.** The Enhanced IDE controller allows you to have a maximum of four hard disk drives in a system. This limitation is overcome by the SCSI controller that allows you to have up to 31 devices, depending on the type of controller used. The latest Ultra-3 SCSI standard supports up to 32 devices.

☒ **A** is incorrect because EIDE isn't faster; rather, it's slower that most SCSI versions. **C** is incorrect because the SCSI devices are connected in daisy-chain fashion and EIDE devices have to be configured as master and slave. **D** is incorrect because it's the SCSI controller that requires the IRQ and I/O address. These resources are typically automatically assigned by the system BIOS.

24. ☑ **B.** There are four available addresses in this SCSI 2 system. SCSI 2 interfaces support a total of eight addresses. One of these addresses is occupied by the controller, leaving availability for seven additional devices. Because three of these seven addresses are already used, there are four addresses available.

☒ **A**, **C**, and **D** are incorrect. There are a maximum of seven addresses available in SCSI 1 besides the controller.

25. ☑ **D.** If a SCSI chain is missing the terminator, none of the SCSI devices in the chain will be able to work. The SCSI chain must be terminated to have a fully functional set of SCSI devices connected to a particular SCSI adapter. The SCSI terminator is usually connected to the last device in the chain on the free SCSI connector.

☒ **A** is incorrect because not only the last device but none of the SCSI devices connected to the chain will be able to work. **B** is incorrect because there are other SCSI devices in the computer connected to another SCSI adapter. **C** is incorrect because the SCSI hard disks are connected to a separate SCSI adapter.

26. ☑ **D.** SCSI address 6 is the highest priority of the four addresses given. The order of SCSI priorities are 7, 6, 5, 4, 3, 2, 1, and 0.

☒ **A** is incorrect because address 3 is the lowest priority of the addresses given. **B** is incorrect because address 4 is lower priority than address 6. **C** is incorrect because address 5 is a lower priority than address 6.

27. ☑ **B.** Most SCSI chains come with a passive terminator. These terminators are frequently inadequate to terminate a large or busy SCSI chain. You'd want to change terminators before taking more drastic measures.

☒ **A** is incorrect because if the chain was working properly before you added an additional device, this is a significant clue as to the situation with the chain. You could easily terminate one of the devices to verify the terminator is functioning. **C** is incorrect because if the chain is operating intermittently, this would indicate that all of the SCSI devices are probably working properly and that you have a termination problem. **D** is incorrect because the cable would generally not cause intermittent malfunctions.

28. ☑ **B.** The most likely problem is that you're having power sags or surges that are causing your system to become unstable. Before you replace the power supply, it'd be wise to invest in a UPS and surge suppressor.

☒ **A** is incorrect because a malfunctioning power supply isn't the best answer until you've installed the UPS and surge suppressor. If the problem continues, you'd then suspect the power supply. **C** is incorrect because installing a safety ground wouldn't help you address power regulation problems. **D** is incorrect because the motherboard doesn't appear to be malfunctioning at this point given the symptoms. It would be reasonable to suspect the motherboard if the power supply has been replaced and the problem continues.

29. ☑ **D.** Most new digital cameras support USB connections, which is fast and reliable.

☒ **A** is incorrect because an Apple FireWire controller isn't as common in digital cameras as USB. FireWire would require an additional controller to be installed in the computer and isn't commonly installed in PCs unless requested.

B is incorrect because none of the currently popular digital cameras include a printer port for data transfer. **C** is incorrect because this option would be more expensive than using the existing USB connection in your computer. The card reader would, however, be faster than a USB connection for picture transfers.

30.   ☑   **B.** The least expensive would be to use a PCI slot if one is available. PCI modems are very inexpensive and readily available.

☒   **A** is incorrect because you could replace the motherboard, but it'd be more expensive than adding a separate modem card. **C** is incorrect because parallel port modems are extremely rare and not as reliable as internal modems. **D** is incorrect because USB modems are more expensive than PCI modems. They work as well and offer the same reliability, but they're simply more expensive.

31.   ☑   **A.** The ATH command is the Hayes-compatible command to hang up an existing call in progress. The Hayes command set was introduced by Hayes Communications many years ago and is the de facto standard for modem communications and protocol.

☒   **B** is incorrect the ATZ command resets the modem to its initialized state. This would hang up the modem and cause all settings to be reset. **C** is incorrect because the +++ command is used to signal to the modem that a command is coming and to deal with the next text it receives as a command rather than data. **D** is incorrect because ATDT is the command to dial a number. You'd enter ATDT and the phone number to make a modem connection.

32.   ☑   **B.** FPD and CRT monitors are, for the most part, interchangeable on desktop PC systems. Most FPD monitors accept the output of standard video cards.

☒   **A** is incorrect because you don't need to replace the video card. **C** is incorrect because FPD monitors are plug compatible with CRT monitors. **D** is incorrect because you wouldn't need a converter to connect an FPD monitor.

33.   ☑   **B.** Adding a SCSI controller would allow you to add a SCSI chain of devices. You can expand up to the number of devices supported by the controller; typically 8, 16, or 32 devices depending on the controller and standard you use.

☒   **A** is incorrect. You wouldn't need to remove the EIDE devices to add a SCSI chain. **C** is incorrect because EIDE controllers have a limit of four devices that can be added to them. Two devices can be added to the primary and two to the secondary. **D** is an option, but if you're expanding your system, SCSI will offer you more flexibility and improved performance over EIDE.

34. ☑ **A.** RAID 0 or disk striping is a performance enhancement but not fault tolerant. RAID 0 spreads a single disk volume across multiple physical disks and allows for rapid disk access.

☒ **B** is incorrect because RAID 1 is called *disk mirroring* and is fault tolerant. RAID 1 uses a minimum of two disks. All writes to the first disk are mirrored to the second disk in real time. **C** is incorrect because RAID 3 is a fault tolerant technology that works similarly to RAID 0 and adds an additional disk to store information for recovery purposes. RAID 3 is called *disk striping* with parity. **D** is incorrect because RAID 5 technology uses multiple disks and spreads redundancy information across the volumes used in the disk array.

35. ☑ **B.** A PCI network card would offer the highest performance on most systems.

☒ **A** is incorrect because you could use an ISA card for a network adapter, but it would degrade CPU performance and not be as efficient as PCI. **C** is incorrect because AGP is currently only used for video adapters. **D** is incorrect because EIDE is a disk interface standard and wouldn't be suitable for a network adapter.

36. ☑ **B.** In general, smaller capacity memory cards cost less than larger capacity memory cards. This memory is usually just as fast as larger memory cards but takes more slots for the same memory density as higher density memory cards.

☒ **A** is incorrect because a single 256MB memory card will probably cost more than four 64MB memory cards. **C** is incorrect for the same reason that A is incorrect. **D** is incorrect because 96MB isn't a standard memory configuration and not commercially available.

37. ☑ **A.** The addition of a CD-R has probably overloaded the power supply of the system. You'd want to evaluate whether older expansion cards could be replaced with newer cards that used less power or you'd want to upgrade the power supply.

☒ **B** is incorrect. The symptoms given don't indicate that the hard drive or any devices have malfunctioned. **C** is incorrect because the BIOS is working correctly because there was no indication that the CD-R was malfunctioning. It's good practice to check the version and/or upgrade the BIOS of a system whenever you install a new component in the system. **D** is incorrect because a CD-R and hard drive are a normal configuration for a modern PC.

38.   ☑   **A.** The power supply and motherboard would need to be replaced in a system that was upgraded from a Pentium III to a Pentium 4. The voltages on Pentium III systems aren't compatible with Pentium 4 systems, and the motherboards aren't compatible.

☒   **B** is incorrect because you can't merely replace the motherboard; you'll also need to replace the power supply. **C** is incorrect because the Pentium III and Pentium 4 sockets aren't interchangeable. **D** is incorrect because you can upgrade this system; it'll require a new power supply and motherboard.

39.   ☑   **C.** To upgrade from a slower processor in the same family, you can generally just replace the processor. All other components should function normally. On a motherboard that requires bus speeds to be set manually, you may also have to change bus jumpers. This is explained in the motherboard manual.

☒   **A** is incorrect because you can upgrade the processor in this situation. **B** is incorrect because the BIOS should work properly, but it's good practice to upgrade the BIOS whenever you make changes to the configuration. **D** is incorrect because you can upgrade in this situation.

40.   ☑   **B.** If the system requires a new video controller, you should upgrade to the newest controller technology available. AGP has become the new standard for video cards on PCs.

☒   **A** is incorrect because you could replace the PCI card with another PCI card, but you'd be better served upgrading to AGP. **C** is incorrect because USB video adapters aren't commonly available for monitors. USB video adapters are available for video capturing. **D** is incorrect because you probably won't encounter a system that has MCA and AGP video adapter slots. MCA is a very old standard and not commonly used in PC systems.

41.   ☑   **A.** Level 1 cache is usually integrated in the CPU package and is intended to enhance processor data access. Level 1 cache is small when compared to other memory resources on the system.

☒   **B** is incorrect because level 1 cache is usually smaller than other caches on the system. **C** is incorrect because level 3 cache is usually a relatively large amount of memory on the motherboard or integrated in some newer processors. **D** is incorrect because the definition of level 1 cache is given in answer A.

42. ☑ **D.** Level 3 cache is usually a relatively large memory block that's usually included on the motherboard. Level 3 cache helps improve performance by keeping commonly accessed data available for rapid access by the processor.

    ☒ **A** is incorrect because a small amount of memory in the processor is referred to as *level 1 cache*. **B** is incorrect because a small amount of memory on the motherboard may be level 2 cache. Level 2 cache is usually larger than level 1 cache. **C** is incorrect because a block of system memory wouldn't be defined as L1, L2, or L3 cache. Some programs and operating systems allocate a block of main memory for caching purposes. This is usually referred to as a *buffer* or *memory pool*.

43. ☑ **B.** The most likely problem is that the device is too new for the BIOS. Upgrading the BIOS will probably fix this problem. If upgrading the BIOS doesn't work, you can manually configure the BIOS to accept the performance characteristics of the new hard drive. Most drive manufacturers provide this information with the disk drive, or you can access it on the manufacturer's site.

    ☒ **A** is incorrect because you can usually flash update the BIOS, and you don't need to replace the motherboard to do this. **C** is incorrect because you don't know if the hard drive controller has malfunctioned, and you'd want to check the BIOS before suspecting the hard drive internal electronics. **D** is incorrect because formatting the drive occurs after the drive has been properly installed and configured. A nonformatted drive would still be present if the BIOS is working properly.

44. ☑ **B.** This is the most likely problem because some USB 2.0 devices don't operate at USB 1.0 speeds. It's possible that the USB device won't be configurable to the older speed.

    ☒ **A** is incorrect because if the device worked on the new system, it has probably not malfunctioned. **C** is incorrect because a BIOS upgrade won't usually correct a USB compatibility problem. USB devices usually have their own upgrade process. **D** is incorrect because if the other USB devices are working properly, the hub is most likely working properly. It isn't uncommon for older USB hubs to not support the USB 2.0 standard, so you'd want to verify that with the manufacturer.

2

Diagnosing and Troubleshooting Problems

T he fun and exciting part of being an A+ technician is troubleshooting and repairing systems. When troubleshooting a system, you want to evaluate the symptoms to determine what the most likely problem is. Becoming proficient at troubleshooting and repairing takes practice and experience. This is an art that you'll develop as you work with systems. Fortunately, most modern PC systems provide a great deal of information about problems that can usually be used to identify and correct problems.

QUESTIONS

1. Which of the following errors isn't a possible cause of problems associated with the boot process?

   A. Errors with the system board

   B. Errors with the processor

   C. A faulty monitor

   D. Problems with onboard memory

2. In which of the following conditions would you assume that the computer has passed the power-on self-test and that any problem in the system isn't a fatal one?

   A. When you see error 201

   B. When you hear a beep

   C. When you hear a series of several beeps

   D. When you don't hear any beeps

3. Which of the following statements correctly describes the order of tests done on the components during the POST?

   A. Processor, keyboard, memory

   B. Processor, memory, keyboard

   C. Memory, processor, keyboard

   D. Memory, keyboard, processor

4. A customer calls you and tells you that his computer reboots itself when he's working on it. He also tells you that sometimes it just switches off and doesn't reboot. What is the likely cause of the problem?

    A. A loose power connection

    B. A bad CMOS battery

    C. A hard disk failure

    D. A stuck key on the keyboard

5. One of your friends told you he loaded a small application from three floppy disks. The setup program prompted him to restart the computer. When he pressed ENTER to restart the computer, the system couldn't boot and was giving the following error:
    Non-system disk or disk error.
    Replace disk and press any key to continue.

    Which of the following could be the possible cause of the problem?

    A. The application corrupted the operating system on the hard disk.

    B. He left the last disk in the floppy disk drive.

    C. He shouldn't have restarted the computer after installation.

    D. The floppy disks corrupted the floppy drive.

6. The mouse pointer in a computer is stuck on a particular place and isn't moving with the physical movement of the mouse. This is a new serial mouse, and you're sure that there's no resource conflict. You've checked all connections and found no problems. You tried to solve the problem by restarting the computer several times, but on many of these occasions the pointer didn't appear at all. You've also opened the mouse and found that the ball and the rubber rollers look neat and clean.

    What else could possibly be the cause of the problem?

    A. The mouse driver needs to be replaced.

    B. The mouse needs reassignment of IRQ.

    C. Serial mice are no longer supported.

    D. The mouse port is defective.

7. You have an 80486 DX2 computer that was running very slowly. You added two new SIMM modules to this computer to increase its performance. When you started the computer after the upgrade, the BIOS gave you a "Memory size mismatch" error. What should you do to resolve the problem?

   A. Change the size of the memory in the BIOS.

   B. The new SIMM modules may be faulty; replace them.

   C. Insert the SIMM modules in reverse order.

   D. Invert the SIMM orientation in the sockets.

8. Which of the following actions would you take first when you start a computer and find there's no display on the monitor even though its power indicator is on?

   A. Change the video adapter.

   B. Try connecting a compatible, working monitor.

   C. Change the video driver.

   D. Replace the power cord of the monitor.

9. You've installed a new hard disk in the customer's computer and installed Windows 98 Second Edition on it. Prior to this, the customer was using the Windows 3.11 operating system. When you arrive back at your office, you get a call from him saying that every time he starts his computer, ScanDisk starts running. He said that the system runs fine otherwise, and he likes the new features. What could be the cause of the problem?

   A. Windows 98 isn't installed properly.

   B. There are bad sectors on his hard disk.

   C. Windows 98 isn't shutting down properly.

   D. There's a virus on the hard disk.

10. A customer complains to you that he can't hear any sound coming out of his speakers from his sound card. Which of the following would you check first?

   A. The configuration of the sound card driver

   B. The jumper settings on the sound card

   C. The speakers and connecting cables

   D. The sound card

Questions 11 and 12 You've been asked to attend to a computer problem at a customer's site. The customer reported that when he starts his computer, he hears a series of beeps, but nothing is visible on the monitor. He couldn't provide any other information on the phone.

The customer told you that the computer is a Pentium-something processor and has a lot of RAM. He uses the Windows 98 operating system. He has also connected a modem for accessing the Internet and a printer he seldom uses. Besides this, he told you that the mouse has a D-shaped connector.

The following two questions describe the series of events at the customer's site. Answer these questions, selecting the best answer for each.

11. You asked the customer if he counted the number of beeps, but he said he didn't remember. Based on the symptoms given by the customer, what should be your first action?

    A. Observe the problem symptoms yourself.

    B. Replace the video adapter.

    C. Replace the monitor.

    D. Ensure that the video adapter is seated properly.

12. You open the computer case and find that the video adapter has come out of the expansion slot. After you fix it and restart the computer, the monitor starts displaying video output. However, the system can't boot, and the following error displays:
    Boot from ATAPI CD-ROM: Failure...
    DISK BOOT FAILURE, INSERT SYSTEM DISK AND PRESS ENTER.

    You observe that when the POST is complete, the lights on the CD-ROM and floppy drive light up once. Which of the following will you rule out as a possible cause of this problem?

    A. Disconnected hard disk drive

    B. Corrupted operating system files

    C. Misconfigured hard disk drive

    D. Insufficient RAM

13. Windows 98 loads on your client's computer, but you can't find the mouse pointer on the screen. You move the mouse on the mouse pad, but the pointer doesn't appear. What should you do first to resolve this problem?

    A. Clean the mouse ball and its internal rollers.

    B. Restart the computer.

    C. Reinstall the mouse driver.

    D. Make sure the mouse is connected.

14. Your customer is complaining that he's unable to make reliable connections to his ISP. He suspects the modem is defective because the calls aren't going through some of the time and he isn't having problems using the phone line for regular telephone calls. He dials up his ISP and the modem produces the usual sounds, but when the Post-Dial Terminal Screen appears, it displays garbled characters as shown in the following illustration.

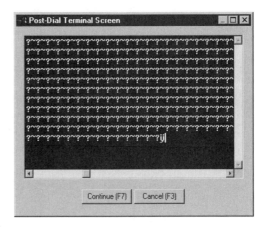

    Which of the following could cause this problem?

    A. Improper dial-up configuration

    B. Incorrect modem driver

    C. Static on the phone line

    D. Bad COM2 port

15. You've been out to work on a customer's computer after a frustrating conversation with him on the phone about the problems he's experiencing. The customer wasn't very helpful on the phone in describing what was wrong with his computer, which caused you to make an additional trip to get components for his computer. After you've made sure that the computer is working fine in every respect, the customer thanks you for your efforts. What would you advise the customer before you leave?

    A. That his bill will be high because the repairs have taken a long time

    B. That he should try to observe fault symptoms before calling customer service

    C. That he should get such repairs done by another company

    D. That he shouldn't mess up his system again

16. You've just installed a new sound card in a customer's PC. The system passes the self-test normally but doesn't boot. Which of the following is the most likely problem?

    A. Defective sound card

    B. Improper IRQ settings on the sound card

    C. Memory failure

    D. Incorrect speaker connections

17. You're a customer-service technician, and you've received a call from a customer indicating that her system passes the memory test but hangs before the CMOS setup prompt. Which component has likely failed?

    A. CPU

    B. Memory

    C. Video card

    D. Expansion card

18. You're replacing a motherboard on a PC system. Which of the following must be checked before installing the new motherboard?

    A. Exact motherboard form factor

    B. Exact motherboard model number

    C. AT power connection compatibility

    D. Exact video card compatibility

19. Your customer is reporting that the PC shuts itself off after running for a brief period of time. The customer reports that she can hear fan noise from the computer's power supply. The behavior is consistent and seems to occur fairly quickly after the machine is turned on. What is the most likely problem?

    A. The motherboard has malfunctioned.

    B. The CPU fan isn't working properly.

    C. The power supply is malfunctioning.

    D. The BIOS is out-of-date.

20. You've been asked to troubleshoot a system that has been turned off for some time. The customer indicates that the date information isn't being kept from day to day. Each time she reboots the system, the date and time aren't correct. What's the most likely suspect?

    A. The BIOS is out-of-date and needs to be upgraded.

    B. The Plug and Play mapper has malfunctioned.

    C. The battery on the motherboard is dead.

    D. The operating system needs to be refreshed from the original distribution.

21. The system you're troubleshooting passes POST most of the time. You notice that it passes POST when the machine has been turned off for a while. However, when it has been running for about an hour, the POST fails at the memory test if the system is restarted. What's the most likely problem?

    A. The BIOS refresh rate is set incorrectly.

    B. A memory chip has a heat problem.

    C. The CPU chip has a heat problem.

    D. This is normal operation for a PC.

22. You boot up a system and receive a "301 POST" error. What does this indicate?

    A. Memory failure

    B. Power supply failure

    C. Keyboard error

    D. Floppy drive error

23. You've been asked to troubleshoot a PC system. The user complains that the mouse stops working when the user goes online with the modem. What's the most likely cause of the problem?

    A. The user is using a serial mouse that has an IRQ conflict with the modem.

    B. The modem is defective and should be replaced.

    C. The mouse is defective and should be replaced.

    D. This is normal behavior for a PC.

24. After you install a new sound card, your system periodically reboots for no apparent reason. What's a likely problem in this situation?

    A. The BIOS doesn't support this sound card.

    B. The IRQ address is set incorrectly.

    C. The power supply is overloaded.

    D. The processor intermix ration is set incorrectly.

25. Which is the primary reason for installing slot covers over blank expansion slots on the back of a system case?

    A. Airflow consideration

    B. EMI considerations

    C. Dust prevention

    D. All of the above

26. Which system component can cause problems to appear in all the system's other components?

    A. Floppy disk

    B. Hard disk

    C. Power supply

    D. RAM drive

27. You notice the amount of time that your laptop operates using the battery has decreased significantly over the past six months. The laptop uses nickel-cadmium batteries. Which of the following steps should you take first to remedy this problem?

    A. Replace the battery with a new battery.

    B. Run the laptop on battery until it shuts off and recharge it. Repeat this a few times to recondition the battery.

    C. Replace the power supply.

    D. The PC is defective and should be serviced.

28. You want to dispose of the battery from your laptop. Which is the best method to do this?

    A. Wrap the battery in a plastic bag, and put it in the trash.

    B. Dispose of the battery using a recycler or hazardous waste disposal site.

    C. Burn the battery in an incinerator.

    D. Dispose of the battery in a sanitized landfill.

29. Your secondary master EIDE controller has failed, and you want to repair the problem in the most cost-effective manner that maintains performance. Which of the following options is the most viable?

    A. Replace the motherboard.

    B. Replace the secondary IDE controller on the motherboard.

    C. Add an additional IDE controller to the ISA bus.

    D. Add an additional IDE controller to the PCI bus.

30. You've just moved your PC, and you notice that the computer automatically shuts down on warm days. What step would you consider to deal with this problem?

    A. Upgrade the CPU fan to a larger unit.

    B. Install a second fan in the PC.

    C. Upgrade the power supply to a larger wattage.

    D. Check for a loose connection in the power cable.

QUICK ANSWER KEY

1.	C	16.	B
2.	B	17.	D
3.	B	18.	A
4.	A	19.	B
5.	B	20.	C
6.	A	21.	B
7.	A	22.	C
8.	B	23.	A
9.	C	24.	B
10.	C	25.	D
11.	A	26.	C
12.	D	27.	B
13.	D	28.	B
14.	C	29.	D
15.	B	30.	B

IN-DEPTH ANSWERS

1. ☑ **C.** A faulty monitor isn't a possible cause of problems associated with the boot process. Similarly, a defective video adapter or a video adapter with an incorrect driver won't cause any problems with the boot process. In any of these cases, the computer will boot properly, but you won't be able to view the display.

   ☒ **A**, **B**, and **D** are all incorrect. Any errors with the system board, processor, or memory are known as *fatal errors* that don't allow the boot process to complete.

2. ☑ **B.** In some PCs, the computer will give a beep signal during the power-on self-test indicating that the computer has successfully passed the POST and that there's no fatal problem with the system. You would want to check the motherboard manual or web site to establish what beep codes are given if a motherboard fails POST.

   ☒ **A** is incorrect because errors starting with 2 are associated with memory. Memory errors are fatal errors that won't allow the computer to boot properly. **C** is incorrect because this indicates a problem with some aspect of the system in most PCs. **D** is incorrect because this indicates that the system board isn't responding at all. The system board either isn't getting power or has developed some fault.

3. ☑ **B.** The computer checks all components during the POST routine, such as the processor, memory, BIOS ROMs, DMA controllers, interrupt controllers, video adapters, keyboard, floppy drive, and hard drive controllers. The order of testing components isn't similar with all BIOS manufacturers, but the key components in question are always tested in the given order. The processor is tested before memory, and memory is tested before testing the keyboard.

   ☒ **A** is incorrect because the keyboard is an external component that's tested when the memory tests have been completed. **C** and **D** are incorrect because these suggest that memory is tested first. In every computer system, the processor is always first to be tested during the POST, irrespective of the manufacturer. Although it isn't listed in any of the answer options, remember that the motherboard itself is the first thing to be tested by the BIOS.

4. ☑ **A.** The most likely cause of the problem is a loose power connection. Loose power connections are caused by a loose power cord or loose power connections on the system board. Any of these can cause the system to reboot and just turn off. Change the power cord, and the problem will be resolved.

☒ **B** is incorrect because the CMOS battery doesn't cause the system to reboot or turn off by itself. **C** is incorrect because the problem is associated with the power source and not with the hard disk or floppy disk. **D** is incorrect because this won't cause the system to reboot.

5. ☑ **B.** The "non-system disk or disk" error is typically caused by a nonbootable floppy disk in the floppy disk drive. Because your friend pressed ENTER immediately after seeing the restart prompt on the screen, the possible cause of the problem is that the floppy disk, which wasn't bootable, was left in the disk drive. The computer searched for the operating system in the floppy disk, and when it didn't find the operating system there, it gave the "non-system disk or disk" error.

☒ **A** is incorrect because had this been the problem, the system would have reported the "missing operating system" error. **C** is incorrect because several applications require a restart to complete installation. This isn't the cause of the current problem. **D** is incorrect because the disk drive can't be "corrupted."

6. ☑ **A.** The mouse driver needs to be replaced. All devices come with device driver files. The cause of the problem could be that you replaced the mouse but didn't install the new mouse driver. The old driver might not be compatible with the new mouse. Loading a new mouse driver will resolve the problem.

☒ **B** is incorrect because the older mouse was working well with the same serial port, and there doesn't seem to be any problem with IRQ assignment. Remember that it's the serial port that needs an IRQ and I/O address assignment, not the device connected to the serial port. **C** is incorrect because serial mice are still supported on nearly all computer systems. **D** is incorrect because it's unlikely that a working port would become defective just by replacing a device. However, serial ports are sensitive and become faulty quickly if proper safety procedures aren't followed.

7. ☑ **A.** Change the size of the memory in the BIOS. Several older computer BIOS programs don't automatically detect changes in the size of the RAM when memory is upgraded. Therefore, you must enter the BIOS setup during computer startup and manually enter the size of the memory. Most newer

BIOS programs automatically detect changes in the size of the physical memory (RAM).

☒ **B** is incorrect because if this were the problem, the error wouldn't have appeared at all. The computer BIOS wouldn't have detected the change in memory size if the SIMMs were faulty. **C** is incorrect because this wouldn't make any difference. **D** is incorrect because you can't reverse the orientation of the SIMM modules.

8. ☑ **B.** The first action you should take in this situation is to try connecting a compatible, working monitor. This would rule out the possibility of the monitor being faulty. Remember that whenever you start troubleshooting or diagnosing a problem, you must start by first trying things that don't require any configuration changes. Because the power indicator on the monitor is on, it's possible that either the monitor is faulty or there's some problem with the video adapter.

☒ **A** is incorrect because this shouldn't be your first action for the given problem. You must not change any component unless you're certain that it's faulty. **C** is incorrect because it's unlikely that the video driver has been corrupted. Moreover, like changing the video adapter, this shouldn't be your first action to resolve the stated problem. **D** is incorrect because you know the monitor is getting power because its power indicator is on.

9. ☑ **C.** Windows 98 isn't being shut down properly. The reason ScanDisk starts running every time the computer starts is that the customer is probably not shutting down the system using the Shutdown option in the Start menu. This causes the operating system to suspect that the hard disk is corrupted, and ScanDisk starts scanning the hard disk for possible errors.

☒ **A** is incorrect because the customer said that Windows 98 runs fine. **B** is incorrect because it's unlikely that a new hard disk has bad sectors. **D** is incorrect because viruses usually don't cause ScanDisk to run on startup.

10. ☑ **C.** The first thing you must check in the given situation is that the speakers are connected properly to the computer and that they're getting power. When you're sure that there's no problem caused by connections and speaker power, you may check other things such as volume control, sound card driver configuration, and hardware configuration such as jumper settings on the sound card.

☒ **A** is incorrect because even if the sound card driver is configured correctly, the sound system won't work if the speakers aren't properly connected or if there's no power. These two things must be checked first. **B** is incorrect because the jumper settings aren't the first things to check unless this is a fresh installation. **D** is incorrect because you must first make sure that the speakers are connected, the speakers are powered, and the controls are working before you replace the sound card.

11. ☑ **A.** The first thing you must do after arriving at the customer's site is to observe the problem symptoms yourself. Because the number of beeps plays an important part in problem diagnostics, you must listen carefully to the beeps produced by the POST. Although this may not tell you the cause of the problem, it's often a good start in diagnostics.

☒ **B** is incorrect because you must make sure that the video adapter is faulty before replacing it. The beeps during the POST routine are caused not only by a faulty video adapter but also by other problems. **C** is incorrect because a monitor problem doesn't produce beeps during the system startup. **D** is incorrect because although this may be the cause of the problem, you can't make this decision until you first carefully check the system startup.

12. ☑ **D.** Insufficient RAM isn't a possible cause of the problem because the system has 64MB of RAM, which is sufficient for running the Windows 98 operating system. The error indicates that the system isn't able to boot from the CD-ROM drive, the floppy drive, or the hard disk.

☒ **A**, **B**, and **C** are incorrect because any of these could be a reason for the error displayed. A disconnected hard disk, corrupted operating system files, or misconfigured hard disk drives could cause the BIOS to fail in loading the operating system. When the BIOS doesn't find the operating system from any of the bootable devices, it'll display the given message.

13. ☑ **D.** Make sure the mouse is connected. The mouse pointer is missing because Windows 98 didn't detect the mouse during startup. The mouse is probably disconnected from the computer. You should first check the mouse connection. If it's disconnected, shut down the computer, connect the mouse, and restart.

☒ **A** is incorrect because the stated problem isn't related to a dirty mouse ball or rollers. **B** is incorrect because the mouse will again fail to appear when restarting the computer if it isn't connected properly. **C** is incorrect because if the mouse driver were corrupted, the mouse pointer would've appeared. An incorrect driver usually causes the mouse pointer to move sporadically across the screen. In certain cases, the mouse pointer may not move at all.

14. ☑ **C.** The garbled characters on the Post-Dial Terminal Screen indicate that there's static on the phone line.

☒ **A** is incorrect because if this were the problem, the modem wouldn't have dialed a correct number, or it may not have dialed at all. **B** is incorrect because an incorrect modem driver won't activate the modem. **D** is incorrect because the modem is sending and receiving signals on this port, indicating that the COM2 port is working well.

15. ☑ **B.** He should try to observe fault symptoms before calling customer service. It's a good idea to advise customers to observe fault symptoms when a computer develops problems. Getting firsthand information contributes to a speedier resolution of the problem either by allowing the customer to obtain a solution to the problem on the phone or by saving the time required to collect facts in order to diagnose the cause of the problem when you arrive at the customer's site for repairs.

☒ **A, C,** and **D** are all incorrect because these are bad customer-service ethics.

16. ☑ **B.** IRQ settings can cause a system to hang during bootup. This is especially true in dealing with ISA-type legacy cards.

☒ **A** is also possible, but check for resource conflicts before deciding that the card is defective. **C** is incorrect because a memory failure will usually be displayed during the memory check. **D** is incorrect because an improper speaker connection wouldn't hang the system.

17. ☑ **D.** If the system passes a memory check and you can see it on the monitor, most likely the central processing unit (CPU), memory, and video are working properly.

☒ **A** is most likely incorrect. The POST is triggered by a command from the CPU. If the POST starts, the CPU will generally be functional. **B** is incorrect because you saw the memory pass the memory test. **C** is incorrect because you saw the memory test on the monitor; therefore, the video card is functioning properly. It's probably a safe assumption that one of the expansion busses is hanging, which is why the system is hanging. A quick way to troubleshoot this problem is to remove all the optional expansion cards and see if the system boots. You'll probably find that an expansion card has malfunctioned, a resource conflict exists, or the motherboard is defective.

18. ☑ **A.** You have several form factors to consider when replacing a motherboard, which are dependent upon the case and power supply connections. If you have a system that'll only accept an AT form factor, you won't be able to use an ATX-type motherboard.

☒ **B** is incorrect because the model number is usually not critical. **C** is incorrect because the type of motherboard you have dictates the power connections. An AT-type case won't accept an ATX motherboard and vice versa. **D** is incorrect because video cards are usually not an issue unless you're replacing a motherboard that does not support an AGP card, and you have an AGP video card.

19. ☑ **B.** The most likely problem is that the CPU fan is malfunctioning. Most motherboards now include temperature protection circuitry if the CPU overheats. This protects the CPU from damage because of overheating.

☒ **A** is incorrect. Although the problem may be a motherboard malfunction, the symptom sounds more like a heat-related problem. If the system starts normally and then shuts down fairly quickly, this indicates a heat problem. **C** is incorrect because power supplies usually have a fan that can be heard because they have an external vent. In this case, the customer is probably hearing the power-supply fan. **D** is incorrect because a BIOS problem usually doesn't just suddenly occur in a system that has been working.

20. ☑ **C.** If a computer system isn't retaining the system date between boots, the battery on the motherboard is almost always the culprit.

☒ **A** is incorrect because the BIOS being out-of-date wouldn't affect the settings being saved in the CMOS. **B** is incorrect because the mapper is called ECSD and is also powered by the battery when the system is turned off. **D** is incorrect because refreshing the operating system wouldn't fix this problem.

21. ☑ **B.** If the POST memory test fails when a system is rebooted after being left on for a while, you most likely have a bad memory unit.

☒ **A** is incorrect and irrelevant because BIOS refresh isn't something that would be affected by temperature. **C** is incorrect; if the CPU had a heat problem, you'd see a more general failure, such as the system locking up repeatedly. You can assume that if the POST starts, the CPU is working properly. **D** is incorrect because most PCs don't need to be rebooted when they're operating normally.

22. ☑ **C.** The 301 error is the code for a keyboard failure. You'd want to check that the keyboard is properly installed. If the problem continues, you'd want to replace the keyboard, and if that doesn't fix the problem, you'll need to replace the motherboard. As an alternative to replacing the motherboard, you may be able to switch to a USB keyboard.

    ☒ **A** is incorrect because memory failure codes are vendor specific, but most BIOS processes provide a plain-language indicator during the memory test. **B** is incorrect; a power supply failure will generally prevent the system from starting correctly, and you wouldn't see a POST error. **D** is incorrect; floppy drives don't provide a default POST error, but the floppy controller does.

23. ☑ **A.** Many older systems have a mouse that's connected to the serial port of the computer. Modems almost always use either an external serial port or they replace one of the ports such as COM1 through COM4. If the mouse and modem use either the same COM port or the matching COM port (COM1/COM3 or COM2/COM4), the mouse will stop working when the other port is used. This will require a rebooting of the computer to correct. It's best to replace the serial mouse with a newer technology mouse such as USB.

    ☒ **B** is incorrect because the modem is working. **C** is incorrect because the mouse is working. **D** is incorrect because this isn't normal behavior for a PC unless an IRQ conflict exists.

24. ☑ **B.** An IRQ problem may cause a system to lock up or periodically reboot. You should check for IRQ or other resource conflicts before deciding the board is bad. This is extremely common when using legacy boards and the ISA bus.

    ☒ **A** is incorrect because the BIOS not supporting a sound card is irrelevant. BIOS settings don't generally affect device installation. **C** is incorrect because the power supply is probably not overloaded and is less likely than a resource conflict. If a resource conflict isn't the problem, you might want to suspect the power supply. **D** is incorrect because there's no such thing as a processor intermix setting except on *Star Trek*.

25. ☑ **D.** All of the reasons listed are why slot covers should always be used over empty slots on the back cover. PCs generate radio frequency noise that can

interfere with other electronic devices. Computers also gather dust, and leaving the slot covers open allows more ways for the computer to collect dust. Case manufacturers also want airflow over all components in the system, and leaving a cover off disrupts the designed airflow of the system.

☒ **A**, **B**, and **C** are all partially correct answers.

26. ☑ **C.** The power supply affects all system components, and a malfunction such as power fluctuations in the power supply will affect all components in the system unit.

☒ **A, B**, and **D** are incorrect because these components operate independently from each other. A malfunction in one won't affect a malfunction in the other. Each of these components draws its power requirements from the power supply in the system unit unless they're externally attached. If they're externally attached, they'll usually have their own power systems.

27. ☑ **B.** Many laptop batteries that use nickel-cadmium will develop a memory about charge levels after extended use. By cycling the battery from fully charged to fully discharged, you may extend the life of these types of batteries. These batteries do wear out. If this doesn't work, you'd want to replace the battery.

Newer batter types such as nickel-metal-hydride don't have a charge memory problem and shouldn't be cycled like this. The most current batteries used in computers are lithium ion, which don't have memory problems with charging.

☒ **A** would be correct if you had already tried the steps in B. Replacing the battery prematurely is expensive and creates potentially unneeded toxic waste. **C** is incorrect; if the battery is charging, then the power supply is working. **D** wouldn't be your first step, most likely the battery needs to be cycled.

28. ☑ **B.** Laptop batteries and batteries in particular contain toxic chemicals that are extremely harmful to the environment. Only dispose of them using approved hazardous waste vendors.

☒ **A** and **D** are incorrect because you shouldn't dispose of a laptop battery using regular trash. **C** is incorrect and extremely dangerous. Lithium and other laptop batteries are extremely toxic and also will explode when heated. This would be extremely dangerous because of the explosive and toxic gas that would be created if the battery were incinerated.

29. ☑ **D.** If an IDE controller fails on the motherboard, you can install an additional controller using an expansion card. This controller would most likely support an additional four devices that in this case would give you the ability to have six IDE devices in the system. Your best performance option would be to use a PCI card.

   ☒ **A** is incorrect because you could replace the motherboard, but it would be more expensive than adding a separate controller. **B** is incorrect because you can't generally replace the IDE controller on the motherboard; it's permanently soldered to the motherboard, and it requires special equipment to be removed and replaced. **C** is incorrect because an ISA bus controller wouldn't maintain performance levels on the system. ISA is considerably slower than PCI.

30. ☑ **B.** Airflow is a critical factor in PC systems. If you relocate a PC or add additional hardware, it's a wise investment to add a second fan to the system. Numerous fan options are available. Most modern motherboards have temperature sensors that automatically power down the system if they overheat. This prevents premature failure of components in the computer system.

   ☒ **A** is incorrect because upgrading the CPU fan may help, but it'll only address the CPU, not the entire system. **C** is incorrect because adding a larger power supply won't improve airflow across the motherboard and expansion cards. **D** is incorrect because a loose power cable might cause random shutdowns but wouldn't be limited to warm days.

CORE HARDWARE/OPERATING SYSTEM EXAMS

3

Power Protection and Safety Procedures

TEST YOURSELF OBJECTIVES

3.01   Preventive Maintenance Products and Procedures

3.02   Power Protection and Safety Procedures

3.03   Environmental Protection Measures

Regular cleaning of computer parts not only extends the computer's life but also is helpful in preventing common problems that may arise from the dust buildup on internal and external components. Dust can increase heat and can cause an electrostatic charge to build up on internal components that may ultimately result in premature failure of the affected component.

Following proper safety procedures is important in preventive maintenance, and you must be careful when handling chemicals and high-voltage equipment such as monitors and power supplies. Power instability causes the majority of problems in computers. Sudden increases and decreases in power voltages must be prevented using surge suppressors and uninterruptible power supplies (UPS).

You can prevent electrostatic discharge (ESD) using ESD wrist straps, and any spare components must be stored in antistatic bags. It's also important to properly dispose of used chemicals and hazardous materials, such as empty toner cartridges and batteries.

QUESTIONS

1. Which of the following computer parts shouldn't be cleaned using soapy water and a damp cotton cloth? Select all correct answers.

    A. Mouse ball

    B. Monitor

    C. Keyboard

    D. Video adapter card

2. You use a computer at home for your personal accounting, Internet access, and e-mail. The computer performance has degraded a little, and you want to download a disk maintenance utility from the Internet and try it on your computer. Which of the following is the most important step you must do to protect your critical data before you decide to run the disk maintenance utility on your hard disk?

    A. Back up the data.

    B. Rearrange the data in folders.

    C. Empty the Recycle Bin.

    D. Set file permissions.

3. You open your computer case to change a jumper on the sound card, and you notice that some of the surfaces have become overly dusty. You want to clean off this dust. Which of the following is the best choice to remove the dust?

    A. Use canned air to blow off the dust.

    B. Use a lint-free towel to clean the dust.

    C. Use isopropyl alcohol.

    D. Use soapy water and a damp cloth.

4. The used computer you purchased last year has never been opened, and you suspect that it's very dirty inside. You notice that a lot of dust has accumulated on the power-supply fans. You want to clean the computer internally. Which is the correct way to clean the insides of the computer system?

    A. Use a nonstatic vacuum to remove any dust.

    B. Use warm water and soap to clean it.

    C. Use isopropyl alcohol to clean it.

    D. Use a lint-free cloth to clean it.

5. Which of the following methods wouldn't be used for maintaining hard disk drives?

    A. Clean with hard disk cleaning disks.

    B. Defragment hard disks regularly.

    C. Use ScanDisk to scan for corrupted files.

    D. Use virus scanning software.

6. You work on your home computer, store some files on floppies, and take them to your office. Because you use the floppy drive frequently, you want to perform a thorough check to ensure that it keeps working well, even though the drive has never created any problem so far. Which of the following procedures is the best way to protect the floppy drive?

    A. Use compressed air and blow out dust from inside the floppy drive.

    B. Use a head cleaner disk cassette to clean the read-write heads of the floppy drive.

    C. Use a cotton swab, rinse it in isopropyl alcohol, and clean the read-write heads.

    D. Don't clean the drive because it's working fine.

7. If you're working on adapter cards without wearing antistatic wrist straps or using any other static prevention method, how much electrostatic voltage is sufficient to damage the chips on the card?

    A. 30 volts

    B. 1,000 volts

    C. 3,000 volts

    D. 20,000 volts

8. Which of the following is an acceptable level of humidity in a room that houses computers and associated peripherals, such as scanners and printers?

    A. 20 percent to 50 percent

    B. 30 percent to 60 percent

    C. 50 percent to 80 percent

    D. 50 percent to 95 percent

9. The customer-support engineer has just left your office after servicing your computer and laser printer. You notice that he has left behind a used chemical bottle. You can't contact the engineer and don't find any Workplace Hazardous Materials Information System (WHMIS) labels or warnings on the bottle or its packaging. You did find a listing of the chemicals in the bottle on a label. Which of the following is your best option to dispose of the bottle?

    A. Throw the bottle in the garbage.

    B. Contact the manufacturer.

    C. Put the bottle in the recycling bin.

    D. Call the Environmental Protection Agency (EPA).

10. One of your friends has purchased a new 1KVA UPS system that'll be able to supply power to two computers, a scanner, and a laser printer. The older 500VA UPS is now free, and he wants to keep it just in case the new one fails. He has asked for your advice on how to store the UPS so that the battery isn't damaged if it isn't used for another six months. Which of the following is correct advice?

    A. Discharge the battery.

    B. Take out the battery, and keep it in a cool, dry place.

C. Keep the UPS connected to power so that it remains charged.

D. Refer to the manufacturer's documentation.

11. You have a computer that's located near a high-voltage transformer. Which of the following should you be concerned about if you want to protect the computer from damage or operational problems, potentially caused by this transformer?

A. Electromagnetic interference

B. Electrostatic discharge

C. Electric shock

D. Magnetic interference

12. The following are some problems related to power circuits and the equipment suggested to prevent them. Identify the equipment that has been inappropriately suggested for the given problem.

A. Electromagnetic interference: A noise filter

B. Sudden rise in AC voltage: A surge suppressor

C. Sudden dip in AC voltage: A UPS

D. Power failures: A Constant Voltage Transformer (CVT)

Questions 13–16 A customer has called you for preventive maintenance. His computer is running Windows XP. The computer uses an EIDE hard disk, a serial mouse connected to the COM1 port, and an internal modem. Additionally, a laser printer is connected to the computer.

Although the customer hasn't told you about any specific problems, you could judge from his tone of voice on the phone that he isn't very happy with his computer.

Your visit to the customer's site reveals several correlated things. These are explained in the following questions. Answer these questions, selecting the best answer for each.

13. The first thing you notice when you start the computer is that after loading the operating system, the computer runs very slowly when you try to open files. You check Windows Explorer and find that the space on the hard disks is nearly 50 percent free. You check the Recycle Bin and find about 150 files

there. You try to open several files, but the system performance doesn't change, and you don't get any errors indicating that any of the files are corrupted. Which of the following utilities will you use to resolve the file access problem?

A. ScanDisk

B. Norton AntiVirus

C. Disk Defragmenter

D. CHKDSK

14. After you've defragmented the hard disk drive, you notice that the power supply fan isn't working. There's a lot of dust on it. You clean the fan using a vacuum cleaner, but the fan still doesn't move. What should you do with the power supply?

A. Replace the power supply unit.

B. Replace the faulty fan with a new fan.

C. Open the power supply, and check the voltage on fan connections.

D. Disconnect the fan because the room is air-conditioned.

15. The customer has a lot of empty toner cartridges stored in one corner of the room. He wants to know what he should do with these cartridges because they're now useless to him. What should be your advice?

A. Throw them in the garbage.

B. Buy toner powder, and refill them himself.

C. Sell them to a refilling company.

D. Any of the above.

16. The customer wants to know what type of fire extinguisher he should install in his computer room. Which of the following types of fire extinguishers would you suggest, considering that the customer is interested in a multipurpose product that would extinguish not only an electrical fire but would also be suitable to extinguish a paper or wood fire?

A. Class A

B. Class B

C. Class C

D. Class ABC

17. You've just purchased a new UPS and want to connect it to your computer
     server. Which of the following devices would you need to connect to the UPS
     to operate the system if maximum battery life is a primary concern?

     A. Laser printer

     B. Monitor

     C. Keyboard

     D. Electrically amplified speakers

QUICK ANSWER KEY

1.	D	10.	D
2.	A	11.	A
3.	A	12.	D
4.	A	13.	C
5.	A	14.	A
6.	D	15.	C
7.	A	16.	D
8.	C	17.	B
9.	B		

IN-DEPTH ANSWERS

1. ☑ **D.** You should never clean any circuit card with soapy water. If you must clean a circuit card, use a vacuum cleaner, air, and approved contact cleaner. Water can cause internal shorts and ruin components.

   ☒ **A**, **B**, and **C** are incorrect. The mouse ball, keyboard, and CRT display of the monitor can be cleaned using a damp soapy cotton cloth. Care must be taken that water isn't dripping from them and they're absolutely dry. Always make sure that all electrical connections are unplugged before servicing any device such as a monitor.

2. ☑ **A.** The most important thing you must do before trying a new utility on your system is to secure the existing data by making a backup. Although chances are rare that any commercially available utility will damage your hard disk, it's always better to take the precaution of protecting your data. The question states that you want to download a utility and run it on your hard disk. The first thing you actually should do is read the documentation of the utility that should be available on the web site. (This should have been your answer, if it were one of the options.) Then if you decide to download the utility and try it on your hard disk, you must make a backup of your data first.

   ☒ **B** is incorrect because this doesn't protect your data. **C** is incorrect because this action doesn't make any difference. **D** is incorrect because it isn't necessary to set file-level permissions to clean up a disk.

3. ☑ **A.** Canned air is the best solution for cleaning the dust out of a computer of the choices given. This air is contaminant free and relatively inexpensive. Residual dust can be vacuumed or blown out of the system. Pay special attention to all fans because dust buildup can cause premature failure of fan motors because of heat retention.

   ☒ **B** is incorrect because you shouldn't use a lint-free towel in a computer. These towels may contain a static charge that could cause ESD damage to components. **C** is incorrect because isopropyl alcohol isn't suitable for cleaning residue. **D** is incorrect because you can't remove the residue on metallic parts with soapy water and a damp cloth.

4. ☑ **A.** You should use a vacuum or compressed air to clean the internal components of a PC. You can also use compressed air to get to places that the vacuum can't reach. You should never use water to clean the internal components of a computer system.

    ☒ **B, C,** and **D** are incorrect. Using any of these methods runs the risk of damaging internal components on the motherboard and circuit cards.

5. ☑ **A.** Hard drives are sealed units, and there's no such device as a hard disk cleaning disk.

    ☒ **B, C,** and **D** are incorrect. These are the tools you'd use to provide maintenance and protection to a hard drive. Defragment hard disks regularly, use ScanDisk for corrupted files, and use virus scanning software. Fragmentation causes hard disks to lose read and write performance. Defragmentation helps by rearranging data in contiguous clusters on the hard disk, thus improving disk access. ScanDisk fixes problems related to corrupted files. Virus scanners are helpful in saving the hard disk from fatal virus programs that might cause loss of system or data files.

6. ☑ **D.** If the floppy drive is working well and hasn't shown any problems, you shouldn't clean it. Cleaning drives reduces the life of read-write heads and must be avoided if you don't have any problem reading or writing to floppy disks. When you actually need to clean the floppy drive heads, you should use a head cleaning disk.

    ☒ **A** is incorrect because you must not use compressed air to clean floppy drives. **B** is incorrect because you don't need to clean a floppy drive when it's working fine. **C** is incorrect because this requires you to dismantle the disk drive, open the disk covers, and expose the read-write heads. This method should never be used for cleaning floppy drives. You must first decide whether the drive needs cleaning. If required, the only correct method is to use a head cleaner disk. Note that this question requires careful reading to determine whether to clean the drive.

7. ☑ **A.** It takes a static charge of only about 30 volts to destroy a computer component. This is known as *hidden* ESD, an amount of ESD that can neither be felt nor be seen but is still present in and around the working area. Whenever you work on computer components such as the motherboard, adapters, and memory chips, you should be careful about static discharge from

your body. As a matter or practice, you should wear antistatic wrist straps while working on these parts.

☒   **B** is incorrect because it requires only about 30 volts of charge to damage semiconductor chips. Most static discharges are nearly 1,000 volts, which is highly damaging for computer components. **C** is incorrect because this much static discharge can cause heavy damage to static sensitive devices. **D** is incorrect because this charge is so high that it can produce an electric spark.

8.   ☑   **C.** The acceptable level of relative humidity in a room that houses computers and associated equipment, such as scanners and printers, is between 50 and 80 percent. A humidity level less than 50 percent is considered extremely dry, and a level of more than 80 percent is extremely humid. Both of these conditions cause ESD buildup in the room and aren't suitable for the normal functioning of computers.

☒   **A** is incorrect because 20 percent humidity indicates extremely dry conditions that cause ESD buildup. **B** is incorrect because although computers can work well if the humidity remains between these limits, these aren't the suggested limits of acceptable humidity. **D** is incorrect because 95 percent humidity indicates an extremely humid room that isn't suitable for the normal functioning of computers.

9.   ☑   **B.** The best option you have in this situation is to contact the manufacturer about disposal methods. The manufacturer will be able to provide you a Material Safety Data Sheet (MSDS) that'll explain the risks in working with the chemical and disposal procedures. If you aren't able to contact the manufacturer, search the Internet for information about WHMIS hazardous materials handling and disposal for the chemicals listed.

☒   **A** is incorrect because hazardous chemicals shouldn't be thrown in the garbage. They're harmful to the environment and can cause injuries to anyone encountering them. **C** is incorrect because you shouldn't recycle the bottle until you know the contents and whether it's safe to do so. **D** is incorrect because the EPA will most likely refer you to the manufacturer.

10.   ☑   **D.** The best advice to your friend would be to ask him to check the manufacturer's documentation about how to store the UPS for long periods. Although it's a good idea to keep the UPS online so that the battery remains charged, it might not be suitable for every customer.

☒ **A** is incorrect because it can be hazardous to discharge a battery and store it. Batteries should always be stored in a charged state. **B** is incorrect because this action will result in discharge of the battery after some time. **C** is incorrect because in certain situations it may not be possible to do so. A battery of this size presents a hazard because even though it's usually low voltage, it has a high current rating.

11. ☑ **A.** A high-voltage transformer near a computer or your work area can cause electromagnetic interference (EMI) in your computer. EMI can cause operational difficulties when in close proximity to sensitive electronic equipment.

☒ **B** is incorrect because the high-voltage transformer won't be a source of ESD. **C** is incorrect because if a transformer is installed properly, there will be no wires or wiring that will be accessible and hazardous. **D** is incorrect because high-voltage equipment won't create an electromagnetic field and won't generate magnetic fields.

12. ☑ **D.** The incorrect equipment in the list is the Constant Voltage Transformer (CVT). The CVT doesn't provide backup power when the power fails. It's used only to maintain a constant AC voltage output when the AC voltage varies.

☒ **A** is incorrect because a noise filter can be used to prevent EMI or noise in power lines. **B** is incorrect because a surge suppressor is capable of containing sudden increases and decreases in input AC voltage. **C** is incorrect because a UPS is capable of handling several power problems such as surges, spikes, and EMI, as well as providing backup power in case of a power failure.

13. ☑ **C.** If you read the question carefully, you'll see the cause of the slow hard disk access. The hard disks are nearly 50 percent empty, but the Recycle Bin has a large number of files in it, indicating that the customer is deleting files frequently. Therefore, the likely cause of the problem is that the hard disk is fragmented. Running Disk Defragmenter will help improve disk access performance.

☒ **A** is incorrect because ScanDisk will only check for corrupt files and lost links in the file allocation table (FAT), and the question states that there are no corrupted files. **B** is incorrect because there's no mention of any kind of virus. The problem is related only to slow performance of the hard disks when files are opened. **D** is incorrect because CHKDSK will check the hard disks for errors but won't defragment them to improve performance.

14. ☑ **A.** Replace the power supply unit. When you have any problems with the power supply unit of a computer, especially at a customer's site, the best course of action is to replace the unit itself. The power supply unit has high voltages inside the case, and it must not be opened to repair the fan or any other component.

☒ **B** is incorrect because the power supply unit should be replaced. You must not attempt to replace the fan. **C** is incorrect because the power supply case must not be opened, especially at a customer's site. **D** is incorrect because even if the room is air-conditioned, the fan in the power supply is required to supply cool air from outside the computer to the internal components to prevent them from heating up.

15. ☑ **C.** The best way to deal with empty toner cartridges is to sell them to a company that can refill them. Toner cartridges are sold in large quantities, and there are several companies that buy old cartridges, refill them, and sell them again. Even if you don't buy the refilled toner cartridges, getting them refilled is an option that prevents waste.

☒ **A** is incorrect because toner cartridges can be refilled and reused. It's important, however, that this job be done either after proper training or by experienced people. **B** is incorrect because refilling toner cartridges requires specialized training, so not everyone should attempt it. Toner powder can spill on clothes, the printer, and all over the floor if not handled carefully. **D** is incorrect because the toner cartridges should be sold to a company that refills them.

16. ☑ **D.** A class ABC fire extinguisher is useful for all types of fires, such as paper and wood (class A), flammable liquids (class B), and electrical fires caused by short circuits (class C). The class ABC fire extinguisher contains dry chemical powder that not only extinguishes the fire but also helps to reduce temperatures.

☒ **A** is incorrect because this type of fire extinguisher isn't suitable for electrical fires. **B** is incorrect because a class B fire extinguisher is suitable for flammable liquids but not for electrical fires. **C** is incorrect because class C fire extinguishers aren't suitable to put out fires caused by paper and wood. If the customer wants a multipurpose product, he should install a class ABC fire extinguisher.

17. ☑ **B.** You would want to have the monitor connected to the UPS to monitor system status if needed during a power failure. You can turn the monitor off during a power failure to prolong the life of the UPS battery.

☒ **A** and **D** are incorrect because you don't need the printer or speakers in a power failure, and they would consume power unnecessarily. **C** is incorrect because keyboards receive their power from the system.

CORE HARDWARE/OPERATING SYSTEM EXAMS

4

Motherboards, Processors, and Memory

TEST YOURSELF OBJECTIVES

Y ou have a wide variety of options for CPUs, memory, and motherboards. This chapter tests your knowledge on the types of options that you'll encounter on the A+ exam. Virtually all of the motherboards you'll encounter also provide a great deal of configuration options to support different operating systems, peripherals, and performance settings. These options are configured and saved in the CMOS of the motherboard.

QUESTIONS

1. One of your friends has a computer system that he wants to upgrade. His system is based on a Pentium III processor and has 128MB of RAM. He wants to upgrade this machine to a Pentium 4 processor with 256MB of RAM. What advice can you give him about this situation?

   A. The memory can be upgraded, but the processor can't be.

   B. The processor and memory can be upgraded.

   C. The processor can be upgraded, but the memory can't be.

   D. Neither the memory nor the processor can be upgraded.

2. The following illustration represents the System Properties dialog box of a computer running Windows 98.

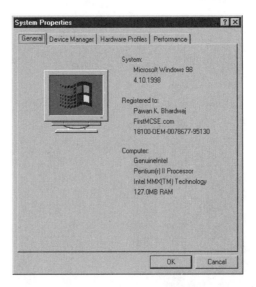

Which of the following is a correct statement regarding the type of processor used in the computer?

A. This is an Intel Pentium MMX processor.

B. This is an Intel Pentium II processor with a 127MB level 2 cache.

C. This is an Intel Pentium II processor with MMX technology.

D. This is an Intel Pentium II clone with MMX technology.

3. What's the maximum L2 cache size on a Pentium 4 processor?

A. 128KB

B. 256KB

C. 512KB

D. 1024KB

4. Which processor uses the PGA 2 socket?

A. Pentium II

B. Pentium III

C. Pentium 4

D. None of the above

5. RAM comes in mainly two forms: static RAM (SRAM) and dynamic RAM (DRAM). Which of the following statements is incorrect regarding these two types of memory?

A. SRAM is commonly used in computers for cache memory.

B. SRAM is faster than DRAM because of its faster access time.

C. Both SRAM and DRAM are used as main memory in the computer.

D. EDO RAM, SDRAM, and VRAM are types of DRAM.

6. Which of the following is a characteristic of DRAM?

A. Small storage capacity

B. Requires periodic refreshing

C. Retains memory when power is turned off

D. Doesn't require refreshing

7. Which type of memory is a special type of memory used for video cards?

   A. SDRAM

   B. Rambus

   C. SoDIMM

   D. VRAM

8. Which of the following statements is correct concerning the parity used by memory in a computer?

   A. Odd parity is used to ensure that the number of 1s in the data stream isn't odd.

   B. Even parity is used to ensure that the number of 0s in the data stream is always even.

   C. Parity is used for error checking, and even and odd parity add 0 and 1, respectively, to the number of 1s in the data stream.

   D. Parity is used for error checking, and odd parity adds 1 to the number of 1s in the data stream if the number of 1s is even.

9. Which of the following statements is a significant advantage of DDR memory?

   A. DDR works at twice the data rate of conventional SDRAM.

   B. DDR uses less power than conventional SDRAM.

   C. DDR has higher storage density than conventional SDRAM.

   D. DDR has no significant advantages over conventional SDRAM.

10. The computer you're using has only a 32-bit Extended Industry Standard Architecture (EISA) input/output (I/O) bus standard. Which of the following types of adapters can't be used in this computer?

    A. 8-bit ISA

    B. 16-bit ISA

    C. 32-bit PCI

    D. 32-bit EISA

11. What is the level 1 cache size of a Pentium 4?

    A. 4KB

    B. 8KB

    C. 16KB

    D. 32KB

12. You're replacing the Baby AT motherboard on an older system. This system has two power connectors labeled P8 and P9. How are the power connectors installed?

    A. Black wires face each other when installed.

    B. Black wires face out when installed.

    C. Red wires face out when installed.

    D. One black wire is in the center, and one is on the end.

13. Which of the following isn't a characteristic of an ATX motherboard?

    A. Communications and I/O connections are integrated on the motherboard.

    B. USB support is included.

    C. It uses a header connection for serial and parallel connections.

    D. It uses a single power supply connection.

14. Which of the following processors includes integrated level 3 cache?

    A. Pentium II

    B. Pentium III

    C. Pentium 4

    D. None of the above

15. What is the data width of the PCI interface?

    A. 8-bit

    B. 16-bit

    C. 32-bit

    D. 64-bit

16. The user wants you to change some of the power management features of the computer. Which of the following should you perform first before configuring the power management settings of the computer?

    A. Set the Frequency/Voltage Control setting.

    B. Check the PC Health Status setting.

C. Note the current settings.

D. Load the optimized defaults.

17. The user has called you about adding a second hard drive in his computer. He got this hard disk from his friend who had recently upgraded his computer with a new larger capacity hard disk. You aren't able to get any information about the number of heads, sectors, or tracks, except that the hard disk has a 30GB capacity. The label on the hard disk isn't readable. Considering that you have to enter the hard disk type in the CMOS settings manually, which of the following settings should you select?

A. Auto Detect

B. Auto Head Detect

C. Auto Sector/Track Detect

D. User Type

18. The current boot sequence of the computer is A:, C:. The user doesn't use the floppy drive frequently, but he wants to keep the drive for emergencies. On the other hand, he doesn't want the system to seek the floppy drive on startup. What will happen if you change the boot sequence from A:, C: to C:, A:?

A. The BIOS will first search the C: drive for the operating system and then the A: drive.

B. The BIOS will always load the operating system from the C: drive.

C. The BIOS will never seek the A: drive for loading the operating system.

D. The BIOS will attempt three times to load the operating system from the C: drive and then seek the A: drive.

19. The user wants you to check the printing quality of the inkjet printer. When you send a page from the word processing program for printing, you notice that the printer software gives an indication of the ink in the print cartridge. In which of the following modes is the parallel port of the computer working? Select all correct answers.

A. ECP mode

B. EPP mode

C. Transfer mode

D. PCL mode

20. The user tells you he stores his important files in this computer. He wants you to set passwords in the system so that no one is able to boot the system without his knowledge. Which of the following methods is most secure for this requirement?

    A. Logon password in Windows 98

    B. Supervisor password in the CMOS settings

    C. User password in the CMOS settings

    D. None of the above

21. What's the ability of a PCI card to take control of the bus and make transfers directly to another PCI card called?

    A. Bus control

    B. Bus mastering

    C. Overclocking

    D. Bus I/O control

22. Which of the following is a characteristic of EDO RAM?

    A. Faster than standard DRAM

    B. Low speed access

    C. Low storage capacity

    D. None of the above

23. Which interface is most commonly used in newer PC systems?

    A. Ultra ATA/100

    B. Ultra ATA/66

    C. Serial ATA

    D. Ultra DMA

24. Which memory package uses 30 pins for connection to the motherboard?

    A. SIMM

    B. DIMM

    C. SoDIMM

    D. RIMM

25. Which memory module is used for subnotebook computers?

    A. SIPP

    B. SIMM

    C. DIMM

    D. MicroDIMM

26. You want to install an AGP 8× video adapter into a system that has a 2× AGP video adapter installed. Which of the following should be checked first?

    A. Verify that the 2× adapter slot can provide the proper voltage.

    B. The pin configurations aren't compatible with earlier versions of AGP.

    C. This will work properly.

    D. The 8× card will only work at the 2× speed.

27. You want to add an older USB 1.1 device to your USB 2.0 hub. How will this impact your system?

    A. The entire USB system will operate at the speed of the slowest USB device.

    B. The entire USB system will operate at its normal speed except the slower USB device.

    C. USB 1.1 devices aren't compatible with USB 2.0 devices.

    D. The USB 1.1 device will operate at the speed of the USB 2.0 hub.

28. What's the purpose of an AMR slot?

    A. To provide an interface between the computer and the phone line

    B. To provide a connection for the computer, audio devices, and the phone line

    C. To provide network and modem connections

    D. None of the above

29. What's the purpose of a CNR slot?

    A. To provide network interfaces

    B. To provide audio interfaces

    C. To provide modem interfaces

    D. All of the above

30. An employee has recently been terminated at your organization. The PC prompts for a password shortly after the power is turned on. You've been unable to guess this password and the ex-employee won't tell you. What should you do to correct this problem?

    A. Inform the employee that he's required to tell you the password.

    B. Replace the motherboard.

    C. Remove the CMOS battery, and reinstall it after a short period.

    D. Call the manufacturer of the motherboard to get the unlock password.

QUICK ANSWER KEY

1.	A	16.	C
2.	C	17.	A
3.	C	18.	A
4.	C	19.	A
5.	C	20.	C
6.	B	21.	B
7.	D	22.	A
8.	D	23.	A
9.	A	24.	A
10.	C	25.	D
11.	B	26.	B
12.	A	27.	B
13.	C	28.	A
14.	D	29.	D
15.	C	30.	C

IN-DEPTH ANSWERS

1. ☑   **A.** The Pentium III and Pentium 4 processors aren't interchangeable. If the motherboard is intended for a Pentium III, it most likely uses an SEC socket for the processor. The Pentium 4 uses a PGA-type socket. The memory can be upgraded depending on the available memory slots on the motherboard.

    ☒   **B** is incorrect because the processor can't be upgraded. **C** is incorrect because the processors aren't interchangeable and the memory is. **D** is incorrect because you can upgrade the memory on most motherboards by adding additional or larger memory modules.

2. ☑   **C.** This is an Intel Pentium II processor with MMX technology. The System Properties dialog box in Windows 98 shows the type of processor being used in the computer. In the given figure, the information displayed about the processor indicates that it's a genuine Intel Pentium II processor. Intel MMX technology indicates that the processor has built-in extensions to support multimedia. All Intel Pentium processors released after the Pentium MMX support the MMX technology. The speed of the processor isn't indicated in this dialog box.

    ☒   **A** is incorrect because the first Intel processor with MMX technology was named *Intel Pentium MMX*. All later processors, including the Pentium II shown in the dialog box, include MMX capabilities. Intel Pentium II and Intel Pentium MMX are two different types of processors. **B** is incorrect because 127MB is the amount of RAM in the system and isn't indicative of the level 2 cache on the processor. **D** is incorrect because the processor is a genuine Intel processor and not a *clone* of Intel Pentium II.

3. ☑   **C.** The Pentium 4 has a maximum L2 cache size of 512KB.

    ☒   **A** is incorrect because the smallest cache size on a Pentium 4 is 256KB. **B** is incorrect because 256KB is a normal L2 cache size for Pentium 4 processors but it is not the maximum supported on the processor. **D** is incorrect because the Pentium 4 does not support a 1024KB cache size.

4. ☑ **C.** Pentium 4 processors are the only processors of the choices given that use the PGA 2 socket.

☒ **A** is incorrect because Pentium II processors use the Slot 1 socket. **B** is incorrect because Pentium III processors use the SECC package. **D** is incorrect because the Pentium 4 uses the PGA 2 socket.

5. ☑ **C.** This statement is incorrect because only DRAM is used as main memory in the computer. Main memory refers to the RAM, and several variants of DRAM are used as main memory or RAM in computers. SRAM, on the other hand, is faster but expensive and is used only as system cache memory.

☒ **A** is an incorrect answer because this statement is true. SRAM is used as system cache. **B** is incorrect because the statement is true. SRAM has a faster access time of approximately 10 nanoseconds (ns). **D** is incorrect because it's true that the given types of RAM are all types of DRAM.

6. ☑ **B.** DRAM requires periodic refreshing to retain memory contents.

☒ **A** is incorrect because DRAM chip storage capacity is large when compared to SDRAM chip storage capacity. **C** is incorrect because, like SRAM, if the power is removed, the contents of memory are lost. The only type of memory that retains its contents is ROM. **D** is incorrect because DRAM chips require periodic refreshing to retain data.

7. ☑ **D.** VRAM is a special type of memory that's optimized primarily for video card applications. VRAM is dual ported and provides the capability receiving data while simultaneously writing data to the video port.

☒ **A** is incorrect because SDRAM is used primarily for video, memory cards, and system memory. **B** is incorrect because Rambus is a memory architecture that's licensed by Rambus Technologies. Rambus memory is a very fast type of DRAM. **C** is incorrect because Small Outline DIMM or SoDIMM is a fast memory that's becoming popular in applications where space is a premium.

8. ☑ **D.** Parity is used by RAM for error checking, and odd parity checks the number of 1s in the data stream and adds 1 if the number of 1s is even. When even parity is used, the number of 1s in the data stream is counted, and 1 is added if the number is odd. This is a question with very confusing options. You must be careful while answering this type of question.

☒   **A** is incorrect because parity is used for error *checking* rather than for *ensuring* that the number of 1s in the data stream remains odd or even. In odd parity, the number of 1s in the data stream should remain 1, and if it doesn't, 1 is added as a parity bit. **B** is incorrect because only 1s are counted for calculating parity, not 0s. **C** is incorrect because the parity bit is either 1 or 0, and it's incorrect to say that both even and odd parity add 0 and 1, respectively, to the data stream.

9.   ☑   **A.** DDR is twice the speed of conventional SDRAM. This is because DDR uses both the positive and negative transitions of the system clock to load and transfer data.

☒   **B, C,** and **D** are incorrect because none of these are an advantage.

10.   ☑   **C.** A computer that has only a 32-bit EISA I/O bus standard supports only 8-bit ISA, 16-bit ISA, and 32-bit EISA adapters. Further, 32-bit PCI adapters need a 32-bit PCI I/O bus architecture on the motherboard and use smaller white-colored PCI slots. A PCI card can't be inserted into an ISA or EISA expansion slot.

☒   **A, B,** and **D** are incorrect because the 32-bit EISA I/O bus supports 8-bit ISA, 16-bit ISA, and 32-bit EISA adapters. The EISA expansion slots can be used to install any of the three types of adapters.

11.   ☑   **B.** The level 1 cache size on a Pentium 4 is 8KB.

☒   **A, C,** and **D** are incorrect because the level 1 cache size is 8KB on a Pentium 4.

12.   ☑   **A.** The Baby AT and AT motherboards used a two-connector power-supply connection. These connectors weren't keyed and could be reversed. Installing these connectors backward can damage the motherboard. If you're working with this type of motherboard, always make sure the black wires face the middle.

☒   **B, C,** and **D** are all incorrect because the black wires always face the middle.

13.   ☑   **C.** The ATX motherboard greatly simplified the installation process. All of the connectors are attached to the motherboard and don't require separate headers or cables like older motherboards. ATX motherboards also provide USB support and use a single power-supply connection.

    ☒ **A, B,** and **D** are incorrect because they're characteristics of an ATX motherboard.

14. ☑ **D.** None of the above. These processors don't include level 3 caching integrated in the processor. Some of the newest processors such as the Intel Xeon processor MP include level 3 caching on the processor. This will become more common with newer generations of processors.

    ☒ **A, B,** and **C** are incorrect because they don't include level 3 caching.

15. ☑ **C.** The PCI bus connector has a 32-bit width. The system bus of newer systems is 64-bit, and to accomplish this translation, the PCI bus requires two data transfer operations to move the entire 64-bit data from the system bus to a PCI device.

    ☒ **A, B,** and **D** are incorrect. The PCI bus connector has a 32-bit data width.

16. ☑ **C.** Before you start changing CMOS settings, it's always good practice to record the current settings. Some motherboards have extensive configuration options, and setting configuration options improperly may cause improper operation of the system. By recording the settings, you're assured of your ability to restore operations of the machine quickly.

    ☒ **A** is incorrect because you wouldn't be changing the frequency or voltage settings of the CMOS unless you're changing the processor on a motherboard. **B** is incorrect because the PC Health Status setting is a feature provided on many motherboards to allow status checking of the system. This allows for diagnosis of some hardware problems without opening the case. **D** is incorrect because you wouldn't want to load the default settings unless you needed to erase existing settings and you needed a place to start configuring the CMOS again.

17. ☑ **A.** If you aren't sure about the type of hard disk, you should select Auto Detect or Auto in the CMOS settings. This enables the BIOS to detect the number of heads, sectors, and tracks automatically. All of the BIOS software manufacturers have this Auto Detect functionality for hard disks.

    ☒ **B** and **C** are incorrect because neither the Auto Head Detect nor the Auto Sector/Track Detect option exists in any BIOS software. These functions are performed by the hard disk Auto Detect feature and aren't available individually. **D** is incorrect because if you're not sure about the number of heads and sectors in the hard disk, you won't be able to configure it correctly. The User Type setting was required in older computers.

18.   ☑   **A.** The BIOS will first search the C: drive for the operating system and then the A: drive. You must be careful about simple questions in the A+ exam that might try to confuse you with the answer options; this is one such question. The boot sequence just tells the BIOS the preferred order of drives for seeking and loading the operating system. If the boot sequence of the computer is changed from A:, C: to C:, A:, then this means the BIOS will seek the C: drive first for locating the operating system, and if it doesn't find it there, it'll search the floppy drive A:.

☒   **B** is incorrect because the BIOS will always *first* attempt to load the operating system from the C: drive. **C** is incorrect because the BIOS will first attempt to load the operating system from the C: drive and then seek the floppy drive if it isn't able to find the operating system on the C: drive. **D** is incorrect because the BIOS will make only one attempt to load the operating system on the C: drive before looking for it on the A: drive.

19.   ☑   **A.** The Enhanced Capability Port (ECP) mode of the parallel ports in a computer allows data to travel in both directions: from computer to printer and from printer to computer. Because the printer is sending the status of ink in the cartridge, data is traveling from the printer to the computer in addition to the print data that's flowing from the computer to the printer.

☒   **B** is incorrect because the Enhanced Parallel Port (EPP) mode is used for devices other than printers and scanners. **C** is incorrect because the transfer mode is a unidirectional mode in which data travels only from the computer to the printer through the parallel port. **D** is incorrect because PCL isn't a printer mode; it's a printer command language. Printer Control Language allows for numerous printing capabilities to exist in modern Hewlett-Packard (HP) and HP-compatible printers.

20.   ☑   **C.** The User password in the CMOS settings ensures that no one except the intended user of the computer who knows the correct password is able to boot the computer. When a user enters an incorrect password, the boot sequence doesn't complete, and the system doesn't load the operating system.

☒   **A** is incorrect because this password doesn't stop the system from booting. The Windows 98 password works only after the system has loaded the operating system. This password isn't secure and won't meet the requirements of the user. **B** is incorrect because this password is meant to secure the CMOS settings only.

Any user who doesn't know the supervisor password can't alter the CMOS settings. This password doesn't prevent any unintended user from booting the system. **D** is incorrect because one correct answer does exist in the given options.

21. ☑ **B.** *Bus mastering* is the capability of a device to take control of the bus to perform direct transfers to other devices. Bus mastering frees the processor from managing these types of tasks.

☒ **A** is incorrect because *bus control* refers to how a bus is controlled and is determined by the design of the bus. **C** is incorrect because *overclocking* is the process of operating a processor at a speed higher than its intended rating. **D** is incorrect because *bus I/O control* is one of the functions of bus mastering, but it isn't bus mastering.

22. ☑ **A.** EDO RAM is anywhere from 5 to 20 percent faster than standard DRAM. This is because EDO RAM allows for a second memory operation to begin before the first one has completed. EDO RAM is popular as main memory and is used in lower-end video cards.

☒ **B** is incorrect because EDO RAM is faster than standard DRAM. **C** is incorrect because EDO RAM storage capacities are the same as DRAM. **D** is incorrect because the correct answer is A.

23. ☑ **A.** Ultra ATA/100 is the most common disk interface used in newer PC systems. It's being replaced by Serial ATA. Ultra ATA is a parallel transfer standard that has bandwidth limits of approximately 100 MBps. Serial ATA transfer speeds start at 150 MBps and are expected to increase significantly over the next few years.

☒ **B** is incorrect. Ultra ATA/66 is an older standard that had a transfer rate of approximately 66 MBps. **C** is incorrect currently. Serial ATA is expected by many industry analysts to become the replacement standard for Ultra ATA/100. **D** is incorrect. Ultra DMA are data access modes that are supported by the ATA standards.

24. ☑ **A.** SIMM memory packages are either 30 or 72 pin. The 30-pin modules are used in old systems and were replaced by 72-pin modules in later generation systems. SIMM modules have been largely replaced by DIMM packages in PC systems.

☒ **B** is incorrect because DIMM modules are 168-pin memory modules. DIMM and SIMM modules aren't interchangeable. **C** is incorrect because SoDIMM stands for Small Outline DIMM modules and is used in PC and PDA systems. This memory uses 144 pins and is considerably smaller than DIMM or SIMM modules. **D** is incorrect because RIMM is a proprietary memory architecture designed by Rambus.

25. ☑ **D.** MicroDIMM is a small memory package intended for subnotebook and similar devices. MicroDIMM is very small and is about 50 percent smaller than SoDIMM packaging.

☒ **A** is incorrect because SIPP is a type of memory package that was used many years ago and had wire pins that were inserted into the memory slot. **B** is incorrect because SIMM memory is large and unsuitable for smaller system applications. **C** is incorrect because DIMM, although smaller than SIMM modules, is still considerably larger than MicroDIMM or SoDIMM packages.

26. ☑ **B.** The 8× AGP standard uses a different connector width than earlier AGP standards. AGP 8× is also referred to as the AGP Pro standard. This standard is for high-end graphics applications and isn't yet commonly used.

☒ **A, C,** and **D** are incorrect and not relevant given the differences in connector sizes between the 2× and 8× AGP standards.

27. ☑ **B.** USB 2.0 accepts USB 1.1 devices, and the connection between the USB 2.0 device and USB 1.1 device will operate at the speed of the USB 1.1 device. All other devices will operate normally.

☒ **A, C,** and **D** are incorrect because connection speeds are negotiated when the device is connected and installed. These connection speeds are independent of each other and based strictly on the capabilities of the devices involved.

28. ☑ **A.** The Audio Modem Riser (AMR) provides a connection between the computer and the phone line. The AMR has no processing power and relies on the computer and operating system to provide processing capabilities. The AMR allows for changing standards to be rapidly configured for modem communications. The downside is that an AMR connection can consume 20 percent or more of the CPU resources for communications when compared to a hardware modem.

   ☒ **B** is incorrect because the AMR doesn't provide output for audio devices such as speakers. **C** is incorrect because the AMR doesn't provide network connections. **D** is incorrect.

29. ☑ **D.** The Communications and Network Riser (CNR) is designed to provide audio, network, and modem interfaces. This allows manufacturers to not provide dedicated circuitry to accomplish these tasks. The CPU provides processing for these functions, and the operating system provides the drivers. This allows for flexibility in operation at the expense of CPU performance.

   ☒ **A, B,** and **C** are partially correct.

30. ☑ **C.** You should remove the CMOS battery from the motherboard, wait ten minutes, and then reinstall it. This will restore the CMOS to the default settings and erase the password.

   ☒ Ordering an ex-employee to give you the password is probably pointless. **A** is incorrect because the ex-employee is under no obligation to tell you. **B** is incorrect because you don't need to replace the motherboard to merely reset the CMOS. **D** is incorrect because unless it's a deeply held secret by all motherboard manufacturers, there's no unlock password.

5

Printers

TEST YOURSELF OBJECTIVES

5.01   Printer Technologies, Interfaces, and Options

5.02   Common Printer Problems

T he various types of computer printers differ in their printing mechanisms, cost, and print quality. Dot-matrix printers use a mixture of pins and ink ribbon to form a character on the paper. They're the least expensive and offer the lowest print quality. Inkjet, DeskJet, and bubblejet printers are nonimpact printers that use ink cartridges, produce better print quality than dot-matrix printers, and can print in color. Laser printers, on the other hand, are very fast—they can print a full page at a time. Laser printers use toner cartridges instead of ink, give the best print quality for black and white, and are the most expensive.

Whatever type of printer is being used, it's important that proper preventive maintenance procedures be followed to avoid problems. Regularly cleaning printers and replacing ribbons, ink cartridges, and toner cartridges not only maintains printing quality at its best but also prevents several printing problems. The most common printer problems are caused by dust, humidity, and poor paper quality. Laser printers are difficult to service, and to resolve a particular problem, you must know the function of each part involved in the printing process.

QUESTIONS

1. Which of the following is used for making an impact on paper in dot-matrix printers and also enables them to create multiple carbon copies?

   A. Rotating daisy wheel

   B. Ink cartridge

   C. Toner powder

   D. Pin-based printers

2. One of your friends is seeking your advice on the types of printers available in the market and how each type of printer would meet his requirements. Which of the following would you suggest as a nonimpact printer that's capable of printing acceptable color prints and isn't very expensive?

   A. Dot-matrix printer

   B. Laser printer

C. Inkjet printer

D. Thermal printer

3. Which of the following printers doesn't exclusively use friction feed rollers for movement of paper?

A. Laser printer

B. Inkjet printer

C. DeskJet printer

D. Dot-matrix printer

4. When you install a printer locally to the LPT1 port of your computer, what should be the maximum length of cable when using an IEEE 1284 cable?

A. 6 meters

B. 8 meters

C. 10 meters

D. 25 feet

5. Your client needs to add an additional printer to his PC. He wants high performance for printing and wants to impact his system to the minimal amount possible. This system is relatively new. What printer technology is most appropriate for him?

A. Install a printer with an IR interface.

B. Install a printer with a USB interface.

C. Install a second parallel port for the printer.

D. Install a serial port printer.

6. In laser printers, the image is transferred from the charged drum to paper using a transfer corona wire. What happens immediately after this process?

A. Cleaning the drum

B. Recharging the drum with a high negative voltage

C. Fusing the toner on the paper

D. Writing the image on the photosensitive drum

7. One of the following statements describes some of the steps involved in the laser printing process. Identify the statement that's incorrect.

   A. In the charging phase, the high-voltage power supply charges the photosensitive drum with a high negative voltage.

   B. In the writing phase, the toner is attracted to the charged drum at the places that don't have a high negative charge.

   C. In the transferring phase, the transfer corona wire applies a small positive charge to the paper that attracts the toner from the drum.

   D. In the cleaning phase, the drum is cleaned using a cleaning blade to remove excess toner.

8. Which of the following statements correctly describes the difference between the primary corona wire and the transfer corona wire in a laser printer?

   A. The primary corona wire charges the paper with a positive charge, and the transfer corona wire transfers high negative voltage to the drum.

   B. The primary corona wire charges the drum with a high positive voltage, and the transfer corona wire transfers a negative charge onto the paper.

   C. The primary corona wire charges the drum with a high negative voltage, and the transfer corona wire transfers a positive charge onto the paper.

   D. Primary and transfer corona wire are mutually exclusive, and a laser printer can have either of them but not both.

9. You've installed a printer on your Windows XP computer. The office has five Windows 98, three Windows XP, and two Windows 2000 computers in your network. Your boss wants your printer to be available for use by all computer users. NetBEUI is used as the network protocol. See the following illustration for details of this setup.

   You're already sharing folders, and File and Printer Sharing is enabled on the computers. Which of the following is the best way to allow all users access to the printer?

   A. Share the printer from the printer's Properties dialog box.

   B. Install print sharing software on all computers.

   C. Use a six-way printer switch.

   D. Do nothing; the printer will be automatically shared because File and Printer Sharing is enabled.

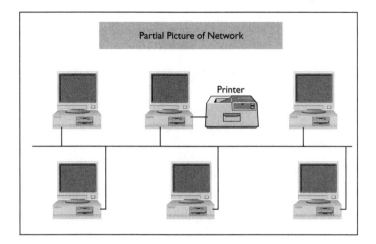

10. Which of the following preventive maintenance procedures will help you keep your dot-matrix printer working well without any expenditure?

    A. Regularly replacing the ribbon cartridge

    B. Regularly cleaning the print head pins

    C. Regularly cleaning the printer parts

    D. Regularly using refilled ribbon cartridges

11. A customer of yours has recently purchased an inkjet printer. He uses his printer only for printing some letters and envelopes. He calls and tells you that the printer has started having frequent paper jams. Which of the following should be your suggestion to the customer to resolve the problem as a first step?

    A. Order a new paper tray.

    B. Try a different type of paper.

    C. Stop printing envelopes.

    D. Replace the paper rollers.

12. The laser printer in your office was purchased two years ago. In recent weeks, this printer has started having several problems. What would be the first step in troubleshooting this problem?

    A. Clean and perform preventive maintenance on the printer per the owner's guide.

    B. Replace the toner cartridge.

    C. Call the manufacturer.

    D. Replace the printer.

13. A laser printer is producing print outputs with a few blotches of toner on one corner of the paper. The printer was cleaned only last week, and you're sure that there's no toner residue inside the printer. Which of the following components of the printer needs replacement?

    A. Drum

    B. Logic board

    C. Cleaning blade

    D. Fuser assembly

14. A laser printer is producing print output that contains the image of previous printing. Which of the following processes do you think is causing the problem?

    A. Fusing

    B. Writing

    C. Cleaning

    D. Developing

Questions 15–17   One of your friends has purchased a secondhand laser printer to replace his bubblejet printer. He needs your help to install this printer on his Windows XP computer. He uses his computer for word processing applications and some graphics design.

The printer he purchased is a black-and-white printer manufactured more than two years ago. He also bought the parallel cable with the printer and the device driver disks that contain printer drivers for Windows 98 and Windows NT 4.

When you arrive at your friend's house, you find that he has already connected the printer to his computer and is trying to print from a word processing program. The following questions describe the various problems you're faced with during your stay at your friend's house. Answer these questions, selecting the best answer for this situation.

15. Your friend is trying to print a page from his word processing program, but the first page doesn't print. The lights of the printer panel flicker a couple of times,

but nothing happens after that. You try to print a test page with the computer, but the printer shows the same symptoms, and nothing prints. You check all connections and find that they're okay. What should you do next to further diagnose the cause of the problem?

A. Replace the printer cable.

B. Check the IRQ assignment of the parallel port.

C. Check the BIOS to see if the parallel port is disabled.

D. Check to see if the correct printer driver is installed.

16. After installing the correct printer driver, you try to print a page from the word processing program, but the paper comes out blank. The printer display on the front panel isn't showing any error message. Which of the following would you rule out as the likely cause of the problem?

A. High-voltage power supply

B. Toner cartridge

C. Primary corona wire

D. Transfer corona wire

17. Once the printer is operational and you're able to print a test page, your friend is happy because you've taken care of all the problems. However, when your friend picks up the printed page from the printer, the toner smears off the page and sticks to his hand. Which of the following parts of the printer should you tell him to replace?

A. Fusing assembly

B. Drum

C. Transfer corona wire

D. High-voltage power supply

18. The output of your laser printer is completely black. You've replaced the toner cartridge, but the problem persists. What's the most likely problem with the printer?

A. Fusing unit malfunction

B. Static discharge malfunction

C. Clogged scavenger bar

D. Defective control unit

19. Your dot-matrix printer is only printing the top half of the characters on each line. Which of the following choices is the likely problem?

A. Defective print head

B. Paper misalignment

C. Platen misalignment

D. Paper-limiting switch malfunction

20. You're printing a report on a dot-matrix printer. The print quality has suddenly become very poor, and you notice fuzz on the paper. What do you need to do to correct this problem?

A. Replace the printer ribbon, and clean the print head.

B. Only replace the printer ribbon.

C. Change to a different type of paper; the bond weight is improper for a dot-matrix printer.

D. Replace the print head because it has malfunctioned.

QUICK ANSWER KEY

1.	D	11.	B
2.	C	12.	A
3.	D	13.	A
4.	C	14.	C
5.	B	15.	D
6.	C	16.	B
7.	B	17.	A
8.	C	18.	D
9.	A	19.	C
10.	C	20.	A

IN-DEPTH ANSWERS

1. ☑ **D.** Dot-matrix printers use metal pins that are activated by a solenoid or spring upon getting signals from the printer main board, also called the *motherboard* or *logic board.* The print head contains the solenoid as well as the pins, which strike the paper through a ribbon. The impact is strong enough to create impressions on multiple carbon copies. For this reason, dot-matrix printers are best suited for accounting applications, such as printing invoices, checks, and account statements.

   ☒ **A** is incorrect because the daisy wheel isn't used in dot-matrix printers. A daisy wheel is a circular-shaped plastic part that prints complete characters, unlike the dot-matrix printer, which uses a matrix of pins to create the shape of the characters. Daisy wheels are used in electronic typewriters and can produce quality text printing. **B** is incorrect because ink cartridges are used in inkjet and bubblejet printers. **C** is incorrect because toner cartridges contain the black powder known as *toner,* which is used in laser printers.

2. ☑ **C.** Inkjet printers are nonimpact printers, are able to produce color prints with an acceptable resolution, and are less expensive than laser printers.

   ☒ **A** is incorrect because this printer falls in the impact printer category and isn't able to produce good-quality color resolution. **B** is incorrect because although these printers are nonimpact printers and provide good resolution, they're the most expensive of the choices. **D** isn't a good choice because thermal printers are most frequently used for point-of-sale devices and don't provide high-quality output.

3. ☑ **D.** The dot-matrix printer doesn't exclusively use friction-feed rollers for moving the paper inside the printer from the paper tray or for moving it out after printing. These printers can use the continuous form-feed or the tractor-feed mechanism for moving the paper in and out of the printer. This method uses two wheels, one on the left and another on the right side of the printer. The wheels have spokes or stubs that fit into the corresponding holes in the continuous roll of paper, and the paper moves when the wheels rotate. The paper is usually perforated to mark the end of the page and can be torn off when a page completes printing.

☒ **A, B,** and **C** are incorrect answers because the laser printer, inkjet printer, and DeskJet printer all use friction-feed rollers for pulling the paper inside the printer from the paper tray and for moving it out when the printing is complete.

4. ☑ **C.** The LPT1 port is a parallel port on the computer. The maximum length of the IEEE 1284 parallel cable connecting the computer's LPT1 port and the printer shouldn't exceed 10 meters. The longer the cable, the more it becomes susceptible to interference that causes printing problems.

☒ **A** and **B** are incorrect because the maximum length of IEEE 1284 parallel cables should be 10 meters. A shorter cable is a better choice, if available. **D** is incorrect because 25 feet is the limit for serial cables.

5. ☑ **B.** Installing a universal serial bus (USB) printer makes the most sense in this configuration. The printer can be connected to the USB port and will operate very efficiently in most applications.

☒ **A** is incorrect because infrared (IR) printers tend to be extremely slow when compared to the other options available. **C** isn't as a good a choice as B. Installing a second parallel port will require opening the computer and installing an additional expansion card. The USB port is already present, and USB printers have become very inexpensive. **D** isn't as good a choice as B because serial printers are becoming harder to find, and they won't operate as quickly as a USB or parallel port printer.

6. ☑ **C.** Immediately after the image is transferred to paper using toner, the paper moves to the fusing assembly in the laser printer. The fusing assembly has heated rollers that melt the toner, which until now is held on the paper with only an electrical charge, and permanently set the toner on the paper.

☒ **A** is incorrect because this is typically the last process in laser printing. When the fusing process finishes, completing the printing process, the drum is cleaned with the help of a cleaning blade to remove excess toner. **B** is incorrect because this is the first process when the laser printer starts printing. **D** is incorrect because the image is *written* to the drum before the developing phase.

7. ☑ **B.** In the writing phase, the toner is attracted to the charged drum at the places that don't have a high negative charge. This step is known as the *developing phase* and not the writing phase, as described here. In the writing phase, the laser beam moves along the drum and creates an image that'll finally appear on the paper. The moving laser beam removes the high negative charge

from selective places on the drum, depending on the signals received from the computer.

☒ **A** is incorrect because the statement is true. The high-voltage power supply charges the drum to nearly –5000 volts (v) direct current (DC). **C** is incorrect because this step is correctly described. During the transfer phase, the image is transferred to the paper, which is positively charged by the transfer corona wire to attract toner from the drum. **D** is an incorrect answer because the statement correctly describes the cleaning step. A cleaning blade removes the excess toner from the drum so that it can be charged again for a new image.

8. ☑ **C.** The primary corona wire charges the drum with a high negative voltage, and the transfer corona wire transfers a positive charge onto the paper. The difference between the primary corona wire and the transfer corona wire is that the former applies a high negative charge of nearly –5000v DC to the drum, and the latter applies a small positive charge to the paper. Whereas the negative charge is used to develop an image on the drum with the help of a laser beam, the positive charge on the paper attracts the toner from the drum. The key to remembering the difference is that the transfer corona wire actually *transfers* the image from the drum to the paper.

☒ **A** is incorrect because the functions of the wires have been interchanged in the statement. The primary corona wire charges the drum with a high negative voltage, and the transfer corona wire charges the paper with small positive voltage. **B** is incorrect because the charges described in the statement have been interchanged. The primary corona wire transfers the high negative charge, and the transfer corona wire administers the positive charge. **D** is incorrect because these wires aren't mutually exclusive. The two corona wires have specific functions in the laser printing process, and all laser printers have both primary and transfer corona wires.

9. ☑ **A.** All local printers can be shared on the network from the Properties dialog box. Click the Start menu, click Control Panel, and then click Printers, which opens the Printers window. Right-click the installed printer, and select Properties. This opens the Properties dialog box of the printer. If File and Printer Sharing is enabled on the computer, a Sharing tab appears in this dialog box. Click this tab, and click Share This Printer to enable printer sharing.

☒ **B** is incorrect because you won't need to install any special software except the printer drivers to enable the computers to use the shared printer. **C** is incorrect because there's no need to install another piece of hardware when the printer can already be shared on the Windows XP operating system. **D** is incorrect because even if File and Printer Sharing is enabled, you have to share the printer from its Properties page.

10. ☑ **C.** Dot-matrix printers are known for repeated problems caused by dirty parts. These printers attract more dust than any other type of printer because of their open print mechanisms, such as the tractor feed and the print heads. It's common practice for users to remove the printer cover and keep it aside when printing. This exposes the printing parts that continuously attract dust, and this dirt collects inside the printer as a result. Furthermore, the special paper used by dot-matrix printers creates and leaves behind a lot of paper particles inside the printer. It's important to regularly clean dot-matrix printers.

☒ **A** is incorrect because although it's good practice to replace ribbon cartridges before they become worn out or run out of ink, this requires spending money. The question asks for the preventive maintenance method that doesn't require expenditure. **B** is incorrect because general cleaning of the dot-matrix printer is more important than cleaning the print head pins. **D** is incorrect because this is against preventive maintenance practices. As far as possible, new ribbons should be used instead of refilled ribbons to maintain high print quality.

11. ☑ **B.** Most paper jam problems are caused by the quality of paper. A possible cause of the paper jam problem in this case is that the customer is using poor quality paper. Changing the paper with another type will help to resolve the problem.

☒ **A** is incorrect because the problem doesn't seem to be caused by the paper tray. **C** is incorrect and unwise advice, and it won't solve the problem. Your job is to resolve the problem and not restrict the customer from using a particular feature of the printer. **D** is incorrect because the paper rollers aren't likely causing the problem. The printer is new and isn't heavily used. The chance of the rollers already being worn out is very unlikely.

12. ☑ **A.** If the printer is two years old, chances are the printer hasn't had preventive maintenance performed on it. Consult the owner's manual and perform the prescribed preventive maintenance. This will probably minimally require vacuuming all accessible areas to remove any paper residue and toner. This will fix many printer problems. If this doesn't fix the problem, the next step would be to replace the toner cartridge in most cases.

☒ **B** is incorrect until the printer has been serviced. Replacing the toner cartridge is a good choice after servicing the printer. **C** is incorrect unless you're unable to resolve the problem following the previous steps. **D** is incorrect because laser printers will last for years if properly serviced and maintained.

13. ☑ **A.** If there's a small nick on the drum, the toner will collect there and then transfer to the paper. Even the cleaning blades don't clean this excessive toner on the damaged part of the drum. Replacing the drum will resolve the problem.

☒ **B** is incorrect because the logic board isn't causing the problem but rather the drum that transfers toner onto the paper is causing it. **C** is incorrect because if the cleaning blade isn't functioning properly, the print output appears like ghosted images. **D** is incorrect because if the fuser assembly doesn't work, the toner doesn't stick to the paper but comes off if you rub your hand on the printed paper.

14. ☑ **C.** It's evident from the problem symptoms that the drum isn't being cleaned properly before it's recharged with a new print image. The drum must be free of any previous image that was charged on it with toner before it gets another image. The leftover toner on the drum from previous images is causing these prints to get mixed up with future prints.

☒ **A** is incorrect because the fusing process is responsible for melting the toner onto the paper once the image has been transferred to paper in the form of toner. **B** is incorrect because this process involves creating a fresh image on the drum. If the leftover toner on the drum from a previous image hasn't been completely cleaned, the new image will contain an impression of the previous image. **D** is incorrect because during the developing process, the toner is applied to the drum in areas that have been *touched* by the laser beam.

15. ☑ **D.** The most likely cause of the problem is that the printer is using the incorrect printer driver. There's a strong possibility of an incorrect printer driver because the user was using a bubblejet printer and most likely didn't install a new printer driver or may have installed an incorrect printer driver for the new printer.

☒ **A** is incorrect because if the printer cable were faulty, there would've been no printer activity at all. **B** is incorrect because the user was printing on a bubblejet printer connected to the same port. **C** is incorrect because the parallel port was in use with the bubblejet printer.

16. ☑ **B.** The blank page could be caused by failure of any of the given components. However, most laser printers give a toner empty or toner low error message when the amount of toner in the cartridge reaches a low level. Although there are several low-end laser printers that don't warn about low toner, printers that have a display usually are high-end laser printers that show an error message when a problem is detected in the printer.

☒ **A, C,** and **D** are incorrect answers because any of these parts could be the cause of the blank page output. If the high-voltage power has failed, the primary corona wire won't be able to charge the photosensitive drum. If the primary corona wire has failed, the drum won't get charged. If the transfer corona wire has failed, the toner won't transfer to the paper from the drum.

17. ☑ **A.** The problem symptoms indicate that the toner isn't being fused or melted properly onto the paper before the paper comes out of the printer. This causes the toner particles to come off the paper when you touch it. Fuser rollers are heated up, and when the paper passes through these rollers, the toner should melt and permanently stick to the paper.

☒ **B** is incorrect because the function of the drum is to create and transfer the image to the paper. The fusing assembly does the final toner conditioning. **C** is incorrect because if the transfer corona wire were defective or broken, there would be no image on the paper at all. **D** is incorrect because the creation of the image and its successful transfer to paper indicate that there's no problem with the high-voltage power supply. The image is created on the drum by charging it with a high voltage of nearly −5000v DC.

18. ☑ **D.** The control unit manages all the functions of the printing process in a laser printer. If the control unit malfunctions, any number of symptoms can occur. Commonly, this error may be caused by a defective toner cartridge. Once you have ruled out the toner cartridge, all that's left is the control unit.

☒ **A** is incorrect because the fusing unit melts the toner onto the paper at the end of the printing process. If the fusing unit had malfunctioned, the toner wouldn't be melted on the paper and you'd have an image on the paper, but it wouldn't be permanent. **B** is incorrect because if the static discharge had malfunctioned, the paper wouldn't have had any printable characters on it because the roller would've retained the ink, and none would have been transferred to the paper. **C** is incorrect because the scavenger bar is intended to scrape any unneeded toner off the printer drum and return it to the toner cartridge for reuse.

19. ☑ **C.** If you're seeing only half a printed character on a page, you should assume that the platen, printer ribbon, or printing surface has become misaligned. Usually you can realign this fairly simply (consult the owner's manual to determine the steps to do this).

☒ **A** is incorrect because when a print head malfunctions, it isn't unusual for the entire head to just stop printing, rendering no meaningful output. **B** is incorrect because a paper misalignment may cause a printing problem but is usually quite evident when you inspect the printer. **D** is incorrect because a paper-limiting switch malfunction might cause your printer to constantly think it's out of paper or has a paper jam, preventing the paper from advancing.

20. ☑ **A.** A sure symptom of a printer ribbon wearing out is fuzz being present on the paper. This fuzz is material being shed from the ribbon. If you replace the ribbon and still observe fuzz on the paper, you probably have a stuck printer pin. Sometimes cleaning the print head will free the print pin. If that doesn't work, you'll need to replace the print head.

☒ **B** is incorrect because replacing the ribbon without cleaning the print head may leave material on the print head and cause it to jam. **C** is incorrect because changing the paper won't prevent printer ribbon deterioration. **D** is incorrect because you don't know if the print head is defective until you change the ribbon and clean the print head.

6

Basic Networking

N etworks are common to most environments now. As an A+ technician, you need to know how to install and configure PC systems for networking. This includes working with the various types of cables, connections, and hardware involved in networking. As an A+ technician, your primary concern is connecting the computer to the network and not supporting the network itself. Nevertheless, having a good understanding of how networks operate will help you to keep your computers connected.

QUESTIONS

1. Which of the following network topologies was used as a backbone extensively, uses coaxial cable, and requires termination at both ends?

    A. Star

    B. Bus

    C. Ring

    D. None of the above

2. Which of the following statements is incorrect concerning the Ethernet Star network in which all the computers are connected to a central hub using twisted-pair cables?

    A. If one of the connected computers goes down, the rest of the network continues to work.

    B. These networks can be expanded without bringing down the network.

    C. The network continues to work even if the hub fails.

    D. Two or more Ethernet networks can be joined in a bus fashion.

3. One of your friends has sought your advice on Ring networks. The following options describe the features of a Ring network. Identify the feature that has been incorrectly listed here.

    A. Difficult to set up and upgrade

    B. Very high signal loss

    C. More prone to failures

    D. Most expensive

4. One of your friends has taken a new job in a small company. This company has eight stand-alone computers. The first task she has been assigned is to connect the computers to make a workgroup. She has sought your help in setting up the network. She's interested in doing this for low cost. Which would you recommend for her?

    A. 100BaseT network

    B. 10BaseT network

    C. 802.5 Token Ring network

    D. 10Base2 network

5. You've been asked to select a suitable networking protocol to implement an Ethernet network in a company that has two departments. The network will have two separate network segments for each of its departments, but selected users in one department should be able to connect to computers in the other department. The selected protocol should be easy to configure and should work well if the network grows to 150 computers. There are no plans to connect the network to the Internet, and the company is using the Windows 98 operating system on all the computers. Which of the following network protocols will meet all these requirements?

    A. NetBEUI

    B. TCP/IP

    C. IPX/SPX

    D. Microsoft DLC

6. The following table specifies the properties of some of the commonly used twisted-pair cables standards.

Cable Type	Speed	Common Usage
CAT 2	10 Mbps	Token Ring networks
CAT 3	16 Mbps	Ethernet networks
CAT 4	20 Mbps	Token Ring networks
CAT 5	100 Mbps	Ethernet networks

Which of the listed cable types has incorrect data?

A. CAT 2

B. CAT 3

C. CAT 4

D. CAT 5

7. A customer is telling you that he's using a 10BaseT Ethernet network in his office. He wants to know why this network is known as a CSMA/CD-based network. Which of the following statements would you use to describe how signals are transmitted in these networks, and what's the first action a device takes before transmitting a packet in a CSMA/CD network?

A. Attempts to possess an empty token

B. Sends a signal to all computers to stop transmitting

C. Listens to the network medium for silence

D. Waits for a random interval of time so that the medium becomes free

8. One of your friends has purchased a second computer for his small home office. Both of the computers have network adapters with RJ-45 connectors. He wants to connect the two computers so that he can copy files from one computer to the other and share the printer that's connected to the existing computer. The older computer has a serial mouse connected to the COM1 port and a modem connected to the COM2 port. He doesn't want to purchase a hub right now but knows that the two computers can be joined with only a twisted-pair cable. Which of the following cables can be used in this situation?

A. Parallel

B. Serial

C. Straight

D. Cross-over

9. You've purchased a second computer for your home office. Both computers include network adapters. You want to connect the two computers to build a small network. Because the network adapters in both computers have RJ-45 connectors, you're sure that you can use UTP cable. So you join the two

network adapters using a cable. Which of the following actions must you perform after installing the cable so that you can test the network?

A. Install the networking protocol.

B. Configure the Dial-Up Networking.

C. Check that the two adapters are communicating.

D. Install the drivers for the network adapters.

10. Which of the following should be unique when you use TCP/IP as your network protocol?

A. DNS server address

B. The IP address

C. Subnet mask

D. The default gateway address

11. The following table specifies several network types and the data speed, cable type, and maximum cable length used in each network.

Network	Speed	Cable Type	Maximum Length
10BaseT	10 Mbps	Twisted pair	100 meters
10Base2	16 Mbps	Thinnet	185 meters
10Base5	10 Mbps	Thicknet	500 meters
100BaseTX	100 Mbps	Twisted pair	100 meters

Which of the following network types has an incorrect specification in the table?

A. 10BaseT

B. 10Base2

C. 10Base5

D. 100BaseTX

12. A user on the network is complaining that he can't print to a shared printer from his Windows 98 computer. You're asked to solve the problem, and you know that all other users can print to the printer. If you suspect that the network might be a problem, which of the following is the best way to start your diagnosis?

A. Check the printer sharing on the computer connected to the printer.

B. Check the configuration of the network adapter.

C. Check Network Neighborhood in the user's computer.

D. Check the configuration of the NetBEUI protocol.

13. Which of the following methods is most commonly used for saving critical data on servers so that it's available in emergency situations?

A. Server clustering

B. Floppy disks

C. Tape backups

D. CDs

Questions 14–16 You've joined a small company as a help desk technician. The main business of the company is to produce graphics designs for major advertising agencies. The company has three departments, namely, accounts, marketing, and production. There are four computers in the accounts department, six computers in marketing, and twelve computers in the production department.

The technician whom you have replaced built the computer network using 10 Mbps hubs and CAT 3 cabling. All computers have network adapters with RJ-45 connectors to connect the computers to the hub and BNC connectors for coaxial cabling.

All computers in the network are using the Windows 98 operating system with NetBEUI as the networking protocol. There's no server in the office, and the three computers that have HP LaserJet 5000 printers are being used as print servers.

The company has just secured a large order, and management has decided to purchase 15 new computers so that the order can be expedited. The following three questions present some problems with this network. Answer these questions, selecting the best answer for each question.

14. The IT manager has received complaints from several users that the network runs very slowly when all users are working on their computers. You're afraid that the problem will become more severe when 15 new computers are added to this network. Which of the following do you think will help increase the network speed without having to change any software configuration?

    A. Change the network adapters from half duplex to full duplex.

    B. Upgrade Windows 98 to Windows NT Workstation.

    C. Replace the CAT 3 cable with a CAT 5 cable.

    D. Split the network into two or more segments.

15. To cope with the increase in business, the company has decided to open another office in a neighboring state. The two offices will be connected by routers using a leased line. Although you won't be involved in setting up the links, your boss has asked you what basic software changes will have to be carried out so that all computers in the local network will be able to access all computers in the neighboring state and make expansion easier in the future. Which of the following should be your answer?

    A. The networking protocol should be changed from NetBEUI to TCP/IP.

    B. The network adapters will need new drivers to access the remote network.

    C. The operating system has to be changed from Windows 98 to Windows NT.

    D. All computers will need two protocols: one for the local network and another for the remote network.

16. The manager now wants to upgrade the network speed from a 10BaseT to 100BaseT network. He has ordered a 100BaseT hub for this purpose. When you find out about this purchase order, which of the following should be your first concern?

    A. The coax cable

    B. The network adapters

    C. The networking protocol

    D. The operating system

17. Your organization has upgraded the old 10BaseT network to a 100BaseT. This has included all hubs and network adapters. Some users are complaining that the network doesn't seem to be faster, and you've been asked to investigate. What's the most likely problem?

    A. The network wiring isn't CAT 5.

    B. 100BaseT networks are unreliable.

   C. The PC configurations haven't been updated for the new speed.

   D. The BIOS is out-of-date on some of these computers.

18. Your home network has been working reliably using a dial-up connection to the Internet. You've just been informed that your neighborhood has cable Internet connections available. The cable connection was made, and you want to share your cable connection with the other computers in your network. When you connect the cable network to your existing hub, you're unable to establish a connection for computers in your network. What's the most likely problem?

   A. Your cable modem doesn't provide NAT or DHCP, and you'll need to add a device that can.

   B. Cable network connections can't be shared with multiple users.

   C. Your ISP has blocked multiple connections.

   D. Your network isn't configured properly for this capability.

19. You want to install a wireless network in your home. Which protocol would be the best choice for this?

   A. 802.3

   B. 803.2

   C. 802.11

   D. 803.11

20. You've been asked to advise the president of your company on the installation of a new network. She indicates that they only want to connect ten or so computers to share files between users. She also wants to share printers and the Internet connection. Which model would you recommend to her?

   A. Server based

   B. Client/server network

   C. Peer to peer

   D. Distributed information system

QUICK ANSWER KEY

1.	B	11.	B
2.	C	12.	C
3.	B	13.	C
4.	A	14.	D
5.	C	15.	A
6.	A	16.	B
7.	C	17.	A
8.	D	18.	A
9.	D	19.	C
10.	B	20.	C

IN-DEPTH ANSWERS

1. ☑ **B.** The bus topology was widely used as a network backbone. This network topology uses coaxial cable and requires that both ends of the cable be terminated.

   ☒ **A** is incorrect because the Star topology isn't used as a network backbone. The Star network neither uses coaxial cable nor requires terminators at the ends. The Star network typically uses twisted-pair cables or fiber-optic cables. **C** is incorrect because the Ring topology isn't used as a backbone. **D** is incorrect because a correct answer is within the given options.

2. ☑ **C.** The network continues to work even if the hub fails. This statement is incorrect because the Ethernet Star network depends on the hub to operate normally. All the computers communicate with one another through the hub, and a faulty hub can bring down the entire network.

   ☒ **A** is incorrect because the statement is true. Failure of one or more computers in a Star network doesn't cause the network to fail. **B** is incorrect because it's possible to expand the network by connecting more computers or other network devices to the network by free ports on the hub. **D** is incorrect because the statement is true. When two or more hubs are cascaded (one hub joined to another using the uplink port), the physical structure becomes a bus network.

3. ☑ **B.** This feature is incorrectly listed in the given options. Ring networks are known for lower signal loss because each computer that participates in the network amplifies the signal before retransmitting it.

   ☒ **A, C,** and **D** are incorrect because the given features are correct. Ring networks are difficult to set up compared to Star and bus networks, they're more prone to failures, and they're expensive because of the special equipment they require.

4. ☑ **A.** You'll probably best meet her requirements recommending the 100BaseT network. This provides expandability and reliability. Star networks are easy to build, maintain, and upgrade. These networks typically use a central

device known as a *hub* that receives signals, amplifies them, and retransmits them on the network. Because each computer is connected to the hub independently, the network continues to function even if one or more computers are shut down or break down because of a problem.

☒ **B** is a valid choice but not the best option. 10BaseT networks are inexpensive but are older and not as upgradable as 100BaseT networks. The costs between the two networks are virtually identical. **C** isn't the best choice. Token Ring networks tend to cost more than 100BaseT networks. Most current network installations are converting to 100BaseT. You'd probably only recommend a Ring for either ideological or compatibility with existing network reasons. **D** isn't the best choice. 10Base2 networks are largely not used anymore and are hard to expand.

5. ☑ **C.** The IPX/SPX-compatible protocol in Windows 98 meets all the requirements in the question. This is because this protocol isn't very difficult to configure, and it's routable. A routable protocol is required when the network is divided into two or more segments, as indicated in the question. You could also use a bridge to connect these two segments. Although IPX/SPX is commonly used in Novell networks, Windows networks commonly use this protocol in small- to medium-sized networks. The only limitation in using this protocol is that you can't connect to the Internet; however, this wasn't a requirement stipulated by the company.

☒ **A** is incorrect because this protocol can be bridged but not routed. It's potentially the slowest of the network options because NetBEUI doesn't work well in large networks and performance would be unacceptably slow. **B** is incorrect because among the given options, this protocol is the most difficult one to configure. Moreover, this protocol isn't required because the company doesn't want to connect to the Internet. **D** is incorrect because this protocol is also not a routable protocol and is used mainly by network printers and to connect to an IBM mainframe computer.

6. ☑ **A.** The CAT 2 cable specifications given in the table incorrectly list the data transfer speed as 10 Mbps. Remember that the CAT 2 cable is limited to a 4 Mbps speed. This cable was typically used in Token Ring networks that had a maximum speed of 4 Mbps, and it's no longer used.

☒ **B, C,** and **D** are incorrect because the given data regarding speed and common usage is correctly specified in the table. The CAT 3 cable supports a speed of 16 Mbps and is commonly used in 10BaseT Ethernet networks. CAT 4 supports up to 20 Mbps and is commonly used in Token Ring networks. CAT 5 is the most common cable type and supports up to 100 Mbps speeds. CAT 5 is used in both Ethernet and Fast Ethernet networks.

7. ☑ **C.** CSMA/CD stands for Carrier Sense Multiple Access with Collision Detect on. In such networks, the computer that wants to transmit a signal first listens to the network medium to see if there's *silence,* which means no other computer is transmitting data. The computer starts transmitting data only if the network medium is silent.

☒ **A** is incorrect because tokens are used in Token Ring networks and not in CSMA/CD networks. **B** is incorrect because the computer only listens for silence on the network medium. The signal sent to all computers to stop transmission is known as a *jamming signal.* This signal is sent when the computer detects that a collision has occurred on the network medium. Collision refers to two computers transmitting at the same time because they weren't able to sense silence because of the large distance between them. **D** is incorrect because this action is taken when a collision is detected on the network medium and a jamming signal has been sent to all computers. All computers wait for a random interval of time before transmitting a signal again.

8. ☑ **D.** The twisted-pair cable (commonly known as UTP cable) comes in only two types, straight and cross-over, both with RJ-45 connectors. The cross-over cable connects two computers without using a hub. It also connects two hubs when expanding the network. Remember that the straight cable can't be used for a *straight* connection between two computers.

☒ **A** is incorrect because the parallel cable can't be used for connecting the two computers in this case because one of the computers has a printer attached to its parallel port. **B** is incorrect because both of the serial ports on the older computer are occupied, one by the serial mouse and the other by the modem. **C** is incorrect because a straight cable is typically used for connecting computers to a hub.

9. ☑ **D.** The first thing you have to do to configure your network is install device drivers (or simply drivers) for your network adapters in both computers. Even if these drivers are already installed, you should check that they're in place.

☒ **A** is incorrect because if the drivers aren't present for the network adapters, the network won't work. Network protocols *bind* to existing network adapters during installation. **B** is incorrect because the Dial-Up Networking doesn't need to be configured for local networking. It's typically configured when you want to connect to the Internet or some other remote network that you can access using your modem. Dial-Up Networking doesn't need a physical network adapter. **C** is incorrect because unless the network adapters and the operating system are configured for networking, the functionality of the network adapters can't be checked.

10. ☑ **B.** No two computers in a network can have the same Internet Protocol (IP) address. This property is unique for each computer. Although it can be assigned to a computer during installation of the operating system, you can change or modify the IP address later. If two computers in the same network have the same IP address, one or both of the computers will usually indicate that an IP address conflict exists and TCP/IP access won't be granted for one or both of the computers.

☒ **A** is incorrect. The DNS server address is usually the same for all computers in the same network. **C** is incorrect because the subnet mask is common for all computers in a network segment. **D** is incorrect because this address is common to all computers in a network segment. The default gateway address is used by a computer in a network segment to access computers in another network segment.

11. ☑ **B.** The specifications for 10Base2 networks are incorrectly listed in the table. The data speed supported by these networks is 10 Mbps instead of 16 Mbps as stated in the table.

☒ **A, C,** and **D** are all incorrect answers because the specifications listed are all correct. 10BaseT networks have a 10 Mbps speed, use twisted-pair cables, and have a maximum cable length of 100 meters. 10Base5 networks have a 10 Mbps speed, use thicknet (thick coaxial) cables, and have a maximum cable length of 500 meters. 100BaseTX networks have a 100 Mbps speed, use twisted-pair cables, and have a maximum cable length of 100 meters.

12. ☑ **C.** The best way to start your diagnosis of a network-related problem in Windows 98 is to check Network Neighborhood. This icon is located on the desktop and gives a firsthand view of the computers and workgroups in the

network. If you don't find any computers in Network Neighborhood or get a message saying "Unable to Browse Network," you should check that the network cables are properly attached to the network adapter. Most network adapters indicate whether the adapter is connected to the hub.

☒ **A** is incorrect because other users are able to print from their computers. **B** is incorrect because this isn't the first thing you should check when an option exists on the desktop to check the computers on the network. **D** is incorrect because the only thing you can check with the NetBEUI protocol is whether it's installed. There's nothing else in the configuration of this protocol that you can check.

13. ☑ **C.** Tape backups are the most commonly used method for saving data so that it's available in case there's an emergency, such as a server breakdown. Data saved on tapes can be restored when the server problem is fixed and the server is brought online again.

☒ **A** is incorrect because clustering is implemented to provide fault tolerance and load balancing. It only stores a copy of the data and isn't the most commonly used method to save critical data for emergencies. **B** is incorrect because floppy disks have a limited storage capacity and aren't suitable for large amounts of server data. **D** is incorrect because CD-ROMs are read-only disks. Instead, CD-Rewritable (CD-RW) could be used for storing data, but again this isn't the most commonly used storage medium.

14. ☑ **D.** When the network is experiencing slow speeds, it's often best to divide the network into two or more segments according to functional requirements. For example, the computers in the accounts department can be separated from those in marketing or production, or both. This helps keep the departmental traffic local to the network segment. Unless required, the local network traffic doesn't travel to other segments.

☒ **A** is incorrect because this will have no effect on the network speed because the hubs usually don't support full-duplex communications. **B** is incorrect because this will have no effect on the network speed. **C** is incorrect because this won't help increase the network speed. The network is a 10 Mbps network, and both CAT 3 and CAT 5 cables support this speed.

15. ☑ **A.** The networking protocol should be changed from NetBEUI to TCP/IP. When two networks are joined by routers, it becomes a routed

network. Because NetBEUI isn't a routable protocol, it can't be used across a routed network. By making the switch to TCP/IP at this time, you'll make it easier to expand later and have the most flexibility for configuration changes.

☒ **B** is incorrect because the device drivers for network adapters don't need to be changed. **C** is incorrect because the computers can access the remote network using the existing Windows 98 operating system. **D** is incorrect because a single protocol can be used to access both local and remote networks. You don't need to add a networking protocol when you add remote networks.

16. ☑ **B.** The network adapters should be your first concern. Most hubs will operate both in 10BaseT and 100BaseT mode. The network adapters, however, may be limited to the 10 Mbps speed unless they're dual speed. Although these network adapters will work with the 100 Mbps Fast Ethernet hub, they'll be able to communicate with only a 10 Mbps speed. You must change the network adapters to either 10/100 Mbps or 100 Mbps adapters.

☒ **A** is incorrect; 10BaseT and 100BaseT networks use UTP, not coax. **C** is incorrect because the installed network protocol will work well with the 100 Mbps network. Network protocols are typically independent of network speeds. **D** is incorrect because the operating system has nothing to do with the speed of the network.

17. ☑ **A.** If your network is an older 10BaseT network, it's likely that your network was wired using CAT 3 cabling. CAT 3 cables are only certified for operation up to 16 MBps and may not operate reliably at the higher speed. You'd need to investigate and replace any older wiring with at least CAT 5.

☒ **B** is incorrect because 100BaseT networks are as reliable as 10BaseT networks but require better cabling for reliable communications. **C** is incorrect because PC configurations are usually not a problem with wide-scale network reliability problems. **D** is incorrect because the basic input/output system (BIOS) will usually not affect network speed because this is determined by the network interface card (NIC), not the BIOS.

18. ☑ **A.** Many cable modems don't provide NAT or DHCP protocol for sharing. You'll typically need to either acquire another device, such as a router, or configure a computer in your network to provide this service. Most cable providers only provide a single IP address as part of the installation.

☒ **B** is incorrect because cable network connections are commonly shared with multiple users. **C** is incorrect because although it's possible, the ISP wouldn't know if the address was being shared by multiple users. **D** isn't correct because your network is configured for multiple users. You need to add a device to allow it to share the cable connection.

19. ☑ **C.** The 802.11 protocol is ideal for a home-based wireless network. 802.11 provides high speed and is relatively inexpensive. 802.11 is also known as Wi Fi and is becoming commonly available in public places. A computer equipped with an 802.11 card is capable of joining multiple networks, making it ideal for a portable computer.

☒ **A** is incorrect because 802.3 is the standard used by 10BaseT and 100BaseT networks. This standard uses twisted-pair cable and isn't wireless. You can connect 802.3 networks to a wireless network using either bridge. **B** and **D** are incorrect because 803.2 and 803.11 aren't valid network protocols.

20. ☑ **C.** A peer-to-peer network is ideal for a small network such as this. You wouldn't have the expense of a server, and you could provide Internet security both on the desktop and using a firewall in a router.

☒ **A** is incorrect because although a server-based network allows for some advantages, the cost of installing and supporting the server may not be worth the benefit. **B** is incorrect because a client/server network is more of an approach than an actual solution. Client/server networks require servers to function. The goal is to minimize the expense of this network environment. **D** is incorrect because a distributed information system is an architectural approach to solving information system implementation on larger networks.

CORE HARDWARE/OPERATING SYSTEM EXAMS

Part II

A+ Operating Systems Technologies

CORE HARDWARE/OPERATING SYSTEM EXAMS

7

Operating System Fundamentals

The operating system is the platform that computer users rely on for interacting with the hardware. Desktop operating systems such as Windows 9x, Windows NT 4 Workstation, Windows 2000 Professional, and Windows XP offer different levels of features and capabilities. Each of these operating systems offers various tools and utilities to manage and organize the system, devices, and data.

As an A+ technician, you'll be expected to be able to install, troubleshoot, and upgrade these types of systems. The skills needed to do this are broad because of the number of different operating systems you're expected to know. Fortunately, the newer operating systems are much more reliable, easy to troubleshoot, and easy to repair than earlier systems. Many of the struggles you'll encounter are a result of user-created problems as opposed to hardware/software incompatibilities.

QUESTIONS

1. Which of the following isn't a function of an operating system?

   A. Providing a user interface

   B. Managing the disk

   C. Interpreting commands and run files

   D. Managing the BIOS

2. A friend has sought your advice on the basic differences between the Windows 98 and Windows XP operating systems. Which of the following statements incorrectly describes the feature similarities of these two operating systems?

   A. Both Windows XP and Windows 98 support Plug and Play.

   B. Both Windows XP and Windows 98 have strong support for multimedia applications.

   C. Both Windows XP and Windows 98 support preemptive multitasking for running multiple applications.

   D. Both Windows XP and Windows 98 support multiprocessors.

3. You've been asked to upgrade a Windows 95 system to Windows XP. The user doesn't want to change anything about how she has her computer set up. She thinks this would cause her to lose time, and she's upgrading the operating system because her boss insists on it. How would you upgrade the system to Windows XP and have the minimum impact on her life?

    A. This isn't possible.

    B. Perform an upgrade from Windows 95 to Windows XP directly. This won't significantly affect how her system operates.

    C. Install a clean version of Windows XP and configure it for multiboot capability.

    D. To upgrade from Windows 95 to Windows XP, you'll first need to upgrade to Windows 98 or Me.

4. A Windows 98 computer has an internal adapter that isn't being recognized by the operating system. The device is shown as an Unknown Device in Device Manager. Which of the following files or utilities isn't involved in preventing the operating system from loading its device driver?

    A. Registry

    B. Automatic skip driver

    C. Application configuration

    D. Device driver

5. You've installed a new application in Windows 98 and accepted all default settings during the installation. If C: is the root drive of the computer, where will you find the folder for this application?

    A. C:\Program Files

    B. C:\Windows

    C. C:\Windows\Program Files

    D. C:\Windows\Application Data

6. You have a Windows XP computer with a 40GB hard disk. The computer technician who set up this computer told you that the hard disk has been divided into two partitions, namely, the C: and D: drives. The C: drive is the

system partition, and the D: drive is the boot partition. Which of the following gives the correct meaning of system and boot partitions?

A. The system partition stores system files, and the boot partition stores boot files.

B. The system partition stores files to boot the system, and the boot partition stores the system files.

C. The boot partition stores the files used during system startup, and the system partition stores Windows setup files.

D. The system and boot partitions have the same meaning.

7. You're using the Windows XP operating system on your computer. Which of the following should you prefer for making changes to system settings that affect how the computer will behave during normal operation?

A. Use Control Panel.

B. Make changes to the BOOT.INI file.

C. Use the Registry Editor program.

D. Use the RUNAS command.

8. Which of the following options would you use to create a bootable floppy disk in a system running Windows 98?

A. Format a floppy disk using the FORMAT A: /Q command.

B. Use the Startup Disk tab in Add/Remove Programs in Control Panel.

C. Use the Startup Disk option in System Tools under the Accessories menu.

D. Use the Maintenance Wizard in the Accessories menu.

9. Assuming that your Windows 98 computer is currently connected to the Internet, which of the following Internet tasks can't be accomplished using Windows Explorer?

A. Visiting your home page

B. Configuring the home page settings

C. Viewing disk contents as a web page

D. Visiting a saved favorite web site

10. The MYFILES folder in the C: drive of your Windows 98 computer has some important files that you don't want disclosed to anyone. The files have been arranged in subfolders named MYACC, MYBANK, and MYCREDIT within the MYFILES folder, as shown in the following illustration.

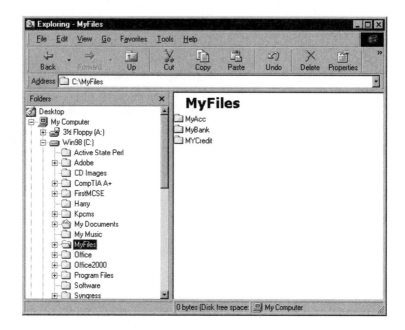

Which of the following commands would you use to set these files up so they're hidden but even when they're visible no one can modify them without changing the settings?

A. ATTRIB C:\MYFILES H R

B. ATTRIB C:\MYFILES +H +R

C. ATTRIB C:\MYFILES +H +R /S

D. ATTRIB C:\MYFILES*.* +H +R /S

11. You're using Windows 2000 Professional on your home computer. Because of space limitations, you've compressed some files using the built-in compression utility. Your computer is connected to the Internet, and you want to secure some of the folders by encrypting them. When you attempt encryption on one

of the folders, you find that the files in the folder get decompressed. Which of the following describes the correct reason for this?

A. The folder wasn't compressed properly.

B. Encryption and compression can't be used on the same disk drive.

C. Encryption and compression can't be used on the same folder.

D. You should encrypt the folder before compressing it.

12. You have some personal account files in your computer that you want to make as safe as possible. Assuming that the system is running the Windows 98 operating system, which of the following attributes are you unable to set on these files using Windows Explorer?

A. Read Only

B. Hidden

C. Archive

D. System

13. Which of the following file systems provides file level security, data compression, data encryption, and auditing file access?

A. HPFS

B. FAT32

C. NTFS 4

D. NTFS 5

14. Which of the files listed is read first during the Windows 9x boot process?

A. IO.SYS

B. CONFIG.SYS

C. AUTOEXEC.BAT

D. NTLDR

15. Which of the following choices is the sequence used to boot Windows 9x/DOS?

A. MSDOS.SYS; IO.SYS; CONFIG.SYS; COMMAND.COM; AUTOEXEC.BAT

B. IO.SYS; MSDOS.SYS; CONFIG.SYS; COMMAND.COM; AUTOEXEC.BAT

    C. IO.SYS; MSDOS.SYS; COMMAND.COM; CONFIG.SYS; AUTOEXEC.BAT

    D. IO.SYS; MSDOS.SYS; CONFIG.SYS; AUTOEXEC.BAT COMMAND.COM

16. The line DEVICE=C:\Windows\HIMEM.SYS is found in which file?

    A. MSDOS.SYS

    B. AUTOEXEC.BAT

    C. CONFIG.SYS

    D. WIN.COM

17. Which of the following files is a carryover from the early Windows environment and is still present for Windows 9*x* compatibility with older applications?

    A. WIN.COM

    B. USER.DAT

    C. WIN.INI

    D. AUTOEXEC.BAT

18. Which file contains the boot selection menu entries?

    A. NTLDR

    B. NTDETECT.COM

    C. NTOSKRNL.EXE

    D. BOOT.INI

19. Which file contains Registry entries for user settings and configuration that can be changed by the user in a Windows XP system?

    A. NTCONFIG.POL

    B. NTUSER.DAT

    C. NTUSER.MAN

    D. USER.DAT

20. A customer reports their hard disk has become very slow after two years of continuous use. They're running the Windows NT operating system on this

computer. Which program would you run to potentially improve performance on this system?

A. SCANDISK

B. DEFRAG

C. CHKDSK

D. None of the above

21. You want to upgrade your Windows XP system from a FAT32 to NTFS. Which method is preferred to accomplish this?

    A. You can't upgrade disks from FAT 32 to NTFS.

    B. Run the CONVERT.EXE command at the command prompt.

    C. Run Disk Management in the Computer Management application to convert the disk.

    D. Run FDISK, reinitialize the drive, and then format it for NTFS.

22. You've added another 80GB hard disk in your system and want to install Windows XP Home Edition. You want to make the computer dual boot between Windows Me and Windows XP. Which of the following file systems should you use on the second disk if you want to access files on the Windows XP partition while running Windows Me?

    A. HPFS

    B. FAT32

    C. NTFS 4

    D. NTFS 5

23. You're experiencing difficulty removing a program using the Add/Remove Programs options in Control Panel. The remove process starts and then fails. The program name still remains in the Add/Remove Programs window and the Start menu. What should you do to remove this program from the Add/Remove Programs window?

    A. You'll need to use the Registry Editor to correct this problem.

    B. You'll need to remove this program by editing the INSTALLED.DAT file.

    C. This error won't occur.

    D. You'll need to install and then uninstall the program again.

24. You're troubleshooting a Windows XP system that isn't starting properly. You have determined that a Windows XP file is missing. You only want to reinstall the missing file. What would you do to get this file from the installation media?

   A. Use the ATTRIB.EXE program to change the settings to read.

   B. Use the EXTRACT.EXE program to extract the file from the CAB files on the installation disk.

   C. You can acquire the file directly from the installation disk.

   D. Reinstall the operating system, and select Repair when prompted.

25. You want to change a setting in the AUTOEXEC.NT file. Which of the following will accomplish that?

   A. Edit the file using EDIT.EXE.

   B. Edit the file using EDIT.COM.

   C. Change the configuration settings for the current session of the command prompt.

   D. You can't edit the AUTOEXEC.NT file because it's a system file.

26. What program automatically scans and attempts to repair Registry problems on a Windows 98 system?

   A. SCANREG

   B. SCANDISK

   C. DEFRAG

   D. The Registry isn't automatically scanned.

27. Which action would you take to view the attributes of the files in a subdirectory you created on a Windows XP system?

   A. Right-clicking on a file in Windows Explorer

   B. Using DIR/A at command prompt

   C. Using DIR/AH at command prompt

   D. Using EDIT.COM

28. Which program is used to view system errors on a Windows XP system?

   A. Security Manager

   B. Task Manager

    C. Log Manager

    D. Event Viewer

29. A user has asked you to help him simplify how his computer works. He's using Windows XP. He wants to quickly access programs without having to use the Start menu all the time. How could you accomplish this in the quickest manner?

    A. You could create shortcuts for him by right-clicking his desktop, selecting New | Shortcut, and then following the configuration options.

    B. You could create shortcuts for him by going to Windows Explorer, creating a new shortcut by selecting New | Shortcut, and then following the configuration options.

    C. You could click the Start menu, select New | Shortcut, and then follow the configuration options.

    D. You could edit the user profile and add shortcuts to his profile.

30. A user has deleted a shortcut by accident. He has called you in a panic because he doesn't remember how to re-create a shortcut. What is the quickest way to fix this problem?

    A. Create a new shortcut and follow the instructions for creating a shortcut.

    B. You can't delete a shortcut.

    C. Use the Add/Remove Programs to recover the shortcut.

    D. Open the Recycle Bin, and drag the shortcut back to the desktop.

QUICK ANSWER KEY

1.	D	16.	C
2.	D	17.	C
3.	D	18.	D
4.	C	19.	B
5.	A	20.	D
6.	B	21.	B
7.	A	22.	B
8.	B	23.	A
9.	B	24.	B
10.	D	25.	B
11.	C	26.	A
12.	D	27.	A
13.	D	28.	D
14.	A	29.	A
15.	B	30.	D

IN-DEPTH ANSWERS

1. ☑ **D.** Managing the basic input-output system (BIOS) isn't a function of the operating system. Basic input and output functions of a computer are handled by the computer BIOS. The operating system utilizes the information provided by the BIOS to communicate with the input/output devices.

   ☒ **A, B,** and **C** are incorrect because these functions are handled by the operating system. The operating system provides a user interface that enables the user to enter commands or run program files and see the results. Disk management is also a function of the operating system that includes tasks such as partitioning and formatting the disk and carrying out routine disk maintenance. Files are run and user commands are interpreted by the operating system, and the results are shown to the user.

2. ☑ **D.** This statement is incorrect because Windows 9*x* systems don't support multiprocessors, and Windows NT, 2000, and XP support multiprocessor systems.

   ☒ **A, B, C** are incorrect because the stated features are supported in both Windows XP and Windows 98. Both operating systems support Plug and Play, have strong support for multimedia applications, and have a similar interface. Both operating systems support preemptive multitasking.

3. ☑ **D.** The path to upgrade would be through Windows 98/Me or Windows NT 4/Windows 2000. There is no way to upgrade directly from Windows 95 to Windows XP. From a practical perspective, it's likely that the system won't meet the compatibility requirements for Windows XP and the installation wouldn't succeed without upgrading at least the video card.

   ☒ **A** is incorrect because it's possible but isn't advised for the reasons given in the correct answer. **B** is incorrect because you can't upgrade directly. **C** is incorrect because the system can be configured to multiboot, but all of her settings and applications wouldn't be accessible in Windows XP unless she reinstalled her applications.

4. ☑ **C.** The application configuration of Windows 98 isn't involved in marking the internal adapter as Unknown Device. The application configuration, as the name suggests, is involved in configuring the applications during installation and during the time they're run.

   ☒ **A** is incorrect because the Registry is involved in preventing the operating system from loading the device drivers successfully. The device configuration is stored in the Registry. **B** is incorrect because this utility in the Windows 98 operating system is used to prevent corrupted or incompatible device drivers from loading during the system startup. **D** is incorrect because it's essentially because the device driver is either corrupt or incompatible with Windows 98, which prevents it to load.

5. ☑ **A.** The default setting for all Windows 9x–compatible applications is to install them in the Program Files folder on the root drive. Because C: is the root drive of the computer running Windows 98, the files will be placed in C:\Program Files. Remember that these are only the default settings, and you can modify these settings during installation if you want to install any application in a different folder.

   ☒ **B** is incorrect because the C:\Windows folder contains system files in Windows 98. **C** is incorrect because this folder doesn't exist. **D** is incorrect because this folder contains settings for Microsoft applications, such as Microsoft Office and Internet Explorer.

6. ☑ **B.** Microsoft terminology defines the partition used to boot the system as the system partition and the partition used to install the Windows system files as the boot partition. The system and boot partitions can be on the same partition of the hard disk, on different partitions of the same hard disk, or on different hard disks.

   ☒ **A** is incorrect because the inverse is true. **C** is incorrect because the Windows setup files are stored in the boot partition. **D** is incorrect because, as specified previously, the system partition is used to start up the system, and the boot partition refers to the partition that contains the Windows directory.

7. ☑ **A.** The easiest and safest way to make changes to the operating system and its utilities is to use Control Panel. Control Panel contains applets for configuring various operating system functions, such as adding and removing programs, adding and removing hardware devices, and setting up Windows components and other utilities, such as setting passwords and configuring

modems and networking. As far as possible, you should use Control Panel to configure systems.

☒ **B** is incorrect because the BOOT.INI file doesn't exist in a system that has only the Windows XP operating system. Furthermore, modifying this file modifies only the boot order of the Windows 2000/XP or dual-boot systems and the location of the operating system to load. **C** is incorrect because using the Registry Editor is recommended only for those settings that aren't possible using Control Panel and other interactive utilities. Incorrect changes in the Registry can create a lot of problems and even render the operating system unable to boot. **D** is incorrect because this command is typically used by system or network administrators in a networked environment when they log onto the computer with less privileged user names and passwords but want to run a program that requires higher privileges.

8. ☑ **B.** A startup disk in Windows 98 can be created from the Startup Disk tab in the Add/Remove Programs window. This utility not only formats the new floppy disk, as desired in the question, but also copies system files to the disk, thus making it bootable.

☒ **A** is incorrect because the /Q switch is used for a quick format of the floppy disk. This doesn't make the disk bootable. To make a bootable disk from the command prompt, you should use the FORMAT A:/S command. **C** is incorrect because there's no option in System Tools to create a startup disk. **D** is incorrect because the Maintenance Wizard also doesn't have an option to create a startup disk.

9. ☑ **B.** Configuring the home page settings can't be accomplished using Windows Explorer. These settings have to be made by using Control Panel, by using Dial-Up Networking or, depending on the version of Internet Explorer, by using the Internet Explorer Tools | Options menu.

☒ **A** is incorrect because you can click the Go menu and select Home Page to visit your home page when you're connected to the Internet. **C** is incorrect because Windows 98 Explorer allows you to display the disk contents as a Web page. This option is in the View menu. **D** is also incorrect because once you're connected to the Internet, you can create and select favorite web sites that you want to connect to bypassing normal navigation features.

10. ☑ **D.** This is the only correct command among the given answer options. The *.* is the wildcard that specifies all the files. The +H sets the hidden attribute on the files, +R sets the read only attribute, and /S tells the operating system to select all the subfolders under the MYFILES folder.

 ☒ **A** is an invalid command because you must specify the + sign with H and R to set the attribute. The + sign sets the attribute, and the – sign removes it. **B** and **C** are incorrect answers because neither of these commands has the correct syntax.

11. ☑ **C.** Encryption and compression can't be used on the same folder. Windows 2000 (and Windows XP Professional) encryption and compression are mutually exclusive. If you want to compress a folder, you can't encrypt it and vice versa. When you encrypt a compressed folder, its contents are first decompressed and then encrypted.

 ☒ **A** is incorrect because when you compress a folder in Windows 2000, it either gets compressed properly or doesn't compress at all. If a problem is encountered during compression, Windows 2000 doesn't process the compression. **B** is incorrect because you can use compression and encryption on the same disk drive as long as the folders are different. **D** is incorrect because this won't work. When you attempt to compress an encrypted folder, the folder will be decrypted.

12. ☑ **D.** The System attribute is set by the operating system. Users can't set or remove the System attribute, which is typically meant to protect files used by the operating system.

 ☒ **A, B,** and **C** are incorrect answers because you can set or remove the Read Only, Hidden, and Archive attributes on any files. For the safety of your personal files, the Read Only and Hidden file attributes should be set. By default, Windows doesn't show the System and Hidden files, which secures these files from accidental deletion.

13. ☑ **D.** The only file system that provides all these features is NTFS 5. NTFS 5 is supported in the Windows 2000 and XP operating systems. It offers features such as file-level security, data compression, encryption, and the ability to audit file access.

 ☒ **A** is incorrect because this file system doesn't offer any of the required features for file protection. **B** is incorrect for the same reason. **C** is incorrect because although it offers file-level security, data compression, and auditing, it doesn't offer file encryption. NTFS 4 is used in Windows NT operating systems.

14. ☑ **A.** IO.SYS is read first during the boot process of a Windows 9*x* system. IO.SYS contains drivers and programming that allows the operating system to interact with the BIOS.

☒ **B** is incorrect because the CONFIG.SYS file loads drivers and memory management functions needed for the operating system to function properly. **C** is incorrect because the AUTOEXEC.BAT file contains instructions to run programs and other operating systems settings used by DOS. **D** is incorrect because NTLDR is a Windows NT/2000/XP file.

15. ☑ **B.** The sequence to boot DOS is IO.SYS; MSDOS.SYS; CONFIG.SYS; COMMAND.COM; AUTOEXEC.BAT.

☒ **A, C,** and **D** are incorrect. IO.SYS reads information from the BIOS and passes it to MSDOS.SYS. MSDOS.SYS loads drivers and other routines needed. CONFIG.SYS contains drivers and memory management configuration directives. COMMAND.COM is the DOS command processor. The AUTOEXEC.BAT file contains program directives and other information to customize the environment.

16. ☑ **C.** The CONFIG.SYS file contains drivers and memory management configuration options. HIMEM.SYS is the memory manager used by DOS and Windows 9*x* systems.

☒ **A** is incorrect because MSDOS.SYS contains drivers and routines needed to load the operating system. **B** is incorrect because AUTOEXEC.BAT is the batch file used by COMMAND.COM to customize the DOS interface and load programs automatically during startup. **D** is incorrect because WIN.COM is the default name of the Windows 9*x* operating system.

17. ☑ **C.** The WIN.INI file was introduced in Windows 3.*x*. This file contains information about configurations and settings and was essential for Windows 3.*x* operations. With the full implementation of the Registry in Windows 95, this file was kept largely for compatibility purposes. It's also present in Windows 98 and Windows Me systems.

☒ **A** is incorrect because WIN.COM is the Windows 9*x* program and is launched automatically when a Windows 9*x* system is loaded. **B** is incorrect because USER.DAT is a Registry file used in Windows 9*x* systems and contains user-specific information. **D** is incorrect because AUTOEXEC.BAT is a DOS batch file and isn't utilized by Windows 9*x*.

18. ☑ **D.** The BOOT.INI file contains the menu entries to boot Windows NT, 2000, and XP. This file can contain multiple boot destinations to allow for booting more than one operating system.

    ☒ **A** is incorrect because NTLDR is the boot loader, which is the first step in the Windows NT, 2000, and XP boot process. **B** is incorrect because NTDETECT.COM is the hardware configuration detection program on a Windows NT, 2000, or XP system. **C** is incorrect because NTOSKRNL.EXE is the kernel program for Windows NT, 2000, and XP systems.

19. ☑ **B.** NTUSER.DAT is the Registry file that contains user settings on a Windows NT, 2000, and XP system. This file stores the profile information that includes desktop settings.

    ☒ **A** is incorrect because the NTCONFIG.POL file is the system policy file on a Windows NT system. This file is also used on some Windows 2000 systems. **C** is incorrect because the NTUSER.MAN file is a mandatory profile that resembles NTUSER.DAT. This file contains settings that users will automatically use when they log in. **D** is incorrect because USER.DAT is a Windows 9*x* file and isn't used by Windows NT, 2000, and XP.

20. ☑ **D.** The problem is likely caused by a disk drive that needs to be defragmented. Defrag or the Disk Defragmenter isn't included with Windows NT 4 systems. It's included with all of the other versions of Windows. You'd need to purchase a third-party defragmentation program to defrag the disk.

    ☒ **A** is incorrect because SCANDISK.EXE is the disk-scanning program that verifies and corrects disk problems. ScanDisk is provided on all versions of Windows 9*x* systems. **B** is incorrect because Defrag or the Disk Defragmenter wasn't shipped with Windows NT 4, so you'd need to buy this program from a third-party vendor. Defrag is provided on Windows 2000 and XP. **C** is incorrect because CHKDSK will find and correct disk errors on Windows 9*x*, Windows NT, 2000, and XP.

21. ☑ **B.** The CONVERT.EXE program allows you to convert FAT16 and FAT32 file systems to NTFS file systems. This utility is run from the command prompt.

☒ **A** is incorrect because Microsoft recommends that Windows XP systems run under the NTFS file system. NTFS provides enhanced features over FAT-based file systems. The current version of NTFS is version 5. **C** is incorrect because Disk Management doesn't provide a method to convert the disk. You must use the DOS program to accomplish this. **D** is incorrect because FDISK isn't used with Windows XP systems.

22. ☑ **B.** The FAT32 file system on the second disk will allow you to access files on the Windows XP disk while running Windows Me. Windows 98 can read only from FAT16 and FAT32 file systems and isn't able to access NTFS disks locally.

☒ **A** is incorrect because the high-performance file system (HPFS) isn't supported in Windows XP, and you won't be able to format the second disk using HPFS. **C** is incorrect because Windows XP doesn't format hard disks with NTFS 4. NTFS 5 is the current version of NTFS. **D** is incorrect because you can't access an NTFS 5 disk locally while running the Windows 98 operating system. You can access shared NTFS drives on the network regardless of the client operating system.

23. ☑ **A.** The programs installed on the system create Registry entries to identify their location and other information. If a program is manually deleted, you may need to edit the HKEY_LOCAL_MACHINE\SOFTWARE\Microsoft\ Windows\CurrentVersion\Uninstall key. Make sure you read about Registry editing on the Microsoft web site before you attempt this. Errors in the Registry editing process can render a system unstable and unusable.

☒ **B** is incorrect because there's no file called INSTALLED.DAT that's used by the Add/Remove Programs program. **C** is incorrect because this error occurs when a program is manually deleted on a Windows XP system. It isn't usually a serious problem, but it's an annoying one. Always use the uninstall procedure specified by the software provider to minimize problems. **D** is incorrect but may work. You can sometimes install a program and then uninstall it to remove an entry. This doesn't always work, however, and it's easier to edit the Registry to fix this problem.

24. ☑ **B.** Installation files for Windows systems are contained in CAB files. CAB files are highly compressed files that contain all the files needed for a system. The EXTRACT.EXE program is the program you'd use to extract the file.

    ☒ **A** is incorrect because you may need to change the attributes of the file once you extract it, and you'd use the ATTRIB.EXE program to accomplish that. The ATTRIB.EXE file doesn't extract files; it changes file attributes. **C** is incorrect because most files on the installation CD are contained in CAB files or are compressed. You need the EXTRACT.EXE file to expand them or extract them from installation files. **D** is incorrect because reinstalling the operating system with the Repair option will reinstall all of the operating systems files that are selected during the repair process.

25. ☑ **B.** You can edit the AUTOEXEC.NT file using EDIT.COM. This editor allows you to easily and quickly modify basic text files. The AUTOEXEC.NT file is used by the DOS emulator on Windows NT, 2000, and XP systems.

    ☒ **A** is incorrect because the text editor is EDIT.COM, not EDIT.EXE. **C** is incorrect because changing the current configuration settings for the command prompt wouldn't permanently change the configuration settings of AUTOEXEC.NT. **D** is incorrect because the AUTOEXEC.NT file is a text file that's loaded when the DOS command processor is loaded.

26. ☑ **A.** The ScanReg program automatically scans and attempts to fix Registry problems each time the system is started on any given day. SCANREG can also be run manually to back up, restore, and optimize the Registry.

    ☒ **B** is incorrect because ScanDisk performs a scan of disk drives and attempts to repair any disk problems it detects. **C** is incorrect because Defrag is the disk defragmenter shipped with most versions of Windows. **D** is incorrect because the Registry is scanned automatically every time the system is restarted on any given day.

27. ☑ **A.** You would open Windows Explorer, select the file, and right-click it. This would allow you to select the Properties option. This will show you the attributes of a file.

    ☒ **B** is incorrect because the DIR/A command will display all files but not their attributes. **C** is incorrect because DIR/AH will show you a list of all hidden files in a directory. **D** is incorrect because EDIT.COM is used to edit text files.

28. ☑ **D.** The Event Viewer is the primary tool to monitor system events and errors. The Event Viewer is included with Windows NT 4, Windows 2000, and Windows XP. This tool provides detailed information about system status for logging and troubleshooting purposes.

    ☒ **A** is incorrect because there's no specific application called Security Manager in Windows XP. Security events do get logged in the Event Viewer, and there's a special category for security. **B** is incorrect because the Task Manager will show you the status of the system at a given moment in time. **C** is incorrect because there's no application called Log Manager included with Windows NT, 2000, or XP. Logs are kept and created either by individual applications, subsystems, or the Event Viewer.

29. ☑ **A.** Windows allows you to create shortcuts on the desktop that can be used to rapidly access programs. Shortcuts make accessing programs easy for users and increase productivity.

    ☒ **B** is incorrect because this procedure would create a shortcut for the user that would reside in a disk directory and wouldn't be visible on the desktop. **C** is incorrect because you can create shortcuts on the Start menu, but this isn't the proper procedure. **D** is incorrect because this isn't the quickest or easiest way to accomplish this task.

30. ☑ **D.** The quickest way to recover a shortcut is to drag it out of the Recycle Bin. Of course, this will only work if he hasn't yet emptied the Recycle Bin. If the Recycle Bin is empty, you will need to re-create it for him.

    ☒ **A** is incorrect because you can create a new shortcut, but this wouldn't be faster than dragging a deleted shortcut out of the Recycle Bin. **B** is incorrect because you can and want to delete unneeded shortcuts. Over time, a user's desktop can become overly cluttered with shortcuts if they don't know how to delete them. **C** is incorrect because Add/Remove Programs won't help you recover a deleted shortcut.

CORE HARDWARE/OPERATING SYSTEM EXAMS

8

Installation, Configuration, and Upgrading

A big part of your job is installing and upgrading operating systems. For the most part, this is a relatively straightforward process. The operating systems that you'll be expected to work on have good installation processes. When working with Windows NT, 2000, and XP, you need to pay strict attention to the Hardware Compatibility List. These operating systems are pretty finicky about what you can install. In many cases, devices that worked properly in Windows 9x won't work at all on Windows XP systems. Verifying that a system to be upgraded has compatible hardware will simplify your life and save you many hours of work.

QUESTIONS

1. You want to verify that a system will operate Windows XP. Which of the following parameters don't meet the minimum system requirements?

   A. Pentium III 300 MHz

   B. 32MB RAM

   C. 10GB of hard disk space

   D. 1× CD-ROM

2. You've found an old copy of the Windows 98 operating system. You're currently running Windows 3.1 on your computer. Which of the following is the first thing you should do before you start installing the new operating system?

   A. Create fresh partitions on the hard disk so that you have two or more partitions.

   B. Reformat the hard disk to a FAT32 file system.

   C. Check the minimum hardware requirements and the Hardware Compatibility List.

   D. Make sure your games will run with the new operating system.

3. You want to prepare a system for installation of Windows XP. This system has a new hard disk that has never been formatted. What step will you need to take to prepare this system for Windows XP installation?

   A. Use FDISK to prepare the disk partitions, and then run FORMAT.EXE to prepare the disk for use.

   B. Use Disk Management to prepare the disk for use.

   C. Windows XP will prepare the disk for use when installation begins.

   D. Use the vendor-provided formatting tools for the hard disk.

4. You've purchased a new Pentium 4 computer and a copy of Windows 2000 Professional. You want to create two partitions on the hard disk. Which of the following is the recommended method for creating the hard disk partitions?

   A. Use the FDISK utility to create all partitions before you start the installation.

   B. Use Disk Management to create the primary and extended partitions.

   C. Create the primary partition using Disk Management before installation, and create the other extended partitions using FDISK.

   D. Create the primary active partition during installation and the other partitions using Disk Management after installation.

5. You want to upgrade your Windows 98 computer to Windows 2000 Professional. Compatibility of the current applications isn't a major issue for you, but you want to make sure that the critical data files are available after the upgrade. Which of the following should be your first concern before you start the upgrade installation?

   A. Consider making a dual-boot system.

   B. Back up your data files.

   C. Learn about uninstalling Windows 2000.

   D. Compress the existing data.

6. You're unable to upgrade to Windows 2000 Professional from which of the following operating systems? Select all correct answers.

   A. Windows 95 OSR2

   B. Windows 98

   C. Windows NT 4 Workstation with Service Pack 4

   D. Windows NT 4 Server with Service Pack 4

7. Which of the following statements is correct regarding the existing formatted partitions and the default action of the setup program when you're running a Windows 2000 Professional upgrade on a Windows 98 system? Select all that apply.

   A. If the system will dual boot with Windows 98 and the partition is less than 2GB, Setup converts it to FAT32.

   B. If the system will dual boot with Windows 98 but the partition is greater than 2GB, Setup converts it to NTFS.

   C. If the system will not dual boot with Windows 98 and the partition is less than 2GB, Setup converts it to FAT.

   D. Whatever the size or formatting of the partition, by default Setup will keep it intact.

8. Ted wants to add Windows 2000 to an existing Windows 98 system. Ted wants to be able to switch between the two operating systems when needed. The computer has the following configuration: the hard disk C: is 10.6GB, hosts the Windows 98 operating system, and is formatted as FAT 32. Drive C: contains word processing programs, Internet software, accounts software, and e-mail programs. Drive C: has approximately 1GB of free disk space left. Drive D: is 10GB, and it contains other important data files and has about 5GB of disk space available. What can you do to make this system dual boot?

   A. Install Windows 2000 on drive C: as a dual-boot configuration.

   B. Install Windows 2000 on drive D: as a dual-boot configuration.

   C. There's inadequate disk space to support both operating systems.

   D. Repartition the drives, and convert them to NTFS.

9. Your system administrator gave you a CD with Windows 2000 Professional and asked you to install it on a new computer. Unfortunately, the administrator has lost the original set of startup disks and has requested you to prepare a set of disks for him. Which of the following commands can you use to create the Windows 2000 startup disks on a computer running Windows 98? Assume that the floppy disk drive is A: and the CD-ROM drive is F: on the Windows 98 computer. The Windows 2000 Setup files are located in the \I386 folder.

   A. F:\I386\WINNT32.EXE /OX

   B. F:\I386\WINNT32.EXE A:

   C. F:\BOOTDISK\MAKEBOOT.EXE A:

   D. None of above; you can't create Windows 2000 startup disks on a Windows 98 computer.

10. Which of the following statements correctly describes the boot sequence of a Windows 2000 computer?

   A. NTLDR loads the operating system. NTOSKRNL loads the graphics mode and runs NTDETECT to detect the hardware.

   B. NTLDR loads the operating system, NTDETECT runs to detect the hardware, and NTOSKRNL loads the graphics mode.

   C. NTLDR runs the POST and loads the operating system, NTDETECT runs to detect the hardware, and NTOSKRNL loads the kernel.

   D. NTLDR loads the operating system, NTDETECT loads the graphics mode, and NTOSKRNL detects the hardware and loads the device drivers.

   Questions 11–13   You've been asked to troubleshoot a Pentium 4 computer that has 128MB of RAM. The computer has a 10.6GB hard disk with two partitions, the second partition was unused. The computer was running the Windows 98 operating system.

   Another technician installed Windows 2000 and left the premises. The user has called complaining of problems, and you're responsible for fixing them. Answer the following three questions based on this scenario.

11. You started the computer but instead of giving you an option for selecting the operating system, the system immediately started loading Windows 2000. Thinking you might not have noticed the option screen, you restarted the system, but it again automatically started Windows 2000. Which of the

following options can you use to view the operating system options to load during startup?

   A. Start the System applet in Windows 2000 Control Panel, and increase the wait time to 20 on the Startup/Shutdown tab.

   B. Windows 98 is possibly deleted from the system, and you must reinstall it.

   C. Boot the system using the Windows 98 boot disk, and modify the BOOT.INI file to correct the timing of the operating system option screen.

   D. Windows 98 should've been installed after installing Windows 2000 Professional, and it must be reinstalled now.

12. The computer is now working properly, and both operating systems can be booted. The user is complaining that the sound doesn't work on the sound card in Windows 2000. So you performed the following:

   You downloaded an updated driver for the sound card from the manufacturer's web site. When you installed it on Windows 2000 and restarted, the computer wouldn't start Windows 2000 and now hangs. Windows 98 works correctly. Which of the following boot options should you use so that the system boots normally and doesn't load the updated driver?

   A. Boot Normally

   B. Step-by-Step Confirmation

   C. Last Known Good Configuration

   D. Enable Boot Logging

13. The sound card is now fixed, and both operating systems work correctly. As you're leaving, the user realizes that the printer he has used isn't available in Windows 2000. There aren't drivers for this printer on the manufacturer's web site for Windows 2000. What can you do to temporarily fix this problem in Windows 2000?

   A. Install the Windows 98 driver in Windows 2000.

   B. Find a similar model printer driver and install that.

   C. Update the printer because it isn't supported by Windows 2000.

   D. There's no temporary fix for this problem.

14. You're attempting to install Windows XP on a newer computer. When you insert the Windows XP installation media in the CD-ROM drive, it isn't booting. This system isn't connected to a network. There are other computers

in the area that you can use that are running Windows 98, Window 2000, and Windows XP. What can you do to install Windows XP on this computer?

A. You can insert the installation media in a working computer and make a boot floppy set for Windows XP from the installation media.

B. You can access the Internet from another computer and download the boot floppy images from the Microsoft web site.

C. Replacing the CD drive with one that's bootable is the only solution in this situation.

D. You can use the installation disks from Windows 2000 to perform the installation.

15. To better prepare yourself for emergency situations, you want to ensure that you're equipped with the tools you might need to restore the system in case of a failure. Which of the listed operating systems doesn't support creating an ERD or recovery floppies?

A. Windows 98

B. Windows NT 4

C. Windows 2000

D. Windows XP

16. You've installed a new Plug and Play PCI network adapter in your Windows 98 computer and restarted. Surprisingly, the operating system didn't detect the network adapter automatically. Which of the following is true?

A. The operating system doesn't support Plug and Play.

B. PCI adapters aren't Plug and Play.

C. The system BIOS doesn't support Plug and Play.

D. Plug and Play software isn't installed.

17. You've just upgraded your Windows 98 computer to Windows XP. When you try to connect to the Internet, the modem doesn't respond. You open Device Manager and find that the modem is listed as an Unknown Device. What should you do with the modem?

A. Replace the modem.

B. Install Windows XP Service Pack 1.

    C. Install an updated driver for the modem.

    D. Reconfigure the Dial-Up Networking.

18. You want to upgrade a Windows XP Home Edition system to Windows XP Professional. Which of the following statements is false?

    A. You'll need to acquire the Windows XP Professional CD and license.

    B. The upgrade doesn't affect licensing. Your existing Windows XP license is valid.

    C. You'll need to activate and register the new Windows XP operating system.

    D. The hardware that's running on your Windows XP Home Edition will work properly under Windows XP Professional.

19. You want to upgrade a high-end Windows NT 4 Workstation system to Windows XP Professional. Which identifies the correct upgrade path for this upgrade?

    A. A direct upgrade exists for this configuration.

    B. You'll need to upgrade to Windows 2000 first to accomplish this upgrade.

    C. You'll need to reformat your drives to work with NTFS 5.

    D. There isn't an upgrade path for this situation. Windows NT 4 is too old.

20. You've just completed the installation of a Windows XP Home Edition operating system. You're concerned that the operating system doesn't reflect the most current software maintenance and release options for Windows XP. Which of the following is the most valid solution for this concern?

    A. Use the Windows Update program to get the latest updates from Microsoft.

    B. Windows XP will automatically attempt to update your computer during the installation.

    C. You'll need to create an update disk to perform an update on a Windows XP computer.

    D. You can use the WINNT.EXE program to get updates from the installation CD.

21. You have a client who is sight impaired. She has just received a new computer with Windows XP and has asked you to help configure the operating system so that she can see text on the screen more clearly. Which option best describes what you need to do to configure her system?

   A. Use Add/Remove Programs to install the Accessibility options from the installation CD.

   B. Use the Accessibility options, available under Accessories on the Start menu.

   C. Configure Accessibility options using the Accessibility icon in Control Panel.

   D. Purchase third-party accessibility software for your client.

22. You've just replaced a malfunctioning AGP adapter on your Windows XP computer. When you log on to Windows XP, you get a warning message telling you that you have 30 days to activate your software. What's the most likely problem?

   A. You'll need to replace the defective adapter with an identical model to eliminate this problem.

   B. You'll need to contact Microsoft via telephone and obtain a new activation number.

   C. You can ignore this message, it's only a warning.

   D. You must reinstall Windows XP when you upgrade a component such as an AGP adapter.

23. Your corporate network is very busy during the day, and you want to configure the Automatic Updates utility to check for updates at 1 a.m. every day. Which of the following choices will make this happen in Windows XP?

   A. Write a batch script to run the update using the Scheduler.

   B. The Automatic Updates utility is exactly that; you have no ability to change the configuration of the Automatic Updates utility.

   C. Click Start | Control | Add or Remove Programs | Set Program Access and Defaults, and follow the wizard to change these settings.

   D. Click Start | Control Panel | System | Automatic Updates, and change the setting in the Settings window.

24. Your Windows XP system doesn't start after you upgraded the operating system using the Windows Update program. Which of the following choices will allow you fix this problem?

    A. Use the Roll Back feature of Windows XP.

    B. Use the Recovery Console of Windows XP to restore the previous version.

    C. Use the Last Known Good Configuration option to restart.

    D. Reboot using the Safe mode of Windows XP.

25. You've just installed a new device in your computer. When you go to the manufacturer's web site and update the driver, you get a warning indicating the driver is unsigned when you attempt to install it. What should you do at this point about the driver?

    A. Install the driver; that's a normal error message.

    B. Don't install the driver; this indicates the manufacturer's web site has been hijacked.

    C. Contact Microsoft Technical Support for the correct driver.

    D. Drivers aren't signed, so this won't happen.

26. You're installing a new adapter in your Windows 98 system. The installation goes uneventfully, and you updated the driver from the Windows 98 distribution media. You just visited the manufacturer's web site and found a driver for this adapter that's newer than the one on your installation media. Which driver should you use?

    A. You should always only use the driver provided with the installation media.

    B. You should use the driver from the manufacturer. The manufacturer knows best.

    C. You should consult the Microsoft Support web site to verify which driver is correct.

    D. You should only use the drivers included with the adapter when you install it.

27. You're receiving a message that your system is running low on resources on a Windows 9x machine. What should you do to remedy this message?

    A. Upgrade the RAM on this system; you're overutilizing memory.

    B. You can ignore this message; it's informational only.

    C. You should reboot the operating system to fix this problem.

    D. This is a Windows XP error and doesn't occur on Windows 9x.

28. You want to move the location of the swap file on a Windows XP system. Which method is preferred to accomplish this?

    A. Set the TEMP environment variable to a new directory.

    B. Click Start | Control Panel | System | Advanced, click the Performance button, and then configure the swap file to the new location.

    C. The swap file is always managed for optimum performance on Windows XP, and you don't need to change it.

    D. You can't change the swap file location on a Windows XP system.

29. You want to install a new application on a client's Windows 98 machine. When you attempt to install the application, you get a message indicating that insufficient disk space exists on the computer. When you discuss this with the user, he can't believe it because he only does a few simple office tasks and uses this computer for Internet research. Which of the choices is the best to correct this problem?

    A. Install additional hard drive space to allow for space for the application.

    B. Decrease the size of the swap file to allocate more space for other applications.

    C. Delete all files in the temporary directory under Windows.

    D. Use the Disk Cleanup Wizard to delete all unnecessary files.

30. Three users are sharing a Windows XP system. Two of the users are complaining that one of the users is "hogging all the disk space." What can you do to rectify this situation?

    A. Delete all old files and set a disk quota using My Computer, selecting a drive, right-clicking the drive, selecting Properties, clicking the Quota tab, and setting a disk quota for users.

    B. Run the Computer Management application in Control Panel, and select Disk Management and then enable Disk Quotas.

    C. Like Windows 9x, Windows XP doesn't support a disk quota scheme.

    D. Only delete old files from the hard disk.

A
QUICK ANSWER KEY

1.	B	16.	C
2.	C	17.	C
3.	C	18.	B
4.	D	19.	A
5.	B	20.	B
6.	D	21.	C
7.	D	22.	B
8.	B	23.	D
9.	C	24.	C
10.	B	25.	A
11.	A	26.	B
12.	C	27.	C
13.	D	28.	B
14.	B	29.	D
15.	D	30.	A

IN-DEPTH ANSWERS

1. ☑ **B.** Windows XP requires a minimum of 64MB of RAM for installation. In practicality, you'll want to have at least 128MB of RAM for acceptable system performance.

   ☒ **A, C,** and **D** are incorrect. All of these components meet the minimum requirements for Windows XP. You or your user won't be happy with this system because it's a very minimal system and will be extremely slow. It's recommended that a Pentium 4 with a minimum of 20GB of diskspace, and at least a 4× CD-ROM be used on a Windows XP system.

2. ☑ **C.** The first thing you should do before installing Windows 98, or any other operating system, on your computer is see if the existing hardware meets the minimum hardware requirements and make sure that it's on the Hardware Compatibility List. This will ensure that you won't face any hardware-related problems during the installation process.

   ☒ **A** is incorrect because you can do this after you determine if your hardware meets the minimum hardware requirements of the new operating system. **B** is incorrect because this is certainly not the first step to perform when you're preparing to install a new operating system. **D** is incorrect because the only thing you should be concerned about before installing Windows 98 is that your computer has the minimum requirements. The games and other entertainment software are a secondary issue.

3. ☑ **C.** Windows XP will do all necessary disk configuration activities during the installation. You can manually initialize a new drive using DOS or other utilities, but this involves an extra step because Windows XP will want to upgrade the disk to the newest file system. Once you've installed Windows XP, you can use Disk Management to change the configuration of any of the disks on the system.

   ☒ **A** is incorrect because you should avoid using FDISK with Windows XP. Windows XP has the newest versions of these utilities, and Microsoft recommends strongly you use the Disk Management tools provided. These tools are much safer and more reliable. **B** is incorrect because you can't use Disk Management until you've successfully installed Windows XP. **D** is incorrect because virtually all disk manufacturers' disks will operate as-is on Windows XP systems and don't require third-party utilities for configuration.

4. ☑ **D.** Create the primary partition during installation and the other partitions using Disk Management after installation. Windows 2000 gives you an option of creating one or all partitions during the installation process, but it's recommended you create only the first partition during the installation, which is necessary to complete the installation process, and when the installation is complete, use the Disk Management console to create and format other partitions. Disk Management allows you to create as many partitions as you want, but the FDISK utility limits the number of primary partitions you can work with. Besides this, Disk Management can format the partitions using the NTFS file system and offer conversion to dynamic disks, some features that aren't available when you use FDISK.

☒ **A** is incorrect because Microsoft doesn't recommend this because of limitations of the FDISK utility. **B** is incorrect because the Disk Management console becomes available only after you've installed the Windows 2000 operating system. **C** is incorrect for the same reason. Disk Management can't be used before the installation of Windows 2000 is complete.

5. ☑ **B.** Because the data files are critical for you, you must back up these files before you run the upgrade install. Although the upgrade install doesn't harm any data files, it's always better to back up important files before upgrading the existing operating system in case of accidental data loss.

☒ **A** is incorrect because the safety of data files is critical, and this should be your first concern. **C** is incorrect because Windows 2000 Setup doesn't include an uninstall option. **D** is incorrect because data compression doesn't ensure the safety of critical data. It only saves hard disk space.

6. ☑ **D.** Remember that you can upgrade to Windows 2000 Professional only from a workstation or desktop operating system and not from a server operating system. You can directly upgrade to Windows 2000 Professional from Windows 95 OSR2, Windows 98/Me, Windows NT 3.51 Workstation, and Windows NT 4 Workstation.

☒ **A, B,** and **C** are all incorrect answers because all these operating systems can be upgraded to Windows 2000 Professional. When you insert the Windows 2000 Professional Setup CD-ROM, the Autorun program on the CD-ROM detects the previous operating system and prompts you to select whether you want to perform a clean install or an upgrade install.

7. ☑ **D.** Whatever the size or formatting of the partition, by default Setup will keep it intact. The setup program doesn't change the file system on any partition when you're dual booting with Windows 98. Instead, you're given an option to make your selection.

☒ **A** is incorrect because the setup program won't convert any partition less than 2GB to the FAT32 file system. **B** is incorrect because the partition won't be automatically converted to NTFS. **C** is incorrect because this action is also not performed automatically.

8. ☑ **B.** You would keep the installation configuration of Windows 98 the same, and when you install Windows 2000, you'll be prompted as to where to put the operating systems files. You would want to select drive D: in this case and a directory. This will put the operating systems files in the location you specified and put the critical boot files on drive C:. This will allow the system to support both operating systems.

☒ **A** is incorrect because you don't have adequate space on drive C: to install Windows 2000. Windows 2000 requires a minimum of 1GB to install in a minimal configuration. You'd utilize all of the remaining disk space on drive C: just with the new operating system. **C** is incorrect because drive D: has adequate space to install the Windows 2000 system files. **D** is incorrect because if you convert the drives to NTFS you will not be able access them from Windows 9x.

9. ☑ **C.** The startup disks for Windows 2000 Professional can be created by running the MAKEBOOT.EXE command, located in the \BOOTDISK folder on the setup CD. Be careful because the question tries to confuse you by stating that the Windows 2000 setup files are in the \I386 folder. The MAKEBOOT.EXE command can be run on any computer running MS-DOS or the Windows operating systems. It's important to note that the setup disks for Windows 2000 Professional and Windows 2000 Server are different.

☒ **A** is an incorrect command because this command is used in Window NT and is no longer valid in Windows 2000. **B** is incorrect for two reasons. First, the WINNT32.EXE command is used for upgrading a previous Windows 2000 operating system to Windows 2000 Professional, and second, you can't specify A: as the destination drive. **D** is incorrect because the MAKEBOOT.EXE command can be used on any computer running MS-DOS or Windows operating systems.

10. ☑ **B.** NTLDR loads the operating system, NTDETECT runs to detect the hardware, and NTOSKRNL loads the graphics mode. When a Windows 2000 computer is started, the POST runs, and NTLDR locates and loads the operating system as specified in the BOOT.INI file. NTLDR then loads the NTDETECT file that detects the installed hardware. After this, NTLDR locates and loads NTOSKRNL, the operating system kernel. Finally, the boot process is handed over by NTLDR to NTOSKRNL, which then loads the device drivers and initializes them as specified in the Registry. In other words, the sequence is NTLDR, NTDETECT, and NTOSKRNL.

☒ **A** is incorrect because NTOSKRNL is loaded after the NTDETECT file. **C** is incorrect because NTLDR doesn't run the POST. The POST is run by the BIOS, and the BIOS locates and runs the NTLDR file, which starts the actual Windows 2000 boot process. **D** is incorrect because neither does NTDETECT load the graphics mode nor does NTOSKRNL detect installed hardware.

11. ☑ **A.** Start the System applet in Windows 2000 Control Panel and increase the wait time to 20 on the Startup/Shutdown tab. In Windows 98 and Windows 2000 dual-boot systems, the boot loader gives you the option of selecting an operating system to load. This option screen is displayed for 30 seconds by default, unless this timing is modified. A possible reason that you aren't able to see the option screen is that this wait time has been set to 0 seconds. This is quite likely because the technician had to restart the system several times and probably didn't want to wait every time while the options screen was displayed. You can modify this wait time on the Startup/Shutdown tab of the System applet in Control Panel after starting the system in Windows 2000 Professional.

☒ **B** is incorrect because there's no indication in the question that Windows 2000 Professional was installed as an upgrade. If the system were upgraded, the question should have stated so. **C** is incorrect because

BOOT.INI is a system file, and its attributes are read-only by default. Unless you change these attributes, you can't modify this file. When a better option exists to correct the problem, you shouldn't alter any files manually. **D** is incorrect because when you want to boot Windows 2000 with any older operating system, it must be the last operating system to be installed.

12. ☑ **C.** When you select the Last Known Good Configuration option, the Windows 2000 computer reverts to the saved configuration that was previously used to boot the system successfully. Any changes made to the system files and the Registry after that will be lost. This startup option is best used when you've loaded a device driver that prevents the system from booting normally after restart.

☒ **A** and **B** are incorrect answers because these options don't exist in Windows 2000 as startup modes. These are Windows 98 startup options. **D** is incorrect because this mode enables you to collect boot information in a log file that you can analyze later to resolve the problem but won't resolve the problem.

13. ☑ **D.** There's no temporary fix for this problem. In all probability, this is a printer that's too old and no longer supported by the manufacturer. This situation is unfortunate, but it does occur from time to time. Encourage the user to replace this printer with a new one.

☒ **A** is incorrect. Drivers aren't interchangeable between operating systems. This may cause the system to hang if Device Manager doesn't catch it and allows it to be installed. **B** is incorrect, but you may be able to find a compatible driver if you investigate enough on the Internet. Some printers are relabeled and there may be a similar driver available, but you shouldn't assume this. **C** is incorrect because there's probably no update for a printer that would include a driver. The problem here is the driver, not the printer.

14. ☑ **B.** The only way to create setup floppies for Windows XP is to download a program from the Microsoft web site that'll create a set when you supply six blank floppy disks. Microsoft has recently announced that floppy installation disks are no longer supported after Windows XP. You'll probably want to update the CD-ROM drive because most of these devices have been bootable for a few years, and it'd be more convenient for future software releases.

☒ **A** is incorrect. There's no program on the Windows XP installation media to make setup floppies. **C** is incorrect because you can create a startup disk set using a program available on the Microsoft web site. **D** is incorrect. Setup disks aren't interchangeable between operating system versions.

15. ☑ **D.** Windows XP doesn't support the creation of an emergency repair disk. Instead, this is managed by Windows XP. There are several recovery options available for Windows XP that can be accessed through the System Recovery Wizard.

☒ **A, B,** and **C** are incorrect because ERD or recovery disk options are available on these other choices. It's important to remember that these disks don't back up data or application disks, only some of the critical system information needed to recover the operating system. To fully prepare for emergency situations, you should regularly back up your system and data files on tape drives.

16. ☑ **C.** The most likely reason for the operating system not being able to detect the new Plug and Play network adapter is that the system BIOS doesn't support Plug and Play. Several older computer BIOSs don't support Plug and Play. To have full Plug and Play functionality in a computer, it's recommended you ensure that the system BIOS, the operating system, and the devices are all Plug and Play compatible.

☒ **A** is incorrect because Windows 98 supports Plug and Play functionality. **B** is incorrect because all PCI adapters are Plug and Play. **D** is incorrect because you don't need to install Plug and Play software separately on a Windows 98 system. Plug and Play support is built in to the operating system itself.

17. ☑ **C.** Install an updated driver for the modem. The modem is listed in Device Manager as Unknown Device because Windows XP didn't recognize it during installation. You should get an updated Windows XP compatible driver for the modem and install it.

☒ **A** is incorrect because you should first try to get and install an updated driver for the modem. **B** is incorrect because unless you're sure that the problem can be addressed by Service Pack 1, you shouldn't install it. The manufacturer of the modem is the right source of an updated driver for the modem. **D** is incorrect because the Dial-Up Networking is dependent on the modem, and if the modem isn't working, this reconfiguration will not resolve the problem.

18. ☑ **B.** Upgrading from Windows XP Home Edition to Professional requires a separate license. Both copies are valid and can still be used, but you must purchase a new or upgrade license to run Windows XP Professional.

    ☒ **A, C,** and **D** are incorrect because these answers are all true.

19. ☑ **A.** You can directly upgrade from Windows NT 4 Workstation to Windows XP. Make sure you've incorporated the latest service packs into Windows NT 4 before you do this upgrade. This will help simplify the process and may help you avoid upgrade problems.

    ☒ **B** is incorrect because you can go directly to Windows XP. **C** is incorrect because the upgrade will automatically update your disk drives to NTFS 5 if they're at NTFS 4. **D** is incorrect because there's a direct path to Windows XP.

20. ☑ **B.** Windows XP attempts to update the software to the latest version during the installation. This can involve a fairly long amount of time on the original Windows XP installations. Later CDs include Service Pack 1 on them. This service pack could take one or two hours to download on a dial-up connection.

    ☒ **A** is incorrect because it's a good idea to run the update immediately after you install the software, but it should automatically run during the installation. **C** and **D** are incorrect because you don't need to create an update disk, and you don't use WINNT.EXE to update your operating system.

21. ☑ **C.** You configure Accessibility options using the Accessibility icon in Control Panel. This allows you to configure all of the Accessibility options that are provided with Microsoft operating systems. These options are minimal, but they're adequate for many impaired people to use. Extensive third-party software and assistive devices are available that should be investigated if you're dealing with users who have accessibility difficulties.

    ☒ **A** is incorrect because Add/Remove Programs doesn't affect accessibility software. It's now installed by default as part of the operating system. **B** is incorrect because the tools are under the Accessories option in the Start menu, but they're configured in Control Panel. **D** is incorrect because you'd want to investigate this if the tools provided aren't adequate but some minimal accessibility tools are provided with Windows XP.

22. ☑ **B.** When you significantly change the configuration of a Windows XP machine, it may trigger the operating system to think it's a new installation.

This is done to prevent software piracy. The only way to acquire a new activation number is contact the Microsoft Activation Center and explain the situation. They'll provide you with a new activation number if they believe your story.

☒ **A** is incorrect. Once you replace the adapter, you may get notified that you need to reactivate even if it's the same model number. Microsoft uses an elaborate algorithm to determine how to detect a new installation has occurred. **C** is incorrect because if you ignore this message, your operating system will stop operating after the grace period. You must register your operating system within 30 days of installation. **D** is incorrect because one of the nice things about the Windows environment is the ease with which controllers can be changed and updated. You'll need to install new drivers, but you won't need to reinstall the operating system.

23. ☑ **D.** You can change the configuration of the Automatic Updates program by selecting Start | Control Panel | System | Automatic Updates and changing the settings in the Settings window. You can also configure other options about how to handle updates in this window.

☒ **A, B,** and **C** are incorrect because you have a great deal of flexibility built into the operating system to deal with system and application updates.

24. ☑ **C.** You can boot the system using the Last Known Good Configuration option if a problem develops after an update. This uses the built-in recovery process in the Windows XP environment. After that, you can attempt to reinstall the update or troubleshoot what has caused the problem.

☒ **A** is incorrect because you can't use the Roll Back feature for drivers until you've booted the operating system. In this case, the system hangs during boot-up. **B** is incorrect because the Recovery Console is helpful in recovering from system startup errors, but you'll have an easier job of fixing this problem using the Last Known Good Configuration option during bootup. **D** is incorrect because Safe mode may work but not in all instances. Start with the Last Known Good Configuration option.

25. ☑ **A.** Driver signing is a method of verifying that you're receiving the most accurate drivers from Microsoft. These files are digitally signed to verify they're authentic. Microsoft generally signs all of its drivers and encourages their

partners do as well. It isn't uncommon for a vendor to provide unsigned drivers, however.

⊠   **B** is incorrect because an unsigned driver isn't an indication of a problem with a driver, only that it doesn't have a signature associated with it. **C** is incorrect because you don't want to contact technical support for this type of problem; it's primarily an administrative one. If you're unsure, contact your network administrator or the manufacturer. **D** is incorrect because this occurs regularly with drivers.

26.   ☑   **B.** Generally, the manufacturer will have more up-to-date drivers than Microsoft. This isn't always the case, and you'll want to verify this by checking the dates of the drivers. You want to use the newest drivers available unless you become aware of a driver with a problem. Microsoft usually provides a set of generic drivers that are developed in conjunction with the manufacturer of the device for many commonly used devices.

⊠   **A** is incorrect because the drivers provided in installation media are frequently the oldest available. You want to try and use the newest drivers in most situations. **C** is incorrect because although you can contact Microsoft, it won't be aware of the latest versions of a manufacturer's drivers in many instances. Contact the manufacturer to inquire about the most recent drivers and their availability. **D** is incorrect because the drivers on installation disks are frequently out-of-date by the time you install them. It's a good practice to use the newest drivers available from the manufacturer.

27.   ☑   **C.** In most cases, a system that reports this is suffering from what's called "memory leaks." Many times old programs don't entirely clear out of memory and can tie up system resources. By restarting the system, you can clear out old data from memory. If the problem continues, you may want to upgrade memory, but it isn't the first thing to try.

⊠   **A** is incorrect because you should try rebooting the system first. **B** is incorrect because you can ignore this message, but it's usually an indication that performance on the system is deteriorating and needs to be addressed. If resource shortages continue, the system may eventually seem to lock up. **D** is incorrect because this message hasn't yet occurred on my machine after almost two years of use. This is a common Windows 9*x* error.

28. ☑ **B.** You can move the swap file to less busy disks by following the steps outlined in this answer. This allows you to spread the workload across multiple disk drives and will ultimately improve performance.

☒ **A** is incorrect because the location of where the system puts temporary files has nothing to do with the location of the swap file. **C** and **D** are incorrect because you can and should manage your swap file configurations on a multidisk system.

29. ☑ **D.** Use the Disk Cleanup Wizard to delete unneeded files on your system. This will scan all of the drives and directories and allow you to systematically delete the large volume of "junk" files that exist on PC systems today. Remember, each web site you visit potentially is stored on your hard disk, and these directories are enormous. Deleting them periodically can do wonders for your disk storage.

☒ **A** is incorrect because you may need to expand disk space, but if you haven't cleaned the existing disk, you may not need to add more disk space. **B** is incorrect because decreasing the size of the swap file may free up some space, but you'll potentially degrade performance of your system in the process. **C** is incorrect because deleting all the files in the temporary directory may free up some space, but usually this is a relatively small amount of space compared to the Internet directories.

30. ☑ **A.** The best thing to do in this situation is to set a disk quota using the procedure described in the answer. This will allow you to restrict disk usage on all users on the system. This will force users to delete files when they're no longer needed.

☒ **B** is incorrect because disk quotas aren't part of the Disk Management subsystem. **C** is incorrect because disk quota schemes are supported in both Windows 2000 and XP. **D** is incorrect because deleting old files is a good idea but will only delay the likelihood of this complaint happening again. You're better off dealing with these types of problems proactively.

CORE HARDWARE/OPERATING SYSTEM EXAMS

9

Diagnosing and Troubleshooting

D iagnosing and troubleshooting operating system problems are some of the most fun you'll have as an A+ technician. The complexity of the newer operating systems when coupled with the new hardware and software that's always showing up virtually guarantees that something will be going wrong somewhere.

Your ability to quickly and correctly diagnose problems in Windows 9*x*, Windows NT 4, Windows 2000, and Windows XP will help you to build a signature presence with the clients you work with.

QUESTIONS

1. You've installed a new adapter in your computer, which is running Windows 98. After the installation, you modified the CONFIG.SYS file manually. When you start the computer, the following error message is displayed:
    Error in CONFIG.SYS line 5.

    Which of the following would you rule out as a possible cause of the error?

    A. The adapter is faulty.

    B. You haven't installed the adapter driver.

    C. The file referenced in CONFIG.SYS doesn't exist in the specified location.

    D. There's a syntax error in CONFIG.SYS line 5.

2. One of your friends upgraded his Windows 98 computer to Windows 2000 a few days ago. He has called you to inform you that his computer doesn't start. You visit him and suspect that the problem is caused by a corrupted startup file. How will you fix a startup problem in his Windows 2000 computer?

    A. Boot the system with a Windows 2000 boot disk, and run the SYS command.

    B. Boot the system using the emergency repair disk, and replace the corrupt files from the CD.

C. Boot the system using the Windows 2000 CD, start the installation, and when prompted, choose the Repair option.

D. Boot the system using the emergency repair disk, and run the SYS command.

3. A computer that's running Windows 98 is exhibiting some boot problems. You want to diagnose the problem that's preventing the system from booting normally. Which of the following utilities are you unable to use for your diagnosis?

A. Device Manager

B. Automatic Skip driver

C. System Configuration utility

D. None of the above

4. One of your colleagues has told you that he was working on the Registry files of his Windows 98 computer, and now his computer doesn't boot. The applications installed on his computer are the same as on your computer, so you copy the Registry from your computer onto a floppy disk, and then copy it onto your friend's computer. What will happen when your friend's computer starts?

A. The computer will boot normally because both computers have the same applications.

B. The computer won't boot because the Windows 98 Registry is computer specific.

C. The computer will boot normally, but the applications will need reconfiguration.

D. The computer will boot only in Safe mode, and some of the applications will work.

5. In which of the following situations will the Windows 98 Safe mode not be helpful in resolving startup problems?

A. When you have a display driver problem

B. When the Safe mode with Networking doesn't work

C. When the Step-by-Step Confirmation mode isn't helpful

D. When the Safe mode with Command Prompt doesn't work

6. You have a dual-boot computer that's running Windows XP and Windows NT 4. You just had to reinstall Windows NT 4 because of a problem with a virus. The installation was successful, and no errors were reported. You shut the system down and attempt to restart the computer running the Windows XP operating system. You're now getting the following error message:

   Windows XP could not start because the following files were missing or corrupted: WINDOWS\SYSTEM32\CONFIG\SYSTEM NTLDR MISSING

   Which of the following will probably correct this problem?

   A. Replace the NTLDR and NTDETECT.COM files from the Windows NT 4 distribution media.

   B. Replace the BOOT.INI file.

   C. Replace the NTLDR and NTDETECT.COM files from the Windows XP distribution media.

   D. None of these choices will fix the problem.

7. A computer running the Windows 2000 Professional operating system is running very slowly. This computer has a Pentium III processor and 32MB of RAM. You've noticed that there's a lot of activity on the hard disk. This hard disk was defragmented two days ago, and when you run ScanDisk, it doesn't report any problems. You suspect that the Windows swap file might be causing the problem. What should you do to resolve the problem?

   A. Delete the WIN386.SWP file, and restart the computer.

   B. Increase the size of PAGEFILE.SYS.

   C. Create another paging file on the hard disk.

   D. Increase the RAM in the computer.

8. You've received a panic call from a customer indicating that her computer has malfunctioned during an upgrade to Windows XP. When you arrive, you see she's getting this message:

   Windows could not start because the following file is missing or corrupt: Windows\System32\Hal.dll

   What should you attempt to fix this problem?

A.   Use the Recovery Console, and use the BOOTCFG command to verify and rebuild your BOOT.INI file.

B.   Edit or create the BOOT.INI file in the Windows XP system files directory.

C.   Use the Last Known Good Configuration option at startup.

D.   Replace the HAL.DLLfile from the distribution media.

9.   Whenever you launch a game program in your Windows 98 computer, it starts, but after some time, the system locks up. This causes problems with other applications that are running. You click several times to exit from the game program, but your mouse doesn't seem to work in the game window. What should you do to exit from the faulty game program?

A.   Press CTRL-ALT-DEL, and click Shut Down.

B.   Press CTRL-ALT-DEL, select the game program in the dialog box, and click End Task.

C.   Press CTRL-ALT-DEL, and click End Task.

D.   Press CTRL-ALT-DEL twice.

10.   You're using a Windows 2000 Professional workstation in your office. You suspect that someone is trying to log on to your computer in your absence. Your network administrator has suggested that you turn on auditing on your system. Which of the following logs would you check in the Event Viewer console to track unauthorized access to your computer once the auditing has been configured?

A.   System logs

B.   Security logs

C.   Data access logs

D.   Application logs

11.   An application in Windows 98 is trying to execute a function that can't be carried out because of a bug in one of the files associated with the application. Which of the following errors is this action likely to produce on the screen?

A.   "Illegal Operation"

B.   "General Protection Fault"

C. "Invalid Working Directory"

D. System will lock up

12. You're sharing the printer attached to your Windows 98 computer with four of your office colleagues in a peer network. Your computer is heavily loaded with several applications, and a large number of data files are on your hard disk. Recently your colleagues have started complaining that sometimes their print jobs aren't printed at all. Your inquiries reveal that none of the users has received any printing errors so far. What should you do?

A. Change the port in the printer's Properties dialog box.

B. Increase the space in your hard disk.

C. Increase the RAM in your computer.

D. Increase the timeout settings in the printer's Properties dialog box.

Questions 13–16   Just after passing your A+ Core Hardware and A+ OS Technologies exams, you accepted a job as a field technician with a major computer vendor in town. After spending a few days in the office learning customer support procedures, you're now ready to work offsite.

The first trouble call you receive is from a customer that purchased his Pentium 4 computer from your company a few months ago. The computer runs the Windows XP Professional operating system. He also purchased a new printer and has attached it to his computer. He's calling with a complaint about some problems that appeared after he installed the printer.

You arrive at the customer's site and find the problems that are presented in the following four questions. Answer each of the questions, selecting the best answer for each.

13. After connecting the printer to his computer, your customer installed a printer driver on his Windows XP computer. He never tested the driver, and when he restarted the computer, it wouldn't start up. Which of the following modes would you use to most quickly restart the computer to troubleshoot the problem?

A. Boot the system using the Last Known Good Configuration option. Then reinstall the printer driver.

B. Boot the system using the Safe mode, and use Device Manager to remove the faulty printer driver.

    C. Boot the system using the Safe mode with Command Prompt, and replace the printer driver files.

    D. Boot the system using the VGA mode so that the printer driver isn't visible to the system.

14. When the boot problem is solved, the system starts normally. Now other users are complaining that they can't print to his printer. The user can print correctly. What's the most likely problem?

    A. The printer hasn't been shared in the network.

    B. The printer driver isn't installed correctly.

    C. The network driver isn't functioning properly.

    D. An incorrect printer port has been assigned to the printer.

15. Your customer seeks your advice on protecting his computer from viruses. He tells you that he's worried about new viruses that might infect his hard disk. The antivirus utility that he's using was purchased six months ago, and you know that it needs to be updated with new virus signature files. Which of the following should you suggest to him as the best source of getting updated files?

    A. Go to the Microsoft web site.

    B. Go to the manufacturer of the antivirus software.

    C. Use the Windows 98 Setup CD.

    D. None of the above. He needs to purchase a new copy of the antivirus utility.

16. Your further diagnostics indicate that your customer's computer might have a virus. You believe this because the machine repeatedly restarts itself for no apparent reason. You've run an updated virus scan on the computer and repaired the operating system, but the problem persists. How would you remove it at this point?

    A. Use the setup program to remove and re-create the existing partition and reinstall the operating system from the distribution media.

    B. Use the Recovery Console to replace the system files.

    C. Reformat the hard disk, and reinstall the operating system and applications.

    D. Restart the computer using a clean boot disk, and run the antivirus software included with Windows XP.

17. After you've detected and cleaned a virus from a computer, the user complains that an application fails to start. Which of the following should be your first step in fixing this problem?

    A. Restart the computer.

    B. Reinstall the application.

    C. Reinstall the operating system.

    D. Fix the application files with the virus recovery utility.

18. You're contemplating upgrading an older system to Windows XP. The system is currently running Windows Me. What can you do to verify that the system will support Windows XP?

    A. Run the Update Advisor from the Microsoft web site.

    B. Systems that run Windows Me are compatible with Windows XP and should upgrade correctly.

    C. Windows Me to XP isn't a valid upgrade.

    D. Ensure that the system meets the minimum memory and disk requirements only.

19. You have a user that has just upgraded from Windows 2000 Professional to Windows XP Home Edition. He isn't happy with Windows XP and wants to revert his system to Windows 2000 Professional. What can you do?

    A. Run the uninstall procedure to recover Windows 2000.

    B. Reinstall Windows 2000 from the installation media.

    C. Boot using the Last Known Good Configuration option, and recover the operating system.

    D. Use the Recovery Console to replace the key system files.

20. You're trying to perform an upgrade to Windows XP and the installation is repeatedly failing. The computer is connected to a network and the Internet. Which of the following should you check first?

    A. The installation media is defective.

    B. The network connection isn't working.

    C. The operating system is running antivirus software that should be disabled.

    D. A device is incompatible with Windows XP.

21. You want to upgrade a computer that's running Windows XP Home Edition to Windows XP Professional. Which of the following statements is true?

    A. This upgrade requires a completely reformatted hard disk.

    B. This upgrade isn't possible in the current release.

    C. All updates from Microsoft will be automatically applied from Windows XP Home Edition.

    D. This upgrade is performed like any other upgrade and presents no difficulties.

22. You've just upgraded from Windows Me to Windows XP. Which of the following is true?

    A. Logon passwords from Windows Me won't be kept.

    B. Logon passwords from Windows Me will be kept.

    C. The Registry will require a restore to keep settings compatible.

    D. None of the above.

23. A user is trying to burn a CD on a Windows XP system. The process is failing repeatedly and the user isn't being allowed to do it. Which of the following is the first thing you should suspect?

    A. The user needs administrative access to do this task.

    B. The CD burner is defective.

    C. The CD burner driver is out-of-date.

    D. CD burners aren't supported under Windows XP.

24. A user is complaining that his word processing application is repeatedly failing, and he gets a message that an error report has been generated. What would be the most likely way to fix this problem?

    A. Reinstall the application.

    B. Update the software from the vendor's web site.

    C. There's no repair for this problem; it's part of Windows XP.

    D. The system has a virus and should be thoroughly scanned.

25. You've just installed a network printer in a small office network. All of the machines are running Windows XP. A user is complaining that when she hits the Print button in her application that files are being printed to an older printer. She wants to print to the newer printer. What is the most likely problem?

    A. The printer driver she's using is out-of-date.

    B. The network printer isn't shared for this user.

    C. The default printer isn't set correctly.

    D. The printer has malfunctioned.

26. You've just upgraded a system to Windows XP and the user has complained that the system is no longer able to access the TCP/IP network that they're connected to. Other users aren't reporting network problems. Which should you check first?

    A. The NIC card has malfunctioned and needs to be replaced.

    B. The NIC driver installation failed during the upgrade.

    C. The network settings need to be manually applied for the Windows XP system.

    D. The network is no longer functioning.

27. A user has just installed Windows XP Home Edition on a system that was running Windows 2000 Professional. The user is complaining that he can no longer access information that exists in his network. The network servers use Windows 2000 Advanced Server in a domain environment. What should you advise the user?

    A. This upgrade isn't recommended, and they should recover Windows 2000 Professional.

    B. The security models used by Windows XP Home Edition and Professional Edition are different, and he should've upgraded to Professional. He'll need to reinstall Windows 2000 and upgrade to Windows XP Professional.

    C. The system should be upgraded to Windows XP Professional to fix this problem.

    D. This problem will never occur if an install is successful.

28. A user is trying to run an older application on a Windows XP system and isn't succeeding. Upon investigation you determine that the application is a Windows 95–based program, and no upgrades are available for this program to run on Windows XP. What can you do to help this user solve this problem?

    A. There's no fix for this problem; the user will need to find an alternative way to accomplish the work.

    B. The user will need to have a FAT area on the disk for this to work.

    C. The user should configure a multiboot environment with Windows 95 to have this work.

    D. The user can attempt to set the compatibility mode in the Properties box and use the Windows Emulator to run this program.

29. You want to remotely manipulate a Windows XP system through a network from your desktop computer. Which of the following statements is true?

    A. Windows XP doesn't have this capability.

    B. You'll need to purchase separate software for this.

    C. You access Remote Desktop on both versions of Windows XP.

    D. You access Remote Desktop only on Windows XP Professional.

30. You've just connected your Windows XP system to your existing cable modem environment and want to increase the security of your system. You installed and updated the antivirus software to the latest version. What additional capability does Windows XP provide to improve security?

    A. Windows XP provides no security enhancements. You must use an outside vendor.

    B. You can configure Windows XP to enable the firewall included with Windows XP.

    C. The antivirus software is adequate to your needs.

    D. You'll need to install an external firewall for improved security.

QUICK ANSWER KEY

1.	A	16.	C
2.	C	17.	B
3.	D	18.	A
4.	B	19.	B
5.	D	20.	C
6.	C	21.	D
7.	D	22.	A
8.	A	23.	A
9.	B	24.	B
10.	B	25.	C
11.	A	26.	C
12.	B	27.	C
13.	A	28.	D
14.	A	29.	C
15.	B	30.	B

IN-DEPTH ANSWERS

1. ☑ **A.** The adapter is certainly not causing the reported error in the CONFIG.SYS file. Such errors are reported when the operating system is unable to process any code specified in a particular line of the CONFIG.SYS file. Usually this error is produced either when a file specified in the CONFIG.SYS line isn't found or when the specified path is incorrect.

   ☒ **B** is incorrect because it's possible that the CONFIG.SYS line 5 is referencing one of the driver files and isn't able to find it. If you've modified the CONFIG.SYS file, which typically is done to load a specific driver file, and you haven't installed the adapter driver, you'll get this error. **C** is incorrect because this may also cause the given error. **D** is incorrect because if there's a syntax error in the CONFIG.SYS file, the operating system won't be able to process that line.

2. ☑ **C.** Boot the system using the Windows 2000 CD, start the installation, and when prompted, choose the Repair option. The corrupted files in Windows 2000 can be replaced by using the setup boot disks and selecting the Repair option. This option prompts you to insert the emergency repair disk. The emergency repair process replaces the corrupted file with an undamaged copy from the original CD and makes the system bootable.

   ☒ **A** is incorrect because the SYS command doesn't work in Windows 2000. You should replace the corrupted startup file from the original CD by following the proper startup process explained previously. **B** is incorrect because the emergency repair disk can't be used to boot a Windows 2000 computer. You should remember that an emergency repair disk in Windows 2000 isn't a bootable disk. **D** is incorrect because neither is the emergency repair disk bootable nor can the SYS command be used to restore startup files in Windows 2000.

3. ☑ **D.** All of the listed utilities can be used to correct problems in the Windows 98 startup environment. This is a typical example of a confusing question that you might get on the A+ exam. All answer options are correct from

the perspective that they can be used for a startup diagnosis, so you must select the best answer *after* carefully reading the question to be sure to choose the option that corresponds to the question asked, in this case, the utility that *can't* be used.

☒   **A** is incorrect because once you boot into Safe mode, you can use Device Manager to fix any problems with device drivers or resource conflicts. **B** is incorrect because this utility is used to locate a problem driver. Windows 98 includes this utility to skip the loading of the driver files for any device that prevents the operating system from loading normally. **C** is incorrect because you can use this utility once you boot into Safe mode to correct problems with the configuration of system devices and to enable or disable components.

4.   ☑   **B.** The computer won't boot because the Windows 98 Registry is computer specific. The Registry is unique to every Windows 9*x* computer. If you copy the Registry files from one computer to another, it's certain that the latter computer won't work. Although both computers have the same applications installed, there might be several other configuration differences between the two computers. As a general rule, you should remember that the Registry from one computer doesn't work on another.

☒   **A** is incorrect because the Registry contains not only application configuration information but also the configuration of the entire computer system, including hardware and software. **C** is incorrect because the computer won't be able to boot normally after copying the Registry. **D** is incorrect because it can't be predicted whether the computer will boot in Safe mode or whether any of the applications will work.

5.   ☑   **D.** When the Safe mode with Command Prompt doesn't work. The Safe mode with Command Prompt starts the Windows 9*x* computer in real mode. If the real mode isn't able to work, which is the most basic mode of starting Windows 9*x*, you won't be able to load the Safe mode because the Safe mode works in protected mode and needs 32-bit device drivers.

☒   **A** is incorrect because the Safe mode can be used to boot a Windows 9*x* computer if there's a display driver problem. If you have a problem with the display driver, boot Windows 9*x* in Safe mode and change the display driver. **B** is incorrect because if this mode doesn't work because of a network driver problem, you can use the Safe mode and change the network settings or network drivers. **C** is incorrect because this mode allows you to load device drivers selectively. When you boot a Windows 9*x* computer in Safe mode, Windows 9*x* loads using the most basic device drivers.

6. ☑ **C.** Replacing the NTLDR and NTDETECT.COM files from the Windows XP distribution media will probably correct this problem. You can do that using the Recovery Console and the FIXBOOT command. This will restore these files to the Windows XP configuration. Most likely the Windows NT 4 installation that you performed replaced these files with Windows NT 4 files. The Windows NT 4 versions of these files don't support the same functionality and features as the Windows XP versions.

    ☒ **A, B,** and **D** are incorrect because these solutions wouldn't fix the problem.

7. ☑ **D.** The problem symptoms indicate that the excessive paging that's taking place on the hard disk is causing the system to slow down. The paging file in Windows 2000 is used by the operating system as virtual memory. Windows 2000 uses this file when the system is low on random access memory (RAM). If you increase the RAM in the computer, the problem will be resolved.

    ☒ **A** is incorrect because the WIN386.SWP file exists in Windows 9*x*, not in Windows 2000. The name of the swap file in Windows 2000 is PAGEFILE.SYS. **B** is incorrect because this won't help resolve the problem. A better way to prevent paging is to increase the amount of RAM in the computer. **C** is incorrect because this is also not an appropriate solution. When you have two or more hard disks, creating a paging file on each disk does help, but increasing the RAM in the computer is a better way to resolve the problem.

8. ☑ **A.** This error message indicates that the BOOT.INI file is either corrupt or missing. In either case, you'll need to either repair it or rebuild it. The Recovery Console provides the BOOTCFG option to do that. There are two commands to do this. BOOTCFG /list will show you all of the entries in your BOOT.INI file. BOOTCFG /rebuild will begin the process of rebuilding your BOOT.INI file by scanning the system disks and creating entries in your boot file for each of the operating systems it finds on your system.

    ☒ **B** is incorrect. You could edit the BOOT.INI file manually, but this isn't the preferred method of fixing problems. **C** is incorrect because using the Last Known Good Configuration option won't boot the system if the BOOT.INI file is improperly configured. **D** is incorrect because the hal.dll file needs to be installed, not copied.

9. ☑ **B.** When you press CTRL-ALT-DEL, the Close Program window opens. You can select the game program that isn't responding and click the End Task

button. You'll notice that after a few moments another dialog box appears that prompts you to click the End Task button again. This happens because the system isn't able to end the program normally.

☒ **A** is incorrect because if you shut down your system, you're likely to lose any unsaved data. Although you'll be prompted again about whether you want to shut down the system, this answer remains an incorrect option. **C** is incorrect because after you press CTRL-ALT-DEL, you should select the game program that isn't responding. Pressing the End Task button will abruptly close whatever program is currently selected in the Close Program dialog box. **D** is incorrect because if you press this key combination twice, the system will abruptly shut down, and you might lose unsaved data without even getting a warning screen.

10. ☑ **B.** The security logs in Windows 2000 Event Viewer keep a record of unauthorized access to your system after the auditing has been configured. Remember that the security logs won't have any records unless auditing is properly configured. To track users trying to log on to your system, you should audit logon success and failure events.

☒ **A** is incorrect because system logs keep a record of system activities, such as system boot time and whether each device driver has loaded successfully. **C** is incorrect because this kind of log doesn't exist in Windows 2000 computers. There are only three types of logs in Windows 2000: system logs, security logs, and application logs. In addition to these logs, Windows 2000 domain controllers have Domain Name System (DNS) logs. **D** is incorrect because this category contains the events written by applications.

11. ☑ **A.** An "Illegal Operation" error is produced when an application or a particular function in the application can't execute because of either a bug or an incorrect path specified somewhere in the application code. These errors can usually be removed either by reinstalling the application or by installing a patch that addresses the underlying bug.

☒ **B** is incorrect because this type of error is produced when an application attempts to carry out a function that isn't permitted by the system. For example, if an application tries to capture memory space that's used either by another application or by the system itself, a General Protection Fault will occur. **C** is incorrect because this error is produced when an application is launched but the working directory is incorrectly specified in the shortcut. **D** is incorrect because the symptoms stated in the question won't cause the system to lock up.

12. ☑ **B.** The symptoms of the problem indicate that the hard disk of the computer where the printer is defined doesn't have enough space to spool the print jobs. When a large number of print jobs are sent to the printer, the computer where the printer is installed holds the print jobs in the print spooler—that is, on the hard disk—until the print device is ready to accept the job. When this happens, however, if there's insufficient space on the hard disk the print job can't be spooled and therefore doesn't print, but no error message is displayed. You should delete any undesired files from your hard disk to free up space for the print spooler.

☒ **A** is incorrect because the printer port isn't causing the problem. If you change the printer port, no one will be able to print to the printer. **C** is incorrect because the problem isn't caused by low memory in your computer. **D** is incorrect because this will also not help resolve the problem. In most cases, the default timeout settings work fine.

13. ☑ **A.** When there's a problem starting up the Windows XP system, you can boot the system using the Last Known Good Configuration option. This loads the operating system from a previously safe situation. In this case, it'd be before the driver was installed. You could then reinstall the driver to determine if that will fix the problem.

☒ **B** is incorrect because this process is slower than the Last Known Good Configuration option. You could use the Safe mode and then fix the driver problem, but this is slower than the Last Known Good Configuration option. **C** is incorrect because replacing the driver files using the command prompt will not reflect the changes in the Registry, and the problem won't be solved. **D** is incorrect because the VGA mode has nothing to do with nondisplay device drivers on the system. The VGA mode is used to fix display problems.

14. ☑ **A.** The printer has probably not been configured to be shared. Printers aren't automatically shared when they're installed. You can enable sharing by opening the printer's Properties and enabling sharing for the printer. You'll need to link all systems that want to use this printer for network sharing to work.

☒ **B** is incorrect because the printer driver is working properly if the host machine is able to print to the printer. **C** is incorrect because you don't have any indication that other network functions aren't working from the symptoms, which makes A the better answer. **D** is incorrect because if the printer prints on the local machine, it's configured properly.

15. ☑ **B.** The best source of updated files for any antivirus utility is the manufacturer of the software. All manufacturers post new virus signature files on their web sites, and usually these files are free to current customers. You should check the web site of the manufacturer regularly to download the latest virus signature files.

☒ **A** is incorrect because Microsoft doesn't keep updates to any antivirus programs on its web site. **C** is incorrect because you won't find any antivirus update files on the Windows 98 Setup CD-ROM. **D** is incorrect because it isn't necessary to purchase a new copy of the antivirus utility. Most antivirus utilities only need to have updated virus signature files. All your friend needs to do is update the virus signature files that can be downloaded from the manufacturer's web site.

16. ☑ **C.** If you've tried reinstalling the operating system and the problem continues, this indicates that you probably have a boot sector virus that isn't being detected by the antivirus software. Replacing the operating system alone won't repair the problem. The boot sector of the disk must be replaced, and the only effective way to do this is to reformat the disk and reinstall the operating system and the applications. This will result in data loss unless you can figure a way to back up data files before you do it. You can be fairly certain that your applications and data files are virus-free because the problem indicates a boot sector issue.

☒ **A** is incorrect because replacing system files won't repair an infected boot sector. **B** is incorrect because the Recovery Console will allow you to repair system files but won't allow you to fix the boot sector of a Windows XP system. **D** is incorrect because the antivirus software included with Windows XP isn't detecting a virus.

17. ☑ **B.** Many viruses will alter the contents of the files on the system. The antivirus software will usually delete these files. If an application file became contaminated, you'd need to install the application from the distribution media

to repair the installation. You may want to uninstall and then reinstall the software using either the setup program provided with the software or the Add/Remove Programs applet included with all versions of Windows.

☒ **A** is incorrect because restarting the computer won't replace a removed application file. **C** is incorrect because the problem resides with the application and not the operating system. **D** is incorrect because the fix of an application usually only deletes the file unless otherwise indicated in the repair process.

18. ☑ **A.** The Update Advisor will scan your computer to determine if all of the installed devices are compatible with Windows XP. Many video adapters aren't compatible with Windows XP and would need to be replaced to operate. Older video adapters will probably not be certified for Windows XP. It'd be a good idea to visit the web site of the video adapter to see if Windows XP drivers are available.

☒ **B** is incorrect. Many devices aren't compatible with Windows XP unless they're certified to operate with Windows XP. Windows Me is a fairly new operating system, but it's much more capable of accepting older devices than Windows XP. **C** is incorrect because you can upgrade directly from Windows Me to Windows XP. **D** is incorrect because verifying memory and disk capacity isn't enough to ensure that the computer meets the Windows XP system requirements.

19. ☑ **B.** You can't revert to Windows 2000 once Windows XP has been installed. You'll need to reinstall the operating system for this to occur. You may need to reinitialize disk drives during the process. It's always good practice to back up your system before you begin any upgrade. This may prevent losing work if an upgrade isn't satisfactory.

☒ **A** is incorrect because the uninstall procedure doesn't work with Windows 2000. **C** is incorrect because the Last Known Good Configuration option is only good when using the same operating system. **D** is incorrect because using the Recovery Console won't replace all of the files needed to run Windows 2000.

20. ☑ **C.** When installing Windows XP, it's important that you disable antivirus software. Windows XP upgrades make a large number of changes to the operating system that may trigger warnings in your antivirus software. The most likely initial suspect in a problem with an upgrade is the antivirus software running on the machine.

☒ **A** is incorrect because the media is the last thing you should suspect in this situation. Media errors will usually be reported during the installation as "errors." **B** is incorrect because you can install Windows XP without a network connection. **D** is incorrect because this is a possibility, but you'd want to check the antivirus software before you suspect an incompatible device. You'll typically get an error message during the install if a device isn't compatible.

21. ☑ **D.** The upgrade from Windows XP Home Edition to XP Professional is a straightforward upgrade and should work with no difficulties.

☒ **A** is incorrect because both version of Windows XP use the same file system format and reformatting won't be required. **B** is incorrect because this is a supported upgrade. **C** is incorrect because updates aren't applied until the operating system is installed.

22. ☑ **A.** Passwords for logon aren't migrated in this upgrade. The two security models are incompatible, so you'll want to apply new passwords when the installation is completed.

☒ **B** is incorrect because passwords aren't retained in this upgrade. **C** is incorrect because Registry settings will automatically be upgraded to Windows XP during the installation. **D** is incorrect because A is correct.

23. ☑ **A.** The burn functions on a CD burner require higher privileges than a normal user is given. This can be applied by the system administrator or the user requires system administrator privileges to use the burner.

☒ **B** is incorrect because the burner shouldn't be suspected until the privileges are established correctly. **C** is incorrect because the driver won't affect privileges. **D** is incorrect because CD burners are supported under Windows XP.

24. ☑ **B.** If the application is repeatedly failing, it's probably a problem with the application not being compatible with the operating system version in use. This is usually indicated by intermittent or sporadic problems with an application. You may also want to verify that the operating system is up-to-date and that all updates have been installed. If the problem persists, you'll probably need to contact the vendor of the application for assistance.

☒ **A** isn't the best choice until you have verified that all software is up-to-date. If you're certain the system is up-to-date, reinstalling the application may fix the problem. This wouldn't be the best first choice, though. **C** is incorrect because you can't yet determine whether the problem is with the operating system or the application. **D** is incorrect because you should first verify that the application and operating system versions are compatible.

25. ☑ **C.** Most applications have a Print button that sends documents to the default printer. This setting can be changed using the printer setup screen or the print options in the operating system.

☒ **A** is incorrect because the printer is working on other computers. You'd want to check the default printer for this user before you suspect a printer driver problem. **B** is incorrect because you don't know if the printer is shared. Printer sharing is done by the host computer, not the client or user computer. Users link to a shared computer. **D** is incorrect because printer malfunctions aren't as likely as the default settings for the user.

26. ☑ **C.** Windows XP attempts to detect networks on the network interface card (NIC) and will configure to a typical setting by default. You'll need to configure the TCP/IP address, subnet mask, and default gateway in a TCP/IP network if automatic addressing such as DHCP isn't available on the network.

☒ **A** is incorrect because a malfunctioning NIC will normally be identified as part of the setup. You should suspect network settings before a hardware malfunction if the network operated before the upgrade. **B** is incorrect because a driver failure will usually show itself in either Device Manager or during the upgrade. **D** is incorrect because you don't have adequate information to determine if the network isn't functioning.

27. ☑ **C.** Windows XP Home Edition systems don't have the ability to join domain environments. You'd need to upgrade to Windows XP Professional for this to be possible. The security models are incompatible.

☒ **A** is incorrect; this upgrade is common and supported by Microsoft. **B** is incorrect because you can upgrade from Windows XP Home Edition to Professional without going back to Windows 2000. You can make this upgrade normally. **D** is incorrect because this problem does occur when a user attempts to join a Microsoft domain.

28. ☑ **D.** Windows XP allows for emulation of earlier versions of operating systems including Windows 95. This allows Windows XP to support older applications, saving software investments. This isn't always possible but does work in many instances.

☒   **A** is incorrect because you can use the emulator for older versions of Windows. **B** is incorrect because you won't need to use FAT for a program running under the Windows XP emulator. **C** is incorrect because you can emulate Windows 95 with the emulator. If you can't configure the emulator to work, you could attempt a multiboot, but this isn't a recommended multiboot option with Windows XP.

29.   ☑   **C.** Remote Desktop allows users to assist each other through a network. For this to work, one user must invite the other user to assist. The inviting system is referred to as the "client" and the invited user is referred to as the "expert." The expert can manipulate the desktop of the client system as if they were a local user of the system.

☒   **A** is incorrect because Windows XP supports this capability. **B** is incorrect because this software is included as part of Windows XP. **D** is incorrect because both Windows XP Home Edition and Professional support this function.

30.   ☑   **B.** Windows XP provides a firewall that can be activated to provide additional security. This firewall prevents attempts to gain access and blocks unauthorized connections.

☒   **A** is incorrect because Windows XP provides a large number of security enhancements. **C** is incorrect because Windows XP includes a time trial version of McAfee antivirus software. **D** is incorrect because although adding an external firewall will help protect a network, it may not be needed in a single computer installation.

10

Networks

N etworks are an important part of almost every computer environment. Understanding the basic concepts of networks will help you more effectively support your customers and improve your worth as a technician. The A+ exam tests across a wide range of networking concepts in both the core and OS exam. You won't be expected to know deeply how to repair complicated network problems, but you can expect to need to know how to configure and repair basic network problems on client PCs.

QUESTIONS

1. You're using two Windows 98 computers at home and want to network them so that you can share files and a common printer connected to one of the computers. You've purchased two network adapters, and you've just completed installing the network adapters and drivers on both computers and connecting the two computers using a cross-over UTP cable. Where should you start configuring the network?

   A. From the My Computer icon on the desktop

   B. From the Network applet in Control Panel

   C. From Device Manager in System Properties

   D. From the Network Neighborhood icon on the desktop

2. You want to configure the TCP/IP properties in your Windows XP computer, and your network administrator has told you that you have a DHCP server on the network. The following statements describe some of the properties of a DHCP server. Identify the incorrect statement.

   A. The DHCP server assigns IP addresses and subnet masks automatically to DHCP clients.

   B. The DHCP server can assign the addresses of DNS and WINS servers.

   C. The DHCP server often assigns the IP addresses for a predetermined time called a "lease."

   D. The DHCP server machine is either a Windows NT server or a Windows 2000 server.

3. You want to share some of your folders on a small Windows 98 peer network. Which of the following options do you have to control access to the shared drives and folders?

    A. Read Only and Full Access

    B. Full Access and Modify

    C. Read Only and Take Ownership

    D. Read Only and Full Control

4. You and your friend have just joined a small company and have been given two new Windows 98 computers. You're working jointly on a training project, and you want to share one of the folders related to the project with your colleague. When you open the Properties dialog box of the folder in Windows Explorer, you find that the Sharing tab doesn't exist. You check the Network Properties in Control Panel, but the Sharing tab doesn't exist there either, as shown in the following illustration.

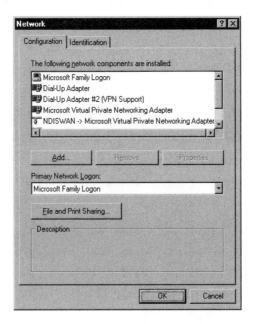

    You check your friend's computer and find the same problem there. When you try to connect to the shared folders on other older computers, you don't have any problems. What could be the reason?

A. Networking software isn't properly installed.

B. File and Printer Sharing hasn't been enabled.

C. There's a problem with the network drivers.

D. An incorrect network protocol is being used.

5. You're being asked to troubleshoot a Windows XP Professional computer system that's attached to a network that has Windows 2000, Windows 98, and Windows XP systems on it. You're able to see network shares and are able to browse computers that are internal to your network using Internet Explorer. You're unable to view web sites on the Internet. What's the most likely problem occurring in this situation of the following choices?

A. The default gateway settings are incorrect on your computer.

B. The TCP/IP suite isn't loaded properly on your computer.

C. Client Services hasn't been installed on your computer.

D. Your network connection isn't working.

6. You're working on a computer that appears to be malfunctioning. You're able to view systems using a web browser if you type in the IP address of the computer. When you type in the web site name, you get an error from the browser. What's the most likely problem?

A. Internet Explorer isn't configured properly.

B. Your computer's TCP/IP suite is corrupt.

C. The address of the DNS server is improper.

D. The default gateway is malfunctioning.

7. You're working on a Windows XP Professional system that's connected to a LAN. The owner of the system is concerned that some users may gain access to her computer and read confidential files. Specifically she's worried about anyone who is logged on using the temporary accounts used by contractors. This network doesn't contain a domain controller. Which configuration option will allow some users to be excluded from her system?

A. Enable Simplified Sharing to limit access to specified users.

B. Disable Simplified Sharing to limit access to specified users.

C. Windows XP Professional doesn't have a mechanism to do this without a domain.

D. No changes are needed on this computer to accomplish the task.

Questions 8–10   You've been asked to report at a customer's site where your company installed a small Windows 98 peer-to-peer network. There seems to be some connectivity issues and sharing problems.

When you arrive at the customer's site, you find they're using a bus network with a thin coaxial cable. After making sure there are no issues related to cabling or termination, you start working on one of the computers.

You discover that the network, although very small, is using the TCP/IP network protocol. The manager of the company tells you he uses TCP/IP because he's a bit technically minded and likes to experiment on his network.

You start your diagnosis. Some interesting problems start to surface, as described in the following three questions. Answer these questions by selecting the best answer for each.

8. Because all the computers have manually configured IP addresses, what's the quickest method to learn the IP configuration of computer A?

    A. Check the statistics of computer A from the DHCP server.

    B. Ping from computer B to computer A, and the IP address of computer A will be listed.

    C. Run WINIPCFG from the command prompt of computer A.

    D. Run WINIPCFG A: from the command prompt of computer B.

9. There seems to be an interesting story about two of the computers. The manager of the company tells you he configured the TCP/IP on both of these computers a few days ago. From that time onward, only that computer which is turned on first works on the network. What could be the reason?

    A. Both computers have the same IP address.

    B. Both computers are configured with the same subnet mask.

    C. The computers are using each other's IP address as a default gateway.

    D. None of the above; this is a common problem in bus networks.

10. You're told that one of the computers is working as a print server. An HP LaserJet printer is connected to this computer and is shared by all users. Sometimes it's difficult to manage print jobs when a print job gets stuck. The manager is asking for your suggestions as to how to get around this problem without having to resubmit all print jobs. What should be your answer?

    A. Stop sharing the printer as soon as a job gets stuck, delete the job, and then share the printer again.

    B. Open the Printer dialog box, click the Printer menu, and then click Purge Print Documents.

    C. Open the Printer dialog box, click the Documents menu, and then click Pause Printing.

    D. Open the Printer dialog box, select the stuck print job, and then click Cancel.

11. Which of the following protocols is used for downloading e-mail from an e-mail server on the Internet?

    A. POP3

    B. SMTP

    C. TFTP

    D. FTP

12. Which of the following would you use to configure additional settings for your Dial-Up Networking connection to the ISP, such as automatic logon authentication?

    A. TCP/IP settings

    B. Server types

    C. Scripting

    D. Multilink

13. You're residing in South Asia and have connected successfully to www.website.com, the servers for which are located in the United States. Which of the following utilities will you use to display detailed information of the route used by packets traveling from your computer to the web site?

    A. PING

    B. TRACERT

C. NETSTAT

D. ARP

14. You've been told you need to interactively communicate with an older Unix-based system. This system doesn't support HTTP. Which program would you use to do that?

A. FTP

B. Telnet

C. TFTP

D. Internet Explorer

15. You're all set to attend an interview with an ISP for a position as a technician. The interviewer is likely to ask you some questions to test your knowledge of Internet basics. What will you tell the interviewer if he asks you which of the following protocols is used to browse web sites on the Internet?

A. HTML

B. ASP

C. HTTP

D. SNMP

16. A cable company is providing the Internet connection for your friend's home computer. You've learned from your friend that a coaxial cable is connected from a wall jack in his living room to a cable modem that's connected to the USB port on the back of the computer. Which of the following options do you think your friend is using to make a dial-up connection to the Internet?

A. He double-clicks the Dial-Up Networking icon in My Computer.

B. He double-clicks the Network Neighborhood icon on the desktop.

C. He double-clicks the shortcut to the Internet connection on the desktop.

D. None; a cable modem doesn't require dial-up to connect to the Internet.

17. Which of the following statements is true about Windows XP?

A. Windows XP provides a basic firewall for computer systems connected to the Internet.

B. Windows XP doesn't provide a firewall for computer systems connected to the Internet.

    C. Windows XP Home Edition provides a firewall but Professional doesn't.

    D. Windows XP Professional provides a firewall but Home Edition doesn't.

18. You've just installed a high-speed cable connection to your home network. Your neighbor has indicated he'd like to share your connection and is willing to help you pay for the cost of your network. Which of the following methods would be the most efficient way to accomplish this?

    A. Install a wireless access point and external antenna to your network; install a wireless connection to his network.

    B. This can't be done because it's against FCC regulations.

    C. Run a CAT 5 cable between your network and your neighbor's network.

    D. Run a splitter from your cable feed to your neighbor's house and install a cable modem at his location.

19. You have a Windows XP computer that you want to use to share your Internet network connection with other computers in a small office. This computer is connected to a cable modem and is the only Internet-connected system in the network. How would you share the network connection without moving the cable modem connection?

    A. Install a second NIC card, and use ICS.

    B. Use ICS with the existing network connection.

    C. Install a hub between your cable modem and your computer.

    D. You can't do this with Windows XP.

20. You're concerned that your children will gain access to information on the Internet that's inappropriate for them to access. What can you do to limit access to adult sites using Internet Explorer and Netscape?

    A. Lower the security protection level to prevent access to unauthorized sites.

    B. Configure the Content Advisor or equivalent to use the PICS rating scheme.

    C. Lower the level of trusted web sites to block access.

    D. This isn't possible with web browsers.

21. You want to prevent access to a web site that users in your company seem to be accessing inappropriately. How can you accomplish this if all of the systems are using Windows XP in a peer-to-peer network?

    A. Set the web site as part of the restricted zone on each of the computers that access this site.

    B. Install ICS to limit access to inappropriate sites.

    C. Change the Content Advisor for all users in your network.

    D. You can't restrict access to specific sites using Internet Explorer.

22. You're being asked by a user to confirm that a connection she's making using Internet Explorer to an e-commerce site is secure. How can you check if the site is secure?

    A. You can't ensure that an e-commerce site is secure.

    B. Verify that the web site URL starts with "https" in the address box.

    C. Contact your ISP to verify the security of the site.

    D. Verify that the web site URL starts with "http" in the address box.

23. Your client has just received an e-mail indicating that she needed to remove a virus by deleting a file in her Windows directory. The client has done this, and now some web sites no longer function properly. What's the most likely thing that has happened in this situation?

    A. The browser has been corrupted and must be reinstalled.

    B. A scripting host has been deleted and needs to be reinstalled.

    C. The virus has contaminated the system and needs to be removed.

    D. The operating system has been corrupted and needs to be reinstalled.

24. You want to enable the firewall protection offered under Windows XP. Which of the following will do this?

    A. Run the Network Setup Wizard.

    B. Run the ICS setup program.

    C. Configure the firewall using the installation CD.

    D. The firewall is enabled automatically.

25. You've just successfully configured your Internet firewall on a Windows XP system. You're getting complaints from a remote user that your FTP site is no longer accessible to him. How can you configure this to work properly?

    A. The firewall prevents FTP connections and can't be changed.

    B. Change the settings of the firewall to allow FTP connections.

    C. Tell the user to access the FTP site using Internet Explorer to fix this problem.

    D. Tell the user to upgrade his FTP client because it isn't compatible with Windows XP.

QUICK ANSWER KEY

1.	B	14.	B
2.	D	15.	C
3.	A	16.	D
4.	B	17.	A
5.	A	18.	A
6.	C	19.	A
7.	B	20.	B
8.	C	21.	A
9.	A	22.	B
10.	D	23.	B
11.	A	24.	A
12.	C	25.	B
13.	B		

IN-DEPTH ANSWERS

1. ☑ **B.** Networking on Windows 98 computers is configured from the Network applet in Control Panel. In the Network configuration dialog box, you can add or remove network protocols, enable File and Printer Sharing, and add or remove network services. This is the centralized location to manage networking on Windows 9*x* computers.

   ☒ **A** is incorrect because although you can open Control Panel and find the Network applet from the My Computer icon, this isn't the best answer. **C** is incorrect because Device Manager can't be used to configure network properties. However, you can use it to add, remove, or update network drivers. **D** is incorrect because this icon is available only when networking is fully configured and File and Printer Sharing is enabled. After the configuration is complete, you can right-click this icon to map or disconnect network drives and change network configurations.

2. ☑ **D.** This statement isn't correct because the DHCP server machine doesn't need to be a Windows NT server or a Windows 2000 server. It can be any machine running a network operating system, such as Unix. Windows computers can also get IP addresses from Unix-based DHCP servers apart from Windows NT and Windows 2000 servers.

   ☒ **A, B,** and **C** are incorrect because these statements correctly describe the properties of DHCP servers. **A** is correct because this is the basic function of a DHCP server. **B** is correct because although these entries are optional, they're useful in large networks for resolving host names and NetBIOS names to IP addresses. **C** is correct because the DHCP server uses leases (or durations) determined by the network administrator to efficiently use available IP addresses.

3. ☑ **A.** The only two options for controlling access to shared resources on a Windows 98 computer in a peer network are Read Only and Full Access. These access control security options can be configured in the Sharing Properties page of a particular drive or a folder. Select the Depends on Password option and specify two different passwords for each type of access.

☒ **B** is incorrect because there's no such access control option as Modify in Windows 98. **C** is incorrect because the Take Ownership permission exists on Windows NT and Windows 2000 computers. It isn't available on Windows 98 computers. **D** is incorrect because although Full Control is equivalent to Full Access, this type of access is available only in the Windows NT and Windows 2000 operating systems.

4. ☑ **B.** The reason you can't see the Sharing tab in the Properties dialog box of the folder is that File and Printer Sharing isn't enabled on both of the computers. Because the computers are new, it's possible that the technician who installed Windows 98 didn't enable this feature. Unless file sharing is enabled, you won't be able to share the folders on your computers. It's important to note that you don't need to select both the file and the printer sharing check boxes if you want to share only files. To enable file sharing only, open the Network Properties in Control Panel and click the File and Print Sharing tab. Click the I Want to Be Able to Give Others Access to My Files check box, and click OK. When the computer restarts after this, the Sharing tab will be added in Network Properties and in the Folder Properties in Windows Explorer.

   ☒ **A** is incorrect because there should be no problems with the installation of networking software because you can connect to shared folders on other computers. **C** is incorrect because if you can connect to other computers, there can't be any problem with the network drivers. **D** is also incorrect because if you're able to connect to shared folders on other computers, there should be no problems with the installation of network software, network drivers, or the networking protocol. If you were trying to connect to another computer that uses a different network protocol, both computers would need to have at least one common protocol, but this isn't the case here.

5. ☑ **A.** The default gateway provides you with connectivity to other computer systems outside of your network. If this setting is incorrect or not configured, you'll be able to view resources in your network properly, but you won't be able to use or access resources outside of your network. A gateway is a device that connects one network to another.

   ☒ **B** is incorrect because you can see other TCP/IP resources on your network. If TCP/IP wasn't working properly, you wouldn't be able to communicate with other computers in your network using TCP/IP. **C** is incorrect because Client Services is part of the protocol for accessing shared resources in your network. If Client Services weren't installed, you wouldn't be able to access network shares on other Windows computers. **D** is incorrect because your network has connectivity with other computers in your network. The first step would be to verify that the default gateway settings are configured properly.

6. ☑ **C.** Domain Name Service or Domain Name System (DNS) allows for access of network resources by the URL. If DNS settings aren't proper, you won't be able to perform name-to-address lookups giving you the symptom in this question. Because you can access resources using TCP/IP addresses, you should assume that the DNS server address is wrong or that the server has stopped operating.

☒ **A** is incorrect because the Internet Explorer browser is working properly. If you can access systems using IP addresses, the browser is working correctly. **B** is incorrect because if you can view web sites by the IP address, then the TCP/IP stack is working properly. **D** is incorrect because you can access other systems using TCP/IP that are outside your network. If the default gateway was improperly configured, you wouldn't be able to leave your network and see network resources outside of your network.

7. ☑ **B.** Simplified Sharing allows for easy access to network resources in a network without a domain controller. You have limited security options to block access by users of network resources. By disabling Simplified Sharing on a Windows XP Professional system, you can configure a more flexible security environment that would allow you to block specific users from accessing specified network resources. Simplified Sharing is the default configuration option for Windows XP Home Edition systems and the default for Windows XP Professional systems that don't access a domain controller for security.

☒ **A** is incorrect because Simplified Sharing would be enabled by default in this instance. **C** is incorrect because disabling Simplified Sharing would address this problem. **D** is incorrect because you do need to change the default configuration in this situation to meet the security requirements.

8. ☑ **C.** WINIPCFG provides a quick view of the IP configuration of a computer. Whether the IP addresses are configured manually or are assigned

automatically by a DHCP server, the complete IP configuration can be viewed by running this command.

☒   **A** is incorrect because the DHCP server isn't being used in the network. Even if a DHCP server were in use, you don't need to check the IP configuration of a computer from the DHCP server when you can do it on the local computer. **B** is incorrect because although PING can reveal the IP address of a computer if name resolution is working, it can't be used to view all TCP/IP parameters configured on a computer. **D** is incorrect because this is an invalid command. WINIPCFG can't be used from remote computers.

9.   ☑   **A.** Both computers have the same IP address. Remember that IP addresses are unique to each computer in a TCP/IP network. If two computers have the same IP address, only one of them will be able to use the network. In a small network, like the one in this situation, the computer that's turned on first will work. When you turn on the second computer with the same IP address, an IP address conflict will be detected, and TCP/IP won't initialize on the second computer.

☒   **B** is incorrect because the subnet mask is always the same in the network, whether it's a small network or a large network with several segments. **C** is incorrect because this isn't the cause of the problem. Even if this were true, both the computers should have been capable of using the network. **D** is incorrect because this problem isn't common in bus networks or in networks of any topology. It's certainly not a limitation or drawback of any network topology in particular.

10.   ☑   **D.** This is a simple question, and you shouldn't let the answer options confuse you. The easiest way to prevent a stuck job from holding up other print jobs in the queue is to select it in the Printer window and click the Cancel button. This won't harm the other print jobs in the queue, and users can continue printing their documents.

☒   **A** is incorrect because even if you stop sharing the printer when a print job gets stuck, this won't clear the printer queue. **B** is incorrect because this will cancel all print jobs, and each user will have to resubmit their jobs, which is what the manager is trying to avoid. **C** is incorrect because this will produce no results. The printer might already have paused because of the bad print job stuck in the print queue.

11. ☑ **A.** Post Office Protocol version 3 (POP3) is used to download e-mail from the e-mail servers on the Internet. POP3 is an enhanced version of the older POP.

☒ **B** is incorrect because Simple Mail Transfer Protocol (SMTP) is used to send e-mail, not to download e-mail. **C** is incorrect because the Trivial File Transfer Protocol (TFTP) is a part of the TCP/IP suite used to transfer files between two TCP/IP computers. **D** is incorrect because File Transfer Protocol (FTP) is used to upload and download files to and from Internet FTP servers. FTP is also used for file transfers in private intranets and provides user authentication.

12. ☑ **C.** Scripting provides a method for writing a text file, known as "script," that's passed on to the ISP when a connection has been established. This text file may contain additional options, such as providing a valid username and password, that are processed by remote servers on the Internet.

☒ **A** is incorrect because this button is located in the Server Types tab, and it allows you to select the automatic or manual assignment of IP addresses. **B** is incorrect because these options are typically available and thus can't be called *additional* options. **D** is incorrect because Multilink is used when you have more than one modem and phone line and you want to combine them for better connection bandwidth and faster speed.

13. ☑ **B.** TRACERT stands for "trace route." This utility is a part of the TCP/IP suite that's used to check the route taken by a network packet from the source computer to the destination host. The TRACERT command lists all the IP addresses of all the routers and hosts that the packet passes on its way to the destination. TRACERT is a useful troubleshooting utility and is widely used for diagnosing network problems.

☒ **A** is incorrect because the PING command tests only the connectivity between the source host and the destination. It doesn't trace the path taken from source to destination. The only result it displays is whether the connection exists. PING is also a TCP/IP troubleshooting utility. **C** is incorrect because NETSTAT gives detailed statistical information about TCP/IP and doesn't help in tracing the route. **D** is incorrect because the Address Resolution Protocol (ARP) is used to translate or resolve IP addresses to MAC addresses, also known as the "physical address" or "hardware address," of the machines.

14. ☑ **B.** Telnet is an older interactive protocol that allows for connectivity to systems that aren't using a web-based service such as HTTP. With Telnet you log on to the server and access the computer as if you were a local terminal user. Telnet has largely been replaced by web-based environments such as the World Wide Web. Nevertheless, you'll encounter environments that still use Telnet for communications. One of the biggest problems with Telnet is the lack of security it offers by default. All information including user IDs and passwords are sent unencrypted and can easily be intercepted. Most sites that still use Telnet require the use of an encryption system such as PPTP or SSH.

☒ **A** is incorrect because FTP isn't considered an interactive protocol. FTP allows for users to upload and download files from a system with an FTP server installed. This isn't considered interactive for the purposes of the A+ exam. **C** is incorrect because TFTP is another file transfer protocol similar to FTP. **D** is incorrect because ARP is a maintenance protocol used by TCP/IP-based networks.

15. ☑ **C.** HTTP stands for "Hypertext Transfer Protocol." This protocol is used to transfer pages from web sites to your Internet browser. You can remember this because the URL of a web site starts with "http."

☒ **A** is incorrect because Hypertext Markup Language (HTML) isn't a protocol but rather a language used to build web pages. **B** is incorrect because Active Server Pages (ASP) is also a language used to build web pages. This language is proprietary to Microsoft and has certain advantages over HTML. **D** is incorrect because Simple Network Management Protocol (SNMP) is used to manage network services and isn't involved in transferring information from Internet web sites to web browsers.

16. ☑ **D.** When a cable company provides Internet connectivity, a cable modem is installed, and dial-up is no longer required. The cable company typically provides a continuous connection to the Internet.

☒ **A** is incorrect because double-clicking Dial-Up Networking brings up the configured Dial-Up Connections window and doesn't actually dial any connection. **B** is incorrect because the Network Neighborhood contains the list of shared resources available on a network. **C** is incorrect because no dialing is involved when a cable company provides Internet service. This statement describes the method for dialing the number of the ISP when you have a dial-up connection to the Internet.

17. ☑ **A.** Windows XP provides a basic firewall for connecting computers to the Internet. This firewall allows for incoming systems to be blocked from viewing certain protocols within the TCP/IP suite. The various protocols are accessed by connecting to either TCP or IP and accessing ports in the protocol. The firewall provides the ability to configure these ports to either accept or reject requests for those ports. The firewall isn't a comprehensive product but does provide basic security for the more commonly accessed Internet ports.

    ☒ **B, C,** and **D** are incorrect because Windows XP provides a basic firewall for all versions of Windows XP.

18. ☑ **A.** You can install a wireless access point with an external antenna for connection to other networks that are physically close to your network. This would allow for connections to occur over a longer distance than is normally provided by standard wireless networks.

    ☒ **B** is incorrect because current regulations from the FCC allow for this to occur as long as all equipment in the network is a type accepted for the usage. **C** is incorrect because installing a CAT 5 cable between your network and your neighbor's would present technical difficulties and expense. This may be less expensive than a wireless connection, but it won't be less maintenance and cost overall. Outside cables are usually more expensive than other cables, and the length of the cable run may be longer than is allowed by 10BaseT or 100BaseT networks. You'd also require additional hubs for the connection. This may be more expensive than the wireless option. **D** is incorrect because each cable connection would require special addressing and permission from the cable company. This would also most likely be viewed as a theft of bandwidth from the cable provider or a violation of your agreement with the cable provide. It may also subject you and your neighbor to criminal prosecution.

19. ☑ **A.** Installing Internet Connection Sharing (ICS) on your computer would allow you to share the Internet connection with other computer systems in your LAN. ICS provides the ability to create a DHCP-like environment for other computers as well as serve as a gateway for computers in the network. All of the computers that you want to share will require a network connection to your computer for this to work. Your computer will be the default gateway for the network. You can also activate Internet Connection Firewall to increase security in your network.

☒   **B** is incorrect because the only network connection described in this question was a connection to the cable. You'll need to connect all the computers in your network to your computer. **C** is incorrect because the cable wire can't be shared except through your computer system. **D** is incorrect because Windows XP provides ICS for sharing a single Internet connection.

20.   ☑   **B.** You can use the Content Advisor to block adult and other sites that are inappropriate for younger computer users. The Content Advisor uses the Platform for Internet Content Selection (PICS) to restrict access to adult sites. To override this, you'd need to enter a supervisor password when prompted. PICS is being widely implemented voluntarily by web hosting services.

☒   **A** is incorrect because lowering the security protection level would allow more risky sites to be accessed using the browser. This would make your system more vulnerable to viruses and other unwanted programs. **C** is incorrect because lowering the level of trusted web sites won't prevent access to adult web sites. **D** is incorrect because you can set access levels with the Content Advisor service offered by most web browsers.

21.   ☑   **A.** You can move a web site URL or address into a restricted zone that blocks access. This will prevent users from accessing that web site either directly or through URL redirections. This is a rather tedious process that'll be required on each computer in the network. You may want to install a device or software called a "proxy server" to limit access to a site for your entire network. This may also improve network performance.

☒   **B** is incorrect because ICS doesn't provide the ability to block Internet sites. **C** is incorrect because the Content Advisor won't automatically block a specific site. You'll need to configure the site using the Restricted Site option of Internet Explorer. **D** is incorrect because you can do this for each user of Internet Explorer on each computer. You'd probably want to add a proxy server to prevent access at the network level as opposed to each user.

22.   ☑   **B.** By verifying that the URL starts with "https," you can be assured that the site is somewhat secure. HTTPS uses the Secure Sockets Layer to ensure privacy of information. Many browsers will also show a golden lock in one of the display areas of the browser or a small key. This indicates that an encryption protocol is in use.

☒ **A** is incorrect because most e-commerce sites have some level of built-in security when transactions involve money or credit information. **C** is incorrect because your ISP won't know whether a site is secure except by using the same method you would. **D** is incorrect because a site that only contains "http" isn't secure.

23. ☑ **B.** This is a common hoax that's sent to users via e-mail. Usually this hoax involves deleting a component of the Java Virtual Machine or other scripting host. If a user follows the directions, that host will typically need to be reinstalled.

☒ **A** is incorrect because the browser is still functioning and won't need to be reinstalled. The scripting host will need to be reinstalled. **C** is incorrect because most likely the system didn't get corrupted from a virus in this situation. **D** is incorrect because the operating system isn't corrupted.

24. ☑ **A.** To enable the firewall, you run the Network Setup Wizard and choose the option that your computer is directly connected to the Internet. This automatically enables the firewall. You can then protect your computer using the various options in this program.

☒ **B** is incorrect because ICS setup occurs through the Network Setup Wizard. ICS allows for sharing of network connections and works with the firewall. **C** is incorrect because the firewall is automatically installed when the operating system in installed by default. **D** is incorrect because the firewall isn't automatically enabled.

25. ☑ **B.** The Internet firewall prevents users from accessing resources on your computer unless they're specifically allowed. The default setting for the Internet firewall is to refuse connections to an FTP server on your system. To change this, you'll need to access the Properties window for your network connection and use the Advanced option configure the firewall to allow for connections to an FTP server. The default is for this to be disabled.

☒ **A** is incorrect because you can change settings on the firewall. **C** is incorrect because accessing the FTP server using Internet Explorer still accesses the FTP server through the ports that are used for FTP services. **D** is incorrect because this has nothing to do with the FTP client; it's a firewall security issue.

A+
CORE HARDWARE/OPERATING SYSTEM EXAMS

Part III

Practice Exams

CORE HARDWARE/OPERATING SYSTEM EXAMS

II

A+ Core
Hardware
Practice Exam

QUESTIONS

1. You've selected the NetBEUI protocol for connecting 12 computers in your office. When you configure the network properties in these computers, which of the following information must you supply in order to have a functional network?

   A. Computer name

   B. IP address

   C. Subnet mask

   D. None of the above

2. If you were to have only two IDE hard disks in a system that has two hard disk controllers, which of the following configurations would give you the best performance?

   A. One hard disk as primary master and the other as secondary master

   B. One hard disk as primary master and the other as secondary slave

   C. One hard disk as secondary master and the other as primary slave

   D. One hard disk as primary master and the other as primary slave

3. You've purchased a new ATAPI CD-ROM drive that you want to install in your PC. The PC has only one hard disk controller. Which of the following statements correctly describes why the CD-ROM shouldn't be connected to the end connector of the ribbon cable?

   A. The ribbon cable is too short and can't reach the CD-ROM drive.

   B. The CD-ROM has to act as a secondary hard disk because some bootable CD-ROMs can automatically upgrade the existing operating system.

   C. The hard disk needs to be the master drive, and the hard disk controller can treat the CD-ROM as a slave drive.

   D. All CD-ROMS are preconfigured as slave drives and must be connected to the middle connector of the ribbon cable.

4. Which of the following tools can't be used for preventive maintenance of a personal computer that has two hard disks, a sound card, and a network adapter?

   A. Antistatic wrist strap

   B. Compressed air

   C. Moist rag

   D. Key-ring knife

5. The power supply unit of your PC has an AC input range of 110 to 120 volts. Which of the following DC voltages isn't available from this power supply?

   A. 3.0 volts

   B. –12 volts

   C. +5.0 volts

   D. –3.3 volts

6. Which of the following types of ESD damage isn't visible immediately but rather affects one or more components in such a way that the component may keep functioning normally?

   A. Catastrophic damage

   B. Degradation

   C. Intermittent

   D. None of the above

7. You're sharing your printer with ten other users in a small departmental workgroup running Windows XP. Because you're the supervisor of the team of users in your department, some users share your computer to store important data files containing large document drafts that you have to finalize. In recent weeks, these users have started complaining that printing on your printer has become extremely slow, and yet they find no problem when accessing files from your computer. What's the most likely source of the problem?

   A. Slow network

   B. Decreasing hard disk space

   C. Malfunctioning printer cable

   D. Corrupt printer driver

8. If you were asked to remove a hard disk from a PC that has already been powered off, in what order would you remove the following parts? Refer to the following illustration for a view of the location of the three parts in question.

Removing the Hard Disks

Mounting screws

Power connector

Ribbon cable

A. You'd remove the screws first, then the ribbon cable, and then the power connector.

B. You'd remove the power connector first, then the ribbon cable, and then the screws.

C. You'd remove the ribbon cable first, then the power connector, and then the screws.

D. The order isn't important if the system power is off.

9. Which of the following are the benefits of non-Intel processors, compared to Intel Pentium processors with approximately equal speeds?

A. They're usually less expensive.

B. They have a large L1 cache.

C. They don't require an L2 cache.

D. They don't require heat sinks.

10. Which of the following SCSI controllers has a maximum data transfer speed of 40 Mbps?

A. Fast SCSI 2 -10

B. Fast Wide SCSI 2 -20

C. Ultra-2 SCSI -40

D. Wide Ultra-2 SCSI -80

11. You're planning to install a SCSI adapter that'll be used to replace your EIDE hard disks with four SCSI drives, as shown in the following illustration. Which of the four SCSI devices will have the highest priority in the SCSI chain?

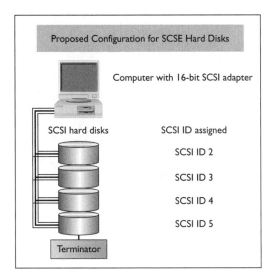

A. Device with SCSI ID 2

B. Device with SCSI ID 3

C. Device with SCSI ID 4

D. Device with SCSI ID 5

12. Your computer dealer has advised you that the computer you're using has an ATX motherboard. Which of the following features are you unlikely to find on this motherboard?

A. Power management controlled by the BIOS

B. Integrated serial and parallel ports

C. USB support

D. DIN-5 connector for the keyboard

13. You've just received a new replacement power supply for an older PC system with an AT motherboard. After the power supply has been mounted inside the computer case, you want to connect it to the motherboard. Which of the following must you be careful to do when making this connection?

    A. The red wires on the two connectors must be kept together.

    B. The black wires on the two connectors must be kept together.

    C. The black wires must be kept on the extreme ends.

    D. The black wire on one connector should face the red wire on the other connector.

14. When your computer is switched on, the power supply fans start running, indicating that it's working properly, the monitor turns on, but nothing is being displayed. What should be your first step to identify the cause of the problem?

    A. Listen to the number of beeps.

    B. Use a different power outlet.

    C. Try changing the memory modules.

    D. Try changing the monitor.

15. After you connect a laser printer on a computer running the Windows XP operating system and install the printer driver, but before sharing the printer on the network, what should be your next step so that other users don't complain of printing problems?

    A. Check that the network is working.

    B. Print a self-test page.

    C. Set permissions for other users.

    D. Install a networking protocol.

16. Which of the following most accurately represents level 1 and level 2 cache?

    A. Level 1 and level 2 are contained on the processor.

    B. Level 1 is in the processor, and level 2 is on the motherboard.

    C. Level 1 and level 2 are on the motherboard.

    D. Level 1 is on the motherboard, and level 2 is in the processor.

17. Which of the following best describes level 3 cache?

    A. Level 3 cache is relatively small compared to level 2 cache.

    B. Level 3 cache is relatively large compared to level 2 cache.

    C. Level 3 cache is closest to the processor.

    D. There's no such thing as level 3 cache.

18. Which of the following configurations is imperative when attaching a third SCSI hard disk to a SCSI controller that already has two hard disks?

    A. IRQ15

    B. I/O address

    C. Terminator

    D. SCSI ID

19. You're working in a publishing company that specializes in computer-aided designs. You're planning to double the memory capacity of your computer. Currently your system has 256MB of RAM installed. The computer has four memory slots for expansion, and they're already being used. This is a relatively new computer system. Finances aren't much of an issue. Which of the following is the most cost-effective solution for doubling your memory size?

    A. Replace two of the memory modules with larger capacity memory modules.

    B. Replace all four of the memory modules with larger memory modules.

    C. Replace one of the memory modules with a larger capacity memory module.

    D. You can't expand the memory of the computer; it's already full.

20. Which of the following printers can be called a "network printer" and is installed as a separate node on the network?

    A. Any printer that's installed on a Windows XP computer and shared with other users

    B. Any printer that's installed on a Windows 98 computer and shared with other users

    C. Any printer that's installed on a Windows 2000 server and shared on the network

    D. A printer that supports networking protocols such as TCP/IP and has a network interface

21. A computer has gathered a lot of dust inside the case, and you want to clean it. Which of the following methods would you use if you don't want the dust to settle on other parts and accessories while cleaning?

    A. Dusting cloth

    B. Compressed air

    C. Vacuum

    D. Water

22. A company wants to connect its 100BaseTX networks that are in two separate buildings. These buildings are 200 meters apart. The company wants the data transfer to be as fast as possible. Which of the following cable types would you suggest?

    A. CAT 3

    B. CAT 4

    C. CAT 5

    D. Fiber optic

23. Your user has just installed a new computer in his 100BaseT network and is complaining that the computer isn't seeing the network reliably. The network is TCP/IP, and another user periodically complains that his computer isn't working reliably either. This other user's computer had been working properly before the new computer was added.

    A. The new computer has a TCP/IP address conflict that should be corrected.

    B. The new computer NIC has malfunctioned.

    C. A terminator on the network has malfunctioned causing collisions.

    D. The TCP/IP stack is corrupt on the new computer.

24. The mouse connected to a serial port hasn't been working properly for the past several days. It doesn't move as intended and jumps rapidly from one spot to another on the monitor. Which of the following is a possible cause of the problem?

    A. A crack in the serial cable

    B. The IRQ or I/O address of the serial port

    C. An incorrect mouse driver

    D. Dirty mouse ball and rollers

25. You've just replaced the Pentium III processor on your motherboard with a faster one. When you turn the power on, you notice that your computer screen is displaying unusual patterns and colors and that your computer isn't booting. What's the most likely problem?

    A. The Pentium III processor isn't compatible with your motherboard.

    B. The motherboard needs to have the BIOS upgraded.

    C. The Pentium III processor isn't seated properly in its socket.

    D. The power supply can't handle the power demands of the newer processor.

26. You use your laptop computer at home and at your office. When you're working in your office, you find it difficult to work with the touchpad mouse, the LCD display, and the built-in keyboard continuously for eight hours. Which of the following options would allow you to use external components such as a large monitor or an external keyboard and mouse, considering that you also require network connectivity and sometimes use external hard disks, a scanner, and a printer?

    A. Use the port replicator.

    B. Use the extended port replicator.

    C. Use a full docking station.

    D. Any of the above.

27. You're at a customer's site to fix a video problem. Your troubleshooting has revealed that the monitor is faulty, and there are no problems with the video adapter, connections, or the video configuration of the operating system. You want to disconnect the monitor and tell the customer to send it to your office for replacement. Which of the following is the correct method to accomplish this?

    A. Disconnect the monitor, let it cool down, and pack it in the original packaging.

    B. Disconnect the monitor, discharge it with a screwdriver, and pack it in the original packaging.

C. Disconnect the monitor, discharge it with a jumper wire, and pack it in the original packaging.

D. Disconnect the monitor, discharge it using a steel scale, and pack it in any empty box.

28. Your boss is planning to implement a network in the office complex based on an industry standard, and he has asked you to suggest which topology would be the most suitable for building a network, supporting up to a 100 Mbps data speed, and providing fault tolerance. Which of the following should be your answer?

A. Token Ring

B. Token bus

C. FDDI

D. Token Star

29. Which of the following is a correct statement describing why the onboard L2 cache is faster than L2 cache memory on the motherboard?

A. Onboard cache is another name for the L1 cache, and the L1 cache runs at the speed of the processor.

B. Onboard cache works at the processor speed, and the external L2 cache runs at the speed of the motherboard.

C. Onboard cache is usually smaller than the external L2 cache and, hence, is more efficient.

D. Onboard L2 cache runs at the cumulative speed of the processor and the motherboard, and the external cache runs at the speed of the processor only.

30. Out of the following IRQs, which will have the highest priority?

A. The IRQ used for the system timer

B. The IRQ used by the math coprocessor

C. IRQ 15, when available

D. The IRQ used by the real-time clock

31. Which of the following errors indicates that the ribbon cable on the floppy disk drive isn't connected properly to the motherboard?

A. The light on the floppy disk drive glows continuously.

B. A:\ isn't accessible.

    C. It can't read from the disk.

    D. The disk in the destination drive is full.

32. When comparing paper-feed mechanisms, which of the following statements incorrectly describes an advantage of inkjet printers versus dot-matrix printers?

    A. Inkjet printers use a friction-feed mechanism, and you don't have to worry about the alignment of perforations.

    B. Inkjet printers can print only on fixed-length paper.

    C. You don't have to worry about separating the pages of the continuous paper after printing.

    D. It's possible to print conveniently on envelopes and cards.

33. Which of the following components on the motherboard makes it possible to save CMOS BIOS settings in the computer while the computer's power is turned off?

    A. RAM

    B. Battery

    C. Cache

    D. Hard disk

34. Considering that you're using a Windows XP operating system computer and an SVGA video adapter with high-resolution and high color display settings, which of the following is a possible reason for a flickering display on the monitor?

    A. Display settings in the operating system

    B. Bad monitor cable

    C. Incorrect video driver

    D. Faulty monitor

35. If you were asked to install memory modules in a new Pentium 4 computer, and the motherboard has four sockets for installing synchronous dynamic RAM modules, what number of memory modules would you use to fill up the memory bank?

    A. Two 16-bit DIMMs

    B. One 64-bit DIMM

C. Two 16-bit RIMMs

D. Four 32-bit SIMMs

36. You've turned on your computer and can hear the power supply fan running. The system passes the POST, but you can't hear the hard disk. What could be the cause of the problem?

A. A broken ribbon cable on the hard disk

B. Incorrect type of ribbon cable

C. Incorrect connection of the ribbon cable on the hard disk

D. Disconnected power connection on the hard disk

37. Which of the following statements about Token Ring networks is incorrect?

A. Token bus networks are based on the IEEE 802.5 standard.

B. Token Ring networks such as the 802.5 standard require Multistation Access Units.

C. Token Ring networks have speeds between 4 Mbps and 16 Mbps.

D. Token Ring networks can use coaxial, twisted-pair, or fiber-optic cables.

38. Which of the following parts of a laser printer causes the paper to attract toner from the drum when the image is ready to be transferred?

A. The control unit

B. The transfer corona wire

C. The fusing rollers

D. The cleaning blade

39. SVGA monitors will connect to which of the following types of D connectors?

A. DB-9 male

B. DB-9 female

C. DB-15 male

D. DB-25 female

40. A customer has reported a problem with his computer. You arrive at his site, and he says he doesn't remember if any error codes were displayed on the screen. What should your first step be in resolving the problem?

    A. Try changing suspected components one by one.

    B. Try to reproduce the problem.

    C. Write down the details of the problem.

    D. Ask if the customer has made any changes recently.

41. The dot-matrix printer you're using has been producing print outputs that show a white line across the width of the page on every line. Which of the following parts of the printer needs replacement?

    A. Ribbon cartridge

    B. Tractor feed

    C. Printer driver

    D. Print head

42. A bubblejet printer is producing print outputs that aren't readable. The strange characters printed aren't what the user intended to print, and he has asked for your help. Which of the following can't be a cause of the problem?

    A. Incorrect printer driver

    B. Dirty ink cartridge

    C. Communication problem

    D. Bad parallel port

43. Which of the following components is used in bus networks to prevent signals from bouncing back and forth in the cable?

    A. Vampire tap

    B. BNC T connector

    C. 50-ohm coaxial cable

    D. 50-ohm terminator

44. The company where you work as a help desk technician has installed a Windows 2000 server into their network. Nearly 50 desktop users, including those from the accounting and marketing departments, will be storing their files on this server. Because this is the only server in the office and it's heavily loaded, management wants to minimize the chances of data loss on this server. They've installed a backup tape as part of the configuration. Which of the following additional capabilities should they consider?

   A. Configure the drives for RAID 0.

   B. Configure the drives for RAID 5.

   C. Make sure they acquire a dual-processor system for redundancy.

   D. None of the above will reduce data loss risks.

45. You've just added a second hard disk to your computer. When the cabling is complete and the power supply is connected, you put the computer cover back on. Which of the following should be your first action immediately after switching on the computer?

   A. Check to see that the hard disk is recognized by the BIOS.

   B. Run the FDISK program.

   C. Format the drive.

   D. Test the drive by copying some files onto it.

46. A customer has reported that his inkjet printer, connected to the LPT1 port of his computer, is giving a communication error when he tries to print. He said that the printer power is on, but there's no activity when he sends a print document. Which of the following would you suspect to be the cause of the problem?

   A. The printer driver

   B. The configuration of the word processor

   C. The printer cable and connection

   D. The LPT port

47. Which of the following statements is correct when installing an EIDE hard disk as a primary slave drive?

   A. The drive must be connected to the end connector on the ribbon cable with the jumper set to the slave position.

B. The drive must be the first drive to be installed in the system, and it must hold the operating system.

C. The drive must be connected to the middle connector with the jumper set to the slave position.

D. The primary slave drive can't work unless a secondary master hard disk is present.

48. Antistatic wrist straps prevent the electrostatic discharge that can cause some computer components to fail. In which of the following cases should you not wear them when working on computers and printers?

A. When you're using an antistatic mat

B. When you're sure that you won't touch any static-sensitive device

C. When you're working on high-voltage equipment

D. When you've used antistatic spray

49. A customer is telling you on the phone that none of the 12 computers in his 10BaseT Ethernet network is able to connect to the others. He couldn't give any other information beyond this. Which of the following could be causing the problem?

A. Excessive network traffic

B. Broken cable on one of the computers

C. Faulty hub

D. Missing terminator

50. You've just received a call from your user complaining that he's unable to access the Internet from his computer. He indicates that his computer is part of an existing TCP/IP network and that he can see other computers in his network. He's using a cable modem, and all of the settings appear to be correct for his system. Others are reporting similar access problems accessing the Internet. What's the most likely problem?

A. Incorrectly set default gateway

B. Malfunctioning cable modem

C. A computer virus

D. Corrupted TCP/IP stack

IN-DEPTH ANSWERS

1. ☑ **D.** The NetBEUI protocol is the simplest of all protocols to configure. You have to install only the protocol; no other configuration is necessary. In Windows 98, open the Network dialog box from Control Panel, click Add, select Protocol, and select NetBEUI from the Microsoft list under the list of manufacturers.

   ☒ **A** is incorrect because the computer name is usually specified during the installation of the operating system. However, you may specify a different computer name during network installation. **B** and **C** are incorrect because these addresses are required when installing TCP/IP.

2. ☑ **A.** When the two hard disks are connected to the end connectors of the primary and secondary connectors, they'll become the primary master and secondary master, respectively. When both the hard disks are connected to the ribbon cable of the primary hard disk controller, the one connected to the end connector will become the primary master drive, and the other connected to the middle connector will act as primary slave, provided the configuration jumper is set to the slave position.

   ☒ **B** is incorrect because the secondary slave drive can't work without a secondary master drive. **C** is incorrect because one of the hard disks has to be the primary master. The other hard disk can be either primary slave or secondary master. **D** is incorrect because this will work but will operate with less performance than A.

3. ☑ **C.** The hard disk needs to be the master drive, and the hard disk controller can treat the CD-ROM as a slave drive. The system that has only one hard disk controller must have the hard disk operating as primary master drive. The end connector on the ribbon cable will thus be reserved for the hard disk drive. The ATAPI CD-ROM can be connected to the middle connector, and the hard disk controller can treat the CD-ROM drive as a slave drive.

   ☒ **A** is incorrect because this isn't the reason that the CD-ROM can't be connected to the end connector. **B** is incorrect because the CD-ROM doesn't have to be a secondary master. Moreover, bootable CD-ROMs don't automatically upgrade the existing operating system. *Bootable* simply means that the system can use a CD-ROM to boot up when the boot sequence in the BIOS is appropriately configured or when the BIOS can't find an operating system on the hard disk. **D** is incorrect because all CD-ROMs aren't preconfigured as slave drives.

4. ☑ **D.** A small knife is an improper tool for any kind of maintenance job. A knife is sometimes needed to remove residue on metallic surfaces, but the only type of knife that should be used for this purpose is a rubber knife. A rubber knife is hard enough to remove this residue. A metallic knife must not be used in any case. Note that the question mentions two hard disks, a sound card, and an adapter. Although you must read each question carefully before deciding on an answer, beware of any details or statements such as this that are included just to draw your attention away from the main objective and waste your time.

☒ **A** is incorrect because this is a common safety device used when performing preventive maintenance and repairing computers. Antistatic wrist straps prevent electrostatic discharge from your body. **B** is incorrect because compressed air is used to blow dust off components inside the computer. **C** is incorrect because a moist rag can be used to clean the case, monitor, and keyboard.

5. ☑ **A.** The switching power supply unit of PCs typically gives DC voltages of 3.3, 5.0, and 12 volts. So, 3.0 volts isn't a standard DC output from the power supply unit of the PC.

☒ **B, C,** and **D** are incorrect options because –12 volts, +5.0 volts, and –3.3 volts DC voltage output is available from the power-supply unit. The three standard DC voltage outputs from the power-supply unit are +3.3, +5.0, and +12 volts.

6. ☑ **B.** When ESD damage isn't visible immediately but has harmed one or more components, it's known as "degradation." Although it doesn't damage any specific component immediately, it can cause intermittent problems. This is more harmful than catastrophic damage caused by ESD.

☒ **A** is incorrect because catastrophic ESD damage is visible immediately and damages the component. The affected component has to be replaced. Catastrophic ESD damage is less harmful than degradation because the effect of ESD can be known and the problem can be resolved by replacing the component that failed because of the ESD damage. **C** is incorrect because ESD damage is classified broadly into only two categories: catastrophic and degradation. **D** is incorrect because there's a correct answer for the given symptoms. Note that the notorious options "none of the above," "all of the above," and "any of the above" will appear in several questions on the A+ exam.

7. ☑ **B.** When a printer is shared on the network, print jobs from network computers are first stored on the hard disk of the computer where the printer is installed and shared. If this computer is low on hard disk space, as indicated in the question, the printing will become slow. To resolve this problem, make more free space on your hard disk to expedite print jobs.

    ☒ **A** is incorrect because users aren't finding any problems when accessing shared files on your computer. **C** is incorrect because a bad printer cable won't cause printing to slow down. **D** is incorrect because if the printer driver were corrupted, the problem would show up as incorrect print outputs, such as garbled prints, rather than slow printing.

8. ☑ **B.** The correct order for removal of a hard disk is to first remove the power connector and then the ribbon cable. When the disk is free of cables, you can remove the screws. This order is important because the ribbon cable could be pulled accidentally if the screws were removed first, or the hard disk could be damaged while pulling the power connector or the ribbon cable.

    ☒ **A** is incorrect because you must remove the power connector first. This is done because a little force is required to pull the power connector, and it's best to pull it when the hard disk is held firmly in its cage by mounting screws. **C** is incorrect because the power connector must be removed before removing the ribbon cable. **D** is incorrect because the order of removal does matter, whether or not the system is powered off. You must make sure the system power is turned off before removing the computer case.

9. ☑ **A.** Non-Intel processors are usually less expensive than Intel processors of the same speed. Non-Intel processors come in speeds that closely match the speeds of Intel Pentium processors. However, they're comparatively less expensive than the corresponding Intel processors and can be installed in standard processor sockets.

    ☒ **B** is incorrect because most non-Intel processors have a smaller or equal size L1 cache when processors of equal speeds are compared. **C** is incorrect because the majority of processors use an L2 cache for enhanced performance. **D** is incorrect because all processors, regardless of their speed or manufacturer, require a heat sink for dissipation of the heat generated during the normal working of the computer.

10. ☑ **C.** The maximum data transfer speed of the Ultra-2 SCSI controller is 40 Mbps. The Ultra-2 SCSI is an 8-bit SCSI controller. The wide version of this SCSI controller is a 16-bit controller known as a Wide Ultra-2 SCSI that supports data transfer rates of up to 80 Mbps.

    ☒ **A** is incorrect because the Fast SCSI 2 is an 8-bit controller that supports up to only a 10 Mbps data transfer rate. **B** is incorrect because this SCSI controller is also limited to only a 20 Mbps data transfer rate. However, the Double Wide SCSI 2 version, which is a 32-bit system, does support 40 Mbps. **D** is incorrect because this SCSI controller isn't limited to a 40 Mbps data transfer rate but can support up to 80 Mbps.

11. ☑ **D.** The priorities for SCSI devices by ID are 7-6-5-4-3-2-1-0. SCSI ID 5 will have the highest priority of the devices shown in the SCSI chain. SCSI ID 7 is always given to the controller and is the highest priority device in the SCSI chain.

    ☒ **A, B,** and **C** are incorrect because these SCSI IDs will be lower priority than SCSI ID 5.

12. ☑ **D.** The ATX motherboard has a completely different component layout compared to the Baby AT motherboard. The keyboard connector is also a mini-DIN-5, rather than a DIN-5. Besides these dissimilar features, ATX motherboards have an additional ±3.3v DC power supply and a single power-supply connector to the motherboard.

    ☒ **A, B**, and **C** are incorrect answers because these features *are* present on ATX motherboards. ATX motherboards have power management features that are typically controlled by the system BIOS, they have serial and parallel ports integrated into the motherboard, and they have USB device support.

13. ☑ **B.** When connecting the P8 and P9 power connectors to the motherboard, the black wires on the two connectors must be kept together. This essentially means that these wires will be connected to the center of the connector on the motherboard. Any other orientation of the power connectors won't work.

☒ **A** is incorrect because it's physically not possible to do this. One of the connectors has a red wire (+5v DC), and the other has an orange wire (power good signal) on the end. **C** is incorrect because the computer won't work with this orientation. **D** is incorrect because the black wires on both connectors should face each other.

14. ☑ **A.** When nothing is displayed on the monitor, the first thing you must do is listen to the number of beeps that the computer produces during the POST. These beeps are a clear indication of the type of problem the computer has encountered. For example, if there's only one long beep on some systems, this indicates that the POST has completed and there may be a nonfatal error, such as a bad video adapter or a faulty monitor. You'll want to check the manual for the motherboard to determine what the beep codes are during startup.

☒ **B** is incorrect because there's no problem with the AC power supply because the power supply fan is working. **C** is incorrect because this isn't the first action you should take to resolve an unknown problem. **D** is also incorrect because you must first diagnose the problem properly before changing any parts.

15. ☑ **B.** Whether or not you share the printer with other users, you should print a self-test page immediately after the installation. This ensures that the printer has been installed correctly with the appropriate printer driver. When you're satisfied that the printer installation is done and you can print successfully from your computer, which will be evident from the test page, you can share the printer with other users. The self-test page option is available in the Properties dialog box of all printers.

☒ **A** is incorrect because this isn't the first thing you should do after installing the printer. Network problems, if there are any, can be checked later if a user complains that he isn't able to connect to the shared printer. **C** is incorrect because it's not possible to set permissions for individual users in Windows 98. The printer is either shared by all users or not shared at all. **D** is incorrect because if you're sharing your computer with others on the network, you don't need to install a separate networking protocol for sharing the printer. Note that the answer options seem to distract your attention away from the actual question. You must concentrate on the *first* thing you should do after installing the printer.

16.   ☑   **B.** On most processors, level 1 cache is contained in the processor, and level 2 cache is on the motherboard. Level 1 cache is smaller in size and said to be closer to the processor than level 2 cache.

☒   **A, C,** and **D** are incorrect for the reasons given previously. Some of the newer processors now include level 2 cache in the processor, but for the purposes of the test you can assume that level 2 cache is external to the processor.

17.   ☑   **B.** Level 3 cache is the largest of the three cache sizes in processors. The typical size of level 3 cache is 1MB. Level 3 caching is used to improve the performance of processors by allowing more commonly accessed information to be stored in cache rather than in main memory. Level 3 cache size is currently 1MB on the Pentium Xeon processor.

☒   **A** and **C** are incorrect because level 3 cache is relatively larger than level 1 or level 2 cache sizes. **D** is incorrect because level 3 cache is being added to newer high-end processors.

18.   ☑   **D.** From the given options, the only configuration consideration required by the third SCSI hard disk when attaching it to the system will be the SCSI ID. All SCSI devices in the SCSI chain are identified by a unique SCSI ID, and no two SCSI devices can share the same SCSI ID.

☒   **A** and **B** are incorrect because SCSI devices require SCSI IDs as opposed to IRQ addresses. Similarly, the I/O address is assigned to the SCSI controller, not to individual SCSI devices. **C** is incorrect because the system is already using other SCSI devices, so a terminator must already be present in the SCSI bus.

19.   ☑   **C.** Newer motherboards use SDRAM memory. This allows the memory boards to be of differing sizes so you'd only need to replace one of the memory units with the larger memory module. Unless otherwise instructed by the motherboard manufacturer, you want to install the largest memory module in the first slot. Usually the slots in memory are labeled "DIMM 0" or "DIMM 1" depending on the manufacturer. This also means you're only removing one of the memory modules from the system. This allows you to retain the investment you've made in the other memory modules.

☒   **A** is incorrect because it isn't the best choice. You can replace two of the modules, but you'll lose the memory capacity of one of those modules. **B** is the most expensive choice and doesn't increase benefits. If possible, you'd want to keep the memory already installed on your system and only replace one of the memory boards. **D** is incorrect because you can always replace memory in installed slots up to the limit of memory capability for the motherboard. Most new motherboards support two or more gigabytes of memory expansion on the motherboard.

20. ☑ **D.** Although any printer can be considered as a network printer when it's shared on the network, the only printer that can become a node on the network is one that has a built-in network interface card. True network printers are those that are connected directly to the hub or switch as a node and can either be accessed directly using a networking protocol such as TCP/IP or through a print server. These types of printers usually require special drivers to be installed on the systems that use them or require the addition of a TCP/IP printing application on the workstations that'll use them.

☒ **A, B,** and **C** are incorrect because a printer can't be called a "network printer" only because it's shared on the network.

21. ☑ **C.** The best way to remove dust is to use a vacuum cleaner to suck up the dust settled on the internal components of the computer. This is the preferred method because the vacuum cleaner will remove the dust without allowing it to settle on other parts. Vacuum cleaners come with a variety of nozzle sizes, and an appropriate nozzle to use is one that can reach most of the areas inside the computer.

☒ **A** is incorrect because cleaning with a dust cloth will cause dust removed from one component to settle on other components. **B** is incorrect because when you blow dust off a component using compressed air, the dust will settle on other internal components of the computer, as well as on the external devices, such as the mouse, mouse pad, keyboard, and speakers. **D** is incorrect because dust inside the computer should never be removed using water or a damp cloth.

22. ☑ **D.** The fiber-optic cable is the best cable for connecting networks that are separated by large distances. Apart from providing high data speeds, this cable is also immune to magnetic and electromagnetic interference because the data travels in the form of optical (light) signals. Moreover, this cable can be used in lengths up to 2,000 meters without any attenuation of signal.

☒   **A** and **B** are incorrect because these cables don't support the 100 Mbps data speeds required by the 100BaseTX networks. **C** is incorrect because although this cable can support up to 100 Mbps data speeds, it's not suitable because it's prone to magnetic and electromagnetic interference. CAT 5 also can't be used in distances greater than 100 meters.

23.   ☑   **A.** The most likely problem is an address conflict between the two computers because no two devices can have the same TCP/IP address in a network. Usually one or both devices will stop working when an address conflict occurs. The best way to resolve this is to change the address to an unused address that's available for the network. A key symptom in this situation if you don't get an error message from one or both operating systems is that when the one computer joins the network, the second computer won't get network access.

☒   **B** is incorrect because the NIC shouldn't be suspected as the problem until the TCP/IP settings are correct. **C** is incorrect because 100BaseT networks don't use terminators. The devices themselves act as terminators when connected to the network. **D** is incorrect because you shouldn't suspect the TCP/IP stack until you've configured the protocol properly for the new computer system.

24.   ☑   **D.** The mouse usually moves on a mouse pad that isn't covered and thus collects dust. This dust is picked up by the rubber ball on the bottom of the mouse and is transferred to internal rollers inside the roller compartment. This causes the mouse pointer to "jump" across the screen. Cleaning the rubber ball and rollers inside the roller compartment will solve the problem.

☒   **A** is incorrect because if the serial cable were cracked, the mouse wouldn't work at all. **B** is incorrect because this doesn't cause the specified problem. However, a resource conflict can occur causing a total failure if more than one device is using the same resources. For example, if a modem and a mouse were using the same IRQ, only one of them would be able to work at a time. **C** is incorrect because if this were the case, the mouse wouldn't have worked at all. Note that the question says, "The mouse hasn't been working *properly* for the past several days."

25.   ☑   **C.** The processor isn't seated properly in the socket. You want to make sure that the processor is fully seated in the processor socket. If the processor

isn't seated properly, the system won't function properly and the symptoms described (or similar ones) will occur.

☒　**A** is incorrect because the processor internal clock will operate at the maximum speed of the processor in most instances. The external or bus speeds will be limited by the motherboard capabilities, but the processor will usually operate at its rated speed. When upgrading a processor, you may have to change jumpers on the motherboard to accept the new speed of the processor. **B** is incorrect because although the BIOS may need to be upgraded, this hasn't been established yet based on the symptoms of the problem. **D** is incorrect because the power supply is probably working properly if the fan is running. Generally, upgrading a processor won't overload a power supply.

26.　☑　**C.** The full docking station provides access to most components and peripherals that a regular desktop system uses. When using a docking station, you simply have to plug your laptop computer into the docking station and restart it. The laptop disables the built-in components for which it finds an alternative attached to the docking station.

☒　**A** is incorrect because the port replicator has limited functionality and doesn't allow all of the external components mentioned in the question to be used externally. **B** is incorrect because the extended port replicator will also not be an appropriate alternative in the given situation. **D** is incorrect because only a docking station can facilitate connection to all the external devices mentioned in the question.

27.　☑　**A.** The original packaging must be used because it's specially designed to protect the monitor from damage during transportation. This is all that's required to ship the monitor.

☒　**B, C,** and **D** are incorrect because you should never attempt to discharge a monitor. This is an extremely dangerous procedure, and it requires you to remove the case from the monitor. An A+ technician isn't trained or qualified to deal with the high-voltage power supplies in monitors, and this presents an extreme danger to you. In other words, DON'T REMOVE THE COVERS OF THE MONITOR.

28.　☑　**C.** FDDI stands for "Fiber-Distributed Data Interface." This network topology is based on Token Ring but uses fiber-optic cable that supports a 100 Mbps data transfer speed. The dual-ring FDDI network consists of two rings to provide fault tolerance. If one of the rings breaks down, the other ring takes over, and the network continues to function. You'd want to also use fiber optics in the case of an office complex because the distance limitations aren't as severe in a fiber-based network as in a coax or twisted-pair network.

☒   **A** is incorrect because Token Ring networks support a maximum data transfer speed of 16 Mbps. **B** is incorrect because this network supports a maximum speed of 4 Mbps. Neither Token Ring nor token bus networks provide any kind of fault tolerance. **D** is incorrect because a Token Star network is actually a Token Ring network that uses a Multistation Access Unit (MAU). These networks may or may not support a 100 Mbps speed, depending on whether they use either a CAT 5 cable or fiber-optic cable.

29.   ☑   **B.** Onboard cache works at the processor speed, and the external L2 cache runs at the speed of the motherboard. "Onboard" simply means it's housed in the processor casing and is able to run at the speed of the processor. The L2 cache on the motherboard is able to run only at the bus speed of the motherboard.

☒   **A** is incorrect because the L2 cache isn't another name for the L1 cache. An L2 cache may be either an onboard cache (built inside the processor package) or an external cache (on the motherboard), and the L1 cache is on board. However, it's true that the L1 cache runs at the processor speed. **C** is incorrect because the onboard cache may or may not be smaller than the external cache, and this isn't the reason that the onboard cache is faster than the external cache. **D** is incorrect because the onboard cache runs at the speed of the processor, not the cumulative speed of the processor and the motherboard.

30.   ☑   **A.** The system timer is responsible for synchronizing the processor speed with various components. IRQ 0 is assigned to the system timer, and because it's a critical component of the computer, it's given the highest priority.

☒   **B** is incorrect because the highest priority is given to IRQ 0. **C** is incorrect because although IRQ 15 is the highest IRQ number available, it doesn't have the highest priority. **D** is incorrect because the real-time clock is responsible for maintaining only the actual date and time. The system timer with IRQ 0 is the most important function and, hence, has the highest priority.

31. ☑ **A.** A continuously glowing light on the floppy disk drive indicates that the ribbon cable connecting the floppy disk drive isn't connected properly or is connected in reverse orientation.

    ☒ **B** is incorrect because this error is displayed when there's no disk in the floppy disk drive and you're trying to read from or write to the drive. **C** is incorrect because this error is produced when the system is unable to read from the floppy disk because either the file or the floppy disk is corrupted. **D** is incorrect because this error indicates you're trying to save a file on the floppy disk and there isn't enough free space left.

32. ☑ **B.** It's incorrect to say that inkjet printers can print only on fixed-length paper. Inkjet printers allow you to print on a variety of paper sizes and even on envelopes and cards.

    ☒ **A** is an incorrect answer because it's true that inkjet printers use a paper tray from which friction-feed rollers pull the paper into the printer. **C** is an incorrect answer because inkjet printers usually don't use continuous paper but instead use a stack of paper already cut to size. **D** is incorrect because it's possible to print envelopes and cards using an inkjet printer. The dot-matrix printer typically uses continuous paper with a tractor-feed mechanism, which makes it difficult to print on envelopes and cards.

33. ☑ **B.** The BIOS settings in the CMOS chips are retained in the absence of power to the computer by a battery commonly known as a "CMOS battery." This battery is charged when the computer is powered and supplies power to the CMOS chips when the computer is turned off.

    ☒ **A** is incorrect because the BIOS settings aren't stored in RAM but on CMOS chips. **C** is incorrect because the purpose of cache memory is to keep ready those instructions that the processor might be calling for. **D** is incorrect because, again, the hard disk isn't used for storing CMOS BIOS settings. Moreover, the question asks for a "component on the motherboard," and the hard disk isn't installed on the motherboard.

34. ☑ **D.** A faulty monitor is usually the cause of a flickering display. Because monitors can't be repaired in the field, it's advisable to replace the faulty monitor to resolve the problem.

    ☒ **A** is incorrect because incorrect display settings usually cause problems such as a missing display, an improper display size, and overlapped images. **B** is incorrect because this won't cause a flickering display. **C** is incorrect because if the video driver were incorrect, the operating system wouldn't have been able to utilize full video resolution and color depth.

35. ☑ **B.** The memory bank will be filled up using only one 64-bit DIMM. When installing RAM modules, you must remember that the memory bank doesn't refer to the number of slots on the motherboard but the width of the address bus. Because the Pentium 4 motherboard supports a 64-bit address bus, you'll need at least one 64-bit DIMM to fill up the memory bank.

☒ **A** is incorrect because a DIMM isn't available in a 16-bit bus width. DIMMs have a 64-bit bus width. **C** is incorrect because you need at least four 16-bit RIMMs (16MB × 4 = 64MB) to fill up the memory bank. **D** is incorrect because the question clearly states that the motherboard has slots for synchronous dynamic RAM (SDRAM) and SDRAM typically comes in DIMMs. SIMM modules can't be installed in DIMM slots.

36. ☑ **D.** The hard disk produces sound only when the power is connected to it. If there's no power connection, the hard disk won't turn, and there will be no sound.

☒ **A** is incorrect because a broken ribbon cable will cause data access problems. **B** is incorrect because it's unlikely that the ribbon cable has been changed because it's not mentioned in the question. **C** is also incorrect because this will cause hard disk access problems. In all the ribbon connection problems stated in options A, B, and C, the hard disk will still produce a turning sound when there's a power connection.

37. ☑ **B.** All Token Ring networks require Multistation Access Units (MAUs). The MAU is used only in Token Ring networks that have the star topology. This is also known as a "Token Ring hub." Each computer is connected to the MAU in a star fashion, but the data travels in a ring fashion.

☒ **A, C,** and **D** are incorrect answers because all these statements are true. The Token Ring is based on the IEEE 802.5 standard. A variation is the token bus topology that's defined in IEEE 802.4 and uses coaxial cable instead of twisted-pair cable. Token Ring networks support either 4 Mbps or 16 Mbps data speeds, depending on the type of topology being used. Token Ring networks can use coaxial cable (token bus), twisted-pair cable (Token Ring), or fiber-optic cable (Fiber-Distributed Data Interface).

38. ☑ **B.** The positive charge on the paper attracts the negatively charged toner from the photosensitive drum. The transfer corona wire applies this positive charge on the paper after the image has been *developed* on the drum with toner powder. Because opposite charges attract each other, when the positively charged paper moves under the drum, it attracts the negatively charged toner.

    ☒ **A** is incorrect because the control unit is responsible for managing all functions of the printer process. If the control unit was defective, the entire system would malfunction. **C** is incorrect because the fusing rollers aren't responsible for transferring the toner from drum to paper. The paper moves to the fusing assembly for melting (or *fusing*) of the toner after the image has been transferred to the paper. **D** is incorrect because the cleaning blade is used to clean the drum after the image has been transferred to the paper and the printer is ready to receive a new page for printing.

39. ☑ **C.** The VGA and SVGA video adapters and monitors have DB-15 female connectors, and the pins are divided into three rows. Enhanced Graphics Adapter (EGA) monitors have a DB-9 male connector. These monitors are connected to EGA video adapters that have a female DB-9 connector for attaching the monitor. There are only two rows of pins in DB-9 connectors—five pins in the upper row and four pins in the lower row. Serial ports, CGA video adapters, and CGA monitors also have DB-9 connectors.

    ☒ **A** is incorrect because the EGA monitor has a DB-9 male connector, and a male connector can't be attached to another male connector. **B** is incorrect because the DB-9 female connector is found on EGA monitors. **D** is incorrect because this type of connector is used for LPT1 and LPT2 parallel ports. Serial ports on some computers also use DB-25 connectors.

40. ☑ **B.** If the customer is unable to provide sufficient information, the first step in successfully diagnosing a problem is to try to reproduce the problem. This will allow you to make your own observations. In such cases, the customer can help you reproduce the problem by outlining the steps he followed when the problem occurred.

    ☒ **A** is incorrect because you must not change any component unless you're absolutely sure that the component is faulty. **C** is incorrect because the customer doesn't remember any error codes, so you won't be able to get the details unless you reproduce the problem. **D** is incorrect because if this were the cause of the problem, the customer most likely would've informed you.

41.   ☑   **D.** The defect symptoms indicate that one of the pins of the dot-matrix printer isn't being activated. This causes the print output to look like a continuous white line on paper. Replacing the print head will resolve the problem.

☒   **A** is incorrect because the problem is caused by a missing print head pin and not the ribbon cartridge. **B** is incorrect because tractor-feed problems usually cause paper movement problems. **C** is incorrect because if the printer driver were incorrect or corrupted, either the print output would've been garbled or there would be no print output at all.

42.   ☑   **B.** A dirty ink cartridge is probably not the cause of the problem. Ink cartridges should be suspected when there are problems in the quality of the print output or if there's no printing at all, caused by an empty cartridge.

☒   **A, C,** and **D** are incorrect because any of these problems can cause garbled printing or unreadable characters. An incorrect printer driver, a communication problem between the computer and the printer, or a bad parallel port can all cause garbled print output.

43.   ☑   **D.** A 50-ohm terminator is used to terminate the ends of a coaxial cable in bus networks. The terminator prevents signals from bouncing back and forth on the wire. If the terminators aren't present on the ends of the coaxial cable, the bus network can't function.

☒   **A** is incorrect because the vampire tap is a connector that connects a computer to the coaxial cable. **B** is incorrect because the T connector is used to connect a network adapter to the running coaxial cable. **C** is incorrect because the cable can't be used to terminate itself.

44.   ☑   **B.** Configuring the disk drives for RAID 5, also called "disk striping with parity" will provide a great deal of improvement in data loss. Having a tape backup will allow them to back up key files on a regular basis but won't prevent data loss between backups. RAID 5 spreads the data across multiple disks and also keeps parity information on the data. In the event of a failure of a part of the disk system, the other disks can be used to regenerate the data to the point of failure. This offers the highest protection of the choices offered.

☒   **A** isn't correct. RAID 0 doesn't provide any fault tolerance and is used to enhance performance of disk access. **C** is incorrect because a dual-processor system isn't a fault-tolerant system. Dual-processor systems still rely on the existing disk storage. Dual-processor systems are an overall performance enhancement potentially over a single-processor system. **D** is incorrect because RAID 5 does provide fault tolerance.

45. ☑ **A.** The first thing you must do immediately after installing a hard disk is check whether it's recognized by the computer BIOS. Every PC displays BIOS information upon startup that includes information on hard disks, floppy disks, keyboards, and so on. Although most of the newer BIOSs automatically recognize the hard disk types, it's best to check the BIOS display to make sure that the disk will work properly.

☒ **B** is incorrect because this utility is used to create or delete disk partitions. The question states that the hard disk won't have any partitions. Although it's not possible to use a hard disk without first partitioning it, the question is asking about your first action after switching on the computer. Partitioning has to be done *after* it's verified that the hard disk is being recognized by the BIOS. **C** is incorrect because you must first check that the hard disk is recognized by the system BIOS. Formatting can be done later. **D** is incorrect because the drive has to be formatted before it can be used for copying data.

46. ☑ **C.** The communication error indicates that the computer isn't able to communicate with the printer. This problem is caused by either a loose connection or a detached printer cable. Check to ensure that the printer is connected properly. If the connection is perfect, the cable might have become faulty. Replace the cable and try printing again.

☒ **A** is incorrect because an incorrect printer driver usually doesn't produce a communication error. **B** is incorrect because, again, this won't produce a communication error. **D** is incorrect because the printer had been working earlier.

47. ☑ **C.** The drive must be connected to the middle connector with the jumper set to the slave position. The hard disk is installed as a slave drive by connecting it to the middle connector on the ribbon cable. The configuration jumper on the drive must be set to the slave position. A primary slave hard disk requires that the primary master hard disk be present in the system.

☒ **A** is incorrect because the end connector on the ribbon connector is reserved for the master hard disk. If you connect a hard disk to the end connector with its configuration jumper in the slave position, it won't work.

B is incorrect because the first hard disk in the system is always the primary master, which holds the operating system. **D** is incorrect because the primary slave drive requires a primary master drive, not a secondary master drive.

48. ☑ **C.** Antistatic wrist straps shouldn't be used when you're working on high-voltage devices. Computers, printers, and monitors contain high-voltage parts, including power supplies. Antistatic wrist straps are designed to ease out excessive static voltage through your body. If you wear them while working on high-voltage equipment, there's a chance that any leaking high voltage will pass through your body, giving you a severe electric shock.

    ☒ **A** is incorrect because even when you're using an antistatic mat, you must wear antistatic wrist straps as additional protection against static electricity, provided the device you're working on isn't a high-voltage device. **B** is incorrect because this isn't the criterion for not using an antistatic wrist strap. **D** is incorrect because antistatic spray isn't a substitute for an antistatic wrist strap but additional protection against static discharge.

49. ☑ **C.** The problem is caused by a faulty hub. From the information given by the customer, it's clear that the network is a star network using UTP cables and a hub. If there's a faulty hub, the entire network is down because the computers communicate to one another through the hub.

    ☒ **A** is incorrect because there are only 12 computers in the network, and the network speed is 10 Mbps. Such a small numbers of computers can't cause excessive network traffic. **B** is incorrect because a single broken cable on one of the computers can't bring down the entire network. Because each computer is independently connected to the hub, only the computer that has a broken network cable would have a problem. **D** is incorrect because terminators aren't used in 10BaseT networks. They're used only in bus networks that use coaxial cables.

50. ☑ **B.** The most likely problem is the cable modem. If all of the other systems are visible and other users are reporting the same symptoms, the network is probably working properly. Your best option would be to troubleshoot assuming that either the cable modem has malfunctioned, the connection to the cable modem is bad, or that something has malfunctioned upstream from the cable modem.

☒ **A** is incorrect because everyone in the network seems to be having the same problem. This may be a problem, but unless someone has changed this setting across the entire network, it's unlikely that this is problem. **C** is incorrect because a computer virus wouldn't usually block Internet access. **D** is incorrect because the other components of the network are visible and accessible.

12

A+ Operating Systems Technologies Practice Exam

QUESTIONS

1. Which of the following methods can't be used in Windows 98 to modify Registry entries? Select all correct answers.

   A. The Computer Management Console

   B. Control Panel

   C. The REGEDT32.EXE command

   D. The REDEDIT.EXE command

2. You want to install Windows 2000 Professional on a computer that's currently running Windows 98. This computer has two hard disk partitions named C: and D:. The computer doesn't have a CD-ROM, and you've mapped drive X: on your computer to the CD-ROM drive of another computer. Which of the following is a correct command to start the installation from the MS-DOS command prompt, considering that the destination drive will be the C: drive?

   A. X:\I386\WINNT.EXE

   B. X:\I386\WINNT32.EXE C:

   C. X:\I386\SETUP.EXE

   D. X:\I386\WINNT32.EXE

3. When you open the TCP/IP properties sheet of your network adapter, you find that it's configured to obtain an IP address automatically. You're using a Windows 98 computer, and a DHCP server in your office provides IP addresses to all desktops. Which of the following options would you use to check the IP address of your computer?

   A. Run the WINIPCFG utility.

   B. Run IPCONFIG /ALL at the command prompt.

   C. Click the Binding tab to find out the IP address.

   D. Restart the computer, and check the BIOS.

4. You want to restore some data to a Windows XP machine from a backup that was done on a Windows 98 machine. You've repeatedly tried to perform this operation with no success. The tapes seem to restore properly on a Windows 98 machine. The Windows XP system seems to be able to back up and restore tapes properly. What's the most likely problem?

   A. The backup formats between the systems are always incompatible.

   B. The backup tapes from the Windows 98 machine are compressed.

   C. The Windows XP tape drive is defective.

   D. The Windows 98 tape drive is defective.

5. You're using the Windows XP operating system on your computer. The hard disk of the computer is almost full, even after you've compressed a large number of files. You currently have 20MB of free disk space. When you attempt to copy a 15MB compressed file onto this hard disk, you get an error message saying that the disk space is insufficient. Why does this message appear when there's 20MB of free space on the disk?

   A. The size of the uncompressed file must be counted.

   B. You can't copy compressed files to a compressed folder.

   C. The file is corrupted after compression.

   D. All of the above.

6. You've just arrived at a customer's site to resolve a problem in his Windows 98 computer. The complaint is that the system produces some errors when the customer is working on certain applications. Unfortunately, the customer hasn't noted any of the error codes. What should be your first step when you start your diagnosis?

   A. Start uninstalling the applications one by one.

   B. Gather as much information as you can.

   C. Ask the customer to reproduce all the error codes.

   D. Search the Registry to locate the error codes.

7. You've decided to convert the hard disk of your Windows 98 computer to FAT32 using the Drive Converter utility. Which of the following benefits of this conversion is incorrectly described here?

A. Uses disk space more efficiently

B. Runs programs faster

C. Can be converted back to FAT16

D. Efficient storage of disk data

8. Which of the following commands should you run to install the Windows 98 operating system, assuming that you've already booted the system with the Windows 98 boot disk and the CD-ROM drivers have been loaded to access the setup CD-ROM?

A. WINSETUP.EXE

B. SETUP.EXE

C. WINNT.EXE

D. WINSTALL.EXE

9. Which of the following statements about system files in the Windows 9x, Windows 2000, and Windows XP operating systems is incorrect?

A. System files can be located anywhere in the hard disk.

B. System files are necessary to load and run the operating system.

C. System files are required for loading Plug and Play device drivers and allocating system resources to them.

D. System files are required to configure the system after installing the operating system.

10. Which of the following operating systems provides the easiest upgrade path to Windows XP?

A. Windows 3.1 because of its simple configuration

B. Windows 95 and Windows 98 because they also use the Registry

C. Windows 2000 because the Registry structure is similar

D. Windows NT 3.5 because all device drivers are compatible

11. You have a computer that's configured to dual boot between Windows 98 and Windows 2000. You've installed a new Plug and Play modem while running Windows 98. The modem works fine in Windows 98, but when you

start the computer in Windows 2000, the same modem doesn't respond. Which of the following is correct?

A.   The modem requires installation within Windows 2000 with the same driver.

B.   The modem requires installation within Windows 2000 with a Windows 2000–compatible driver.

C.   The modem can work with only one operating system.

D.   There's an IRQ conflict in the system.

12.   Which of the following options can you use without any configuration to quickly track the processes running on a Windows 2000 Professional computer and the system resources such as memory used by each process?

A.   Task Manager

B.   System Monitor

C.   Event log

D.   Performance console

13.   You're concerned that a Windows XP system you're working in is being exploited by outside hackers. Which of the following utilities might provide you with the most accurate indication that this happened?

A.   Task Manager

B.   System Monitor

C.   Event log

D.   Performance console

14.   Which of the following files in the Windows 98 operating system is used to switch from real mode to 32-bit protected mode during the system startup?

A.   VMM386.VXD

B.   EMM386.EXE

C.   IO.SYS

D.   WIN.COM

15. What happens when Windows 98 isn't able to locate a suitable driver for a new Plug and Play adapter?

    A. You're prompted to locate and install a third-party driver yourself.

    B. You're warned that the adapter won't work and should be removed.

    C. Windows 98 installs a substitute driver.

    D. None of the above.

16. You have four files named FOOT.EXE, FOOT.COM, FOOT.WPD, and FOOT.BAT in one of the folders of a Windows 98 computer. Which of the files will execute when you type FOOT at the MS-DOS command prompt if the folder is in the search path?

    A. FOOT.EXE

    B. FOOT.COM

    C. FOOT.WPD

    D. FOOT.BAT

17. The computer you're using at home was purchased a few years ago with a preloaded version of Windows 98 and several other free applications. During these two years, you've installed many other applications and attached several devices to this computer. You're thinking of cleaning up the system by formatting the hard drive and reinstalling the operating system. In which of the following situations should you reinstall the operating system?

    A. When none of the applications and none of the devices respond

    B. When one of the applications doesn't respond

    C. When one of the devices doesn't work

    D. When the system locks up frequently on launching an application

18. You have two phone lines at home and have purchased an additional modem for your computer. After connecting the modem to a free serial port and configuring the dial-up numbers, you want to combine the two modems to dial the remote access server in your office. Which of the following places in Dial-Up Networking properties will you use to define additional modems?

    A. From the Configure button on the General tab of Connection Properties

    B. From the Multilink tab of Connection Properties

    C. From the Options tab in Modem Properties

    D. From the Connection tab in Modem Properties

19. You installed a new network adapter in your computer running the Windows 98 operating system. You installed the driver files from the floppy disk that came with the adapter. When you restarted the computer, it didn't boot but froze on the Windows 98 startup screen and wouldn't fully load. Which of the following can help you resolve the problem?

    A. Start the computer using boot normally mode, and replace the driver with a Windows 98 generic driver for the adapter.

    B. Start the computer using the Safe Mode with Networking option, and replace the driver files.

    C. Start the computer in Safe mode, and replace the driver using Device Manager.

    D. Start the computer in step-by-step confirmation mode, and when prompted, replace the driver files.

20. You're working in a small company that has six computers configured in a peer network. The only color printer in the office is connected to your computer and is shared with other users. The users work on word processing programs and print several documents every day. The documents average ten printed pages. These users complain that when they come to collect their documents from the printer, they find the documents mixed up by other users. Which of the following will help you quickly address their grievances?

    A. Ask the users to stand by the printer.

    B. Allocate different time slots to each user.

    C. Use separator pages with the documents.

    D. Pause the printer after every print job.

21. The following symptoms are related to some problems in a Windows 98 computer. Which of them doesn't indicate a possible problem with the Windows swap file?

    A. The system locks up frequently.

    B. System response is very slow.

    C. The printer doesn't respond.

    D. The system takes a long time to load applications.

22. Which of the following statements incorrectly describes the function of the BOOT.INI file in the Windows 2000/XP operating systems?

    A. It's responsible for presenting the user with a list of operating systems and the time duration for which the options menu will be displayed.

    B. It displays the Windows 2000/XP startup options when the user presses the F8 key in case there's a startup problem.

    C. It specifies the location of the boot files once the user selects an operating system to load.

    D. It specifies the default operating system in case the user doesn't select a particular operating system.

23. You've just completed an update from Windows 98 to Windows XP. Overall you're happy with the performance and features, but you're noticing that some of your devices are intermittently working improperly and the system sometimes hangs for no apparent reason. Which of the following should you verify first to correct this problem?

    A. The BIOS may not be the most current for that motherboard.

    B. The operating system is corrupt and needs to be reinstalled.

    C. The disk drive is beginning to malfunction and needs to be replaced.

    D. Your system has been attacked by a virus.

24. Which of the following statements correctly describes the reason Windows 2000 Professional or Windows XP Professional is preferred over Windows 98 as a client operating system in a networked environment?

    A. Windows 2000 and Windows XP have better Plug and Play and multimedia support.

    B. Windows 2000 and Windows XP support NTFS permissions and have better processing power.

    C. Windows 2000 and Windows XP can serve as client to Windows 2000 servers.

    D. Windows 2000 and Windows XP are interactive and user friendly.

25. You've made some changes to a Windows 98 computer configuration. The new configuration doesn't work, and it has become evident that there's no other means of repairing the configuration than editing the Registry. What should be your first action before you start changing the Registry values to change the configuration?

    A. Restart the computer.

    B. Back up the existing Registry.

    C. Export the Registry to some other computer.

    D. Set the Registry file attributes to Read Only.

26. You install a SCSI hard disk in your computer that already has an IDE drive. When the adapter and disk drive have been installed, you start your computer and find that Windows 98 doesn't recognize the new drive. Which of the following isn't essential to successfully configuring the SCSI hard disk?

    A. Setting the SCSI ID on the hard disk

    B. Installing the SCSI driver

    C. Assigning an IRQ to the SCSI drive

    D. Running the SCSI utility to partition the disk

27. A Windows 2000 computer isn't starting up, and you think the problem is complex. Which of the following would be your last option before making a decision to reinstall the operating system?

    A. Replace the existing Registry with a good copy from another computer.

    B. Use the Recovery Console to start the computer in the non-GUI interface or command prompt mode.

    C. Use the emergency repair disk.

    D. Try resolving the problem by removing hardware components one by one.

28. You were working on your Windows 98 computer and accidentally deleted some system files. Which of the following files do you think is the most critical for booting Windows 98 and, if missing, would produce a fatal error?

    A. SYSTEM.INI

    B. CONFIG.SYS

    C. HIMEM.SYS

    D. AUTOEXEC.BAT

29. Which of the following antivirus utilities is included with the Windows 2000 operating system?

    A. Norton

    B. Symantec

    C. AVBoot

    D. McAfee

30. A computer is showing the following error when it starts up:
    NTLDR missing. Replace disk and press any key to continue.

    What does this error indicate? Select all correct answers.

    A. The computer has the Windows 95 operating system.

    B. The computer has the Windows NT operating system.

    C. The computer is a dual-boot system with Windows 98 and Windows 2000.

    D. The computer is running Windows 3.11.

31. A network adapter with an appropriate driver is already installed on your Windows 98 computer. As well, networking is installed using the NetBEUI protocol. Which of the following states the correct sequence of actions necessary to connect to shared drives on other computers?

    A. Enable File Sharing in Network Properties, right-click Network Neighborhood, and select Map Network Drive.

    B. Enable File and Printer Sharing in Network Properties, right-click Network Neighborhood, and select Map Network Drive.

C.   Enable File Sharing in Network Properties, click Tools in Windows Explorer, and select Map Network Drive.

D.   Right-click Network Neighborhood, and select Map Network Drive.

32.   There are some files on your Windows 98 home computer that contain important business data. You don't want these files to be visible to anyone else using your computer in your absence. Which of the following is the best way to hide these files when someone uses your computer?

A.   Set the File Properties as Hidden in Windows Explorer.

B.   Copy the files to floppy disks and hide them.

C.   Click View in Windows Explorer, and click As a Web Page.

D.   Set permissions so that only you have permission to view the files.

33.   Assuming that your Internet connection is live, which of the following is an incorrect URL to connect to a web site and won't make a connection?

A.   www.website.com

B.   http://website

C.   http://www.website.com

D.   www.web1.website.com

34.   Which of the following methods can you not use to connect to a shared network drive when you're working on a computer running the Windows 98 operating system?

A.   Right-click My Computer, and click Map Network Drive.

B.   Right-click Network Neighborhood, and click Map Network Drive.

C.   Type **MAP DRIVE F: \\COMPUTERNAME\SHARENAME** from the DOS prompt.

D.   Select Tools | Map Network Drive in Windows Explorer.

35.   You were trying to connect to www.osborne.com when your friend dropped in. He asked you what the popular term is for this Internet address. Which of the following should be your answer?

A.   UDP

B.   URL

    C. UNC

    D. FQDN

36. Which of the following is your best defense against data loss if there's a disaster? Select two answers.

    A. Back up your data regularly on tape drives, and store the tapes offsite.

    B. Back up your data regularly on two servers.

    C. Keep the backup tapes locked inside the server room.

    D. Use a UPS on your computer.

37. You have a Windows XP computer in your office and an Epson Stylus color printer connected to it. There are five more Windows 98 and XP computers in the same office. Your boss has requested that you connect all computers so resources on these computers can be shared. Select the resource that won't be sharable in this environment.

    A. Disk drives

    B. Folders

    C. Printers

    D. Monitors

38. You don't want to upgrade your Windows 98 computer to Windows XP Professional, but you'd like to know if your hardware and software are compatible so you can do the upgrade later. Which option of the WINNT32.EXE setup command will enable you to perform this compatibility check?

    A. /CHECKUPGRADEONLY

    B. /SYSPART<drive_letter>

    C. /CHECKUPGRADE

    D. /COPYDIR < folder_name>

39. One of the computers in your office is a Pentium 166 MHz computer with a 512KB L2 cache, 64MB of RAM, and 560MB of free hard disk space. The computer is currently running the Windows 98 operating system. Which of the following components will cause a problem if you were to make this computer dual boot with Windows 2000 Professional?

A. Processor

B. Cache memory

C. Hard disk space

D. RAM

40. You have a dual-boot system running Windows 98 and Windows 2000 Professional. This system has two hard disks, and each operating system is installed on a different disk. You've converted your Windows 2000 disk (drive D:) from FAT32 to NTFS 5 using the Disk Management utility in Windows 2000, but now you aren't able to see the Windows 2000 disk when running Windows 98. Which of the following options would you use to convert the file system back to FAT32 without losing any data?

A. Run the Reconvert utility in Disk Management.

B. Run CONVERT D: /FS:FAT32 from the command prompt.

C. Format the disk using the FAT file system.

D. None; FAT to NTFS conversion is a one-way process.

41. An internal modem is listed as an Unknown Device in Device Manager in a Windows 98 computer. Which of the following problems could possibly be causing this?

A. An incorrect driver has been installed.

B. The driver files haven't been installed.

C. There's a resource conflict with another device.

D. All of the above.

42. Which of the following types of servers on the Internet is configured to prompt you for a username and password before you're allowed to see the contents on the server?

A. An HTTP server

B. An anonymous FTP server

C. A WWW server

D. A secure web site

43. You were working on a Windows 98 computer and accidentally deleted a file specified in SYSTEM.INI that's required by a legacy device. What will happen when the computer restarts?

    A. Windows 98 won't boot successfully.

    B. The boot process will fail during the GUI mode.

    C. You'll get an operating system error.

    D. Nothing; Windows 98 will boot normally.

44. Most of your work on the Internet involves downloading files from several FTP and web sites. You're planning to set up an additional connection to the Internet. Which of the following options will suit your requirements?

    A. ISDN

    B. PSTN

    C. DSL

    D. POTS

45. A Windows XP computer isn't starting up, and you suspect that it's either the video adapter or the network adapter that might be causing the problem. Which of the following boot options is the best for starting Windows XP on this computer to troubleshoot the problem?

    A. Boot normally

    B. Safe mode

    C. Step-by-step confirmation

    D. Debugging mode

46. One of your friends told you that when you type a URL in the address box of an Internet browser, the name is translated to its IP address. Which of the following services do you think is used to perform this translation?

    A. DHCP

    B. WINS

    C. DNS

    D. ISP

47. One of the web sites you tried to connect to has sent a warning message that Secure Sockets Layer isn't enabled on your computer. Which of the following tabs in Internet Options will you use to enable Secure Sockets Layer?

    A. Security

    B. Content

    C. Advanced

    D. Programs

48. You've been given a new computer that'll be connected to the office network. This computer runs Windows XP Professional. You'll use this computer to design graphics advertisements for the company's clients. Each of the design files takes nearly three days to complete, and you usually don't let anyone touch your design files before they're complete. Your office network doesn't use a Windows domain environment. Which of the following choices will provide you with the highest flexibility for managing the security of your files across the network?

    A. Disabling Simple File Sharing with the NTFS file system

    B. Disabling Simple Network Security with the FAT32 file system

    C. Establishing File Sharing for the directories that contain the files

    D. Separating logon accounts for each user

49. You want to configure the TCP/IP network protocol on your Windows XP computer, which is part of one of the three segments of a network. It's essential that you be able to access shared resources on all computers in the network. Which of the following statements given is incorrect?

    A. The IP address is necessary and shouldn't be in use by any other computer in any segment of the network.

    B. The subnet mask is optional and, when specified, should be unique to the computer.

    C. The default gateway entry is essential because this is a multiple segment network.

    D. The DNS and WINS server entries are optional.

50. You've just installed Windows XP on a new computer system. During the installation, the system has accessed the Internet using a dial-up line and seems to be taking an extraordinary amount of time to complete. What's the likely problem in this situation?

    A. Nothing; this is normal for Windows XP.

    B. The modem has malfunctioned.

    C. Antivirus software is interfering with the process.

    D. None of the above.

IN-DEPTH ANSWERS

1. ☑ **A** and **C.** The Computer Management console and the REGEDT32.EXE command aren't available in the Windows 98 operating system. The Registry can be modified indirectly by changing system settings through Control Panel or by direct editing.

   ☒ **B** is incorrect because modifying computer configuration using one or more of the options in Control Panel is an indirect and safe method to modify the Registry. **D** is incorrect because you can use this command in Windows 98 as well as in Windows 2000 to edit the Registry.

2. ☑ **D.** The Windows 2000 setup files for the Intel platform are located in the \I386 folder on the setup CD-ROM. When installing from within a running Windows 98 operating system, you need to run the WINNT32.EXE file. If "X" is the letter for the network drive mapped to the CD-ROM, the correct command becomes X:\I386\WINNT32.EXE.

   ☒ **A** is incorrect because the WINNT.EXE setup command is used for clean installations that are initiated from a 16-bit operating system, usually DOS. **B** is incorrect because you don't need to specify the destination drive with this command. The setup program will prompt you for the installation drive during installation. **C** is incorrect because SETUP.EXE isn't a valid setup command in Windows 2000. This command is used to start installing the Windows 3.*x* and Windows 9*x* operating systems.

3. ☑ **A.** The WINIPCFG utility in Windows 98 is the best source to find out the IP address assigned to the computer by a DHCP server. This utility can also be used to force the release of an IP address or renew an existing IP address.

☒ **B** is incorrect because this utility isn't available in all versions of Windows 9x. Windows NT and Windows 2000 computers have this utility. When used with the /ALL switch, the IPCONFIG utility displays detailed IP configuration for the computer. **C** is incorrect because the Bindings tab doesn't show the IP address of the computer. This tab lists the protocols to which a service is bound and allows you to set the binding order. **D** is incorrect because the BIOS will not report the IP address of the computer.

4. ☑ **B.** Some versions of backup allow for compression of data during backup. This is done to save space on the tape. To restore the tape you'll need to go to another system that's running the backup version that the tapes were created under, restore them, and then back them up in an uncompressed format. The NTbackup program included with Windows XP doesn't recognize the compression format that's used by MSBackup.

☒ **A** is incorrect because the backup formats between the two systems are compatible as long as compression isn't used. **C** and **D** are incorrect because both tape drives appear to be functioning correctly.

5. ☑ **A.** The size of the uncompressed file must be counted. When you copy a compressed file to a folder in Windows XP, the size of the uncompressed file is taken into account. The uncompressed size of the file you're trying to copy is more than 20MB, and this is why you're getting the error.

☒ **B** is incorrect because this isn't true. Both compressed and uncompressed files can be copied to a compressed folder in Windows XP. **C** is incorrect because Windows XP doesn't corrupt files when compressing them. **D** is incorrect because there's only one correct reason that you aren't able to copy the compressed file. Although it's unlikely that you'll get difficult questions on Windows 2000/XP or Windows 9x file and folder management in the A+ exam, you must be aware of certain well-known features and limitations of these operating systems.

6. ☑ **B.** Gather as much information as you can. When the cause of a problem isn't known and the customer or computer user doesn't remember the error

codes, you should try to gather as much information as you can. If you ask the customer a few questions, such as how the problem started, what particular application produced the errors, and what happened when the errors were displayed, you'd have enough information to start your initial diagnosis.

☒   **A** is incorrect because unless you know the exact cause of the problem, you shouldn't uninstall any applications. **C** is incorrect because the customer might not be able to produce *all* the errors again, as stated in the answer. You should, however, ask the customer if he can reproduce some of the errors because if he can, then he essentially knows how the errors happened, and this will provide valuable information as to the sequence of events leading up to the errors. **D** is incorrect because the Registry contains configuration information and doesn't store any error codes generated by applications.

7.   ☑   **C.** This is an incorrect statement regarding the benefits of the FAT32 file system in Windows 98. The drive, once converted to FAT32, can't be converted back to the FAT16 file system without first repartitioning and reformatting it.

☒   **A**, **B**, and **D** are incorrect because all these features are benefits of the FAT32 file system. A hard disk using the FAT32 file system stores disk data more efficiently than FAT16, the conversion to FAT32 creates several megabytes of additional disk space, and FAT32 is capable of running programs faster.

8.   ☑   **B.** The simple command to start a Windows 98 installation is SETUP.EXE, assuming that you're in the correct folder on the CD-ROM drive that has the installation files. If you're at the C: prompt, you must change to the appropriate folder on the CD-ROM drive so that the SETUP.EXE file can be located and run.

☒   **A** is incorrect because this file doesn't exist and thus is an incorrect command. **C** is incorrect because this file is used in Windows 2000 to start the installation from the DOS prompt. **D** is incorrect because this command doesn't exist for installation of the Windows 98 operating system.

9.   ☑   **A.** This statement is incorrect because the system files are usually located on the boot partition in Windows 98, Windows 2000, and Windows XP. Windows 98 typically uses the WINDOWS directory and Windows 2000/XP use the WINNT folder. The boot partition refers to the partition on the hard

disk that contains these folders. If these files are moved from their original location, the operating system either won't load or won't run properly.

☒ **B, C,** and **D** are incorrect answers because these statements are true. The system files are necessary to load and run the operating system. They're required to load drivers for Plug and Play devices and allocate resources to them. When you install any application programs after the installation of the operating system, the system files are required to successfully complete the configuration of the application.

10. ☑ **C.** Windows 2000 because the Registry structure is similar. Windows 2000 provides the easiest upgrade path to Windows XP because of the similar Registry structure and the fact that a majority of the configuration can be migrated to the new operating system.

☒ **A** is incorrect because you can't upgrade from Windows 3.1 to Windows XP. You must first upgrade Windows 3.1 to Windows 9x or Windows NT and then to Windows XP. In fact, this is the most complex upgrade path. Microsoft recommends that if you have a running Windows 3.1 system, you should perform a clean install instead of an upgrade. **B** is incorrect because the Registry structures of Windows 95 and Windows 98 are similar to each other, but they're entirely different from the Registry structure of Windows XP. **D** is incorrect because the device drivers for Windows NT 3.5, Windows NT 4, Windows 2000, and Windows XP are all different.

11. ☑ **B.** You need to install the modem while running the Windows 2000 operating system and using a Windows 2000 driver. Although both Windows 98 and Windows 2000 support Plug and Play and will detect the modem as soon as a particular operating system is started, in some cases, you might have to load the driver files from the disk supplied by the manufacturer.

☒ **A** is incorrect because the modem drivers might be different for Windows 98 and Windows 2000. **C** is incorrect because most modems are compatible with multiple operating systems and have corresponding device drivers. **D** is incorrect because if there were an IRQ conflict, the modem wouldn't have worked with Windows 98 either.

12. ☑ **A.** The Task Manager in Windows 2000 displays a list of currently active processes on the computer. It also displays the different resources such as

memory and processor usage by individual processes. You can bring the Task Manager up by pressing CTRL-ALT-DEL or by right-clicking the taskbar.

☒ **B** is incorrect because it's used to collect information on processes and won't display any results unless some basic configuration is performed. The configuration involves adding counters for different objects. **C** is incorrect because event logs also collect information on system, application, and security events after proper configuration. **D** is incorrect because the System Monitor discussed is a part of the Performance console. None of these options gives you the quick results required by the question.

13. ☑ **C.** The event logs can be viewed by the Event Viewer to determine activities that have occurred over time on the system. If the system is being hacked by outsiders, you can set the Event Viewer to store the results of access using the security or applications log settings. This would be the best tool to view events that have happened in the past.

☒ **A** is incorrect because the Task Manager will only show you what's currently happening on the system, not what has happened in the past. **B** is incorrect because the System Monitor will allow you to view information about system performance but doesn't show individual events or programs running on the system. **D** is incorrect because the Performance console is part of the tools used to manage a system and uses current information.

14. ☑ **A.** During the Windows 98 startup process, the WIN.COM file locates and loads the virtual memory manager VMM386.EXE. This file loads device drivers into memory and also switches the processor from real mode to 32-bit protected mode. This mode is called the "protected-mode boot" because the system loads and initializes the critical system files and device drivers.

☒ **B** is incorrect because this file is used for memory management and doesn't switch the processor from real mode to protected mode. **C** is incorrect because the IO.SYS file is the file that initializes the loading of the Windows 98 operating system. **D** is incorrect because the WIN.COM file is the first file used after the boot process has entered the protected mode. It loads the VMM386.VXD file.

15. ☑ **A.** When Windows 98 isn't able to locate a suitable driver for any new adapter, it prompts you to locate and install a third-party driver yourself. If

you've received a driver disk with the adapter, you may insert it and install the driver supplied by the manufacturer.

☒ **B** is incorrect because Windows 98 doesn't give any such warning to remove the adapter. **C** is incorrect because a substitute driver isn't installed. **D** is incorrect because one correct answer option does exist.

16. ☑ **B.** When you don't specify an extension with a file at the MS-DOS command prompt, the operating system first looks for the file with a COM extension in its path. If a COM file is found, it'll be executed and the interpreter will consider the task completed. If there's more than one file with the same name but with COM, EXE, and BAT extensions, the interpreter will attempt to find and execute the program file by precedence of COM, EXE, and BAT.

☒ **A** is incorrect because this file is executed if the operating system is unable to locate the FOOT.COM file. **C** is incorrect because this file can't be executed using only the filename. If you're in Windows Explorer, you can execute the WPD file by double-clicking it. **D** is incorrect because this file executes when there are no FOOT.COM or FOOT.EXE files.

17. ☑ **A.** When none of the applications and none of the devices attached to the computer respond, it becomes evident that there's a serious problem with the operating system. Because it's not feasible to diagnose each application or device problem separately, reinstalling the operating system is a good decision.

☒ **B** and **C** are incorrect answers because the decision to reinstall the operating system shouldn't be based on failure of a single application or a single device. A better decision is to diagnose the problem or remove the faulty application or device. **D** is incorrect because in this case you should suspect low system memory, a faulty application, or limited space in the Windows swap file. This problem shouldn't necessitate reinstalling the operating system.

18. ☑ **B.** The Multilink tab in Connection Properties allows you to specify additional modems for use in conjunction with the existing modem. Multilink allows you to combine the bandwidth of two or more lines and get a better connection speed. You should configure the modem before you enable Mulitilink in Connection Properties.

☒ **A** is incorrect because the Configure button on the General tab is used for configuration of modem properties. **C** is incorrect because this tab is in the

Modem Properties sheet and is used to configure dial-up options, such as bringing up the terminal screen before and after dialing. **D** is incorrect because this tab is used to configure port settings and start and stop bits for the modem communication.

19. ☑ **C.** Start the computer in Safe mode, and replace the driver using Device Manager. When a Windows 98 computer refuses to boot normally after installing a driver or after updating an existing device driver, you can use Safe mode to boot the computer. In this mode, Windows 98 loads only basic drivers to run the system. You can then use Device Manager to replace the bad driver files.

☒ **A** is incorrect because this is what you were doing when the system locked up. **B** is incorrect because the computer will load the driver for the network adapter, which is the driver causing the problem. **D** is incorrect because this mode gives you the option of selecting which drivers to load but doesn't prompt you to replace any drivers, as stated in the answer.

20. ☑ **C.** Use separator pages with the documents. This option will help resolve the problem quickly and without much configuration. A separator page with each document will help the users identify their documents, and the chances of pages getting mixed up will be reduced. The Use Separator Page option is available in Printer Properties.

☒ **A** is incorrect because this is a waste of time. **B** is incorrect because this will prevent users from printing important or urgent documents even when the printer is free. **D** isn't a practical option because you'll always have to watch the printer window, which is difficult and won't help resolve the problem.

21. ☑ **C.** If the printer attached to a Windows 9*x* computer doesn't respond, you shouldn't suspect the Windows swap file. There are likely to be other reasons for this problem, such as connections, cables, printer drivers, or a faulty printer. The swap file is used when the system needs additional memory to process user requests or to run application programs.

☒ **A, B,** and **D** are incorrect answers because if the system locks up frequently, if its response is slow, or if it takes a long time to load applications, either the swap file has become corrupt or it has insufficient space to accommodate requests.

22. ☑ **B.** This isn't a function of the BOOT.INI file in Windows 2000/XP. The BOOT.INI file doesn't invoke the startup options menu if the user presses the F8 key when Windows 2000 or Windows XP begins to load.

    ☒ **A, C,** and **D** are incorrect answers because these statements correctly describe functions of the BOOT.INI file. The BOOT.INI file displays the operating system's menu, specifies for how long this menu is to be displayed, specifies a default operating system if the user doesn't make a selection, and tells NTLDR the location of boot files for each operating system.

23. ☑ **A.** This type of problem is common when the BIOS isn't upgraded before the operating system is upgraded. You should visit the motherboard manufacturer's web site to determine how to upgrade the BIOS of your motherboard. It's a good practice to upgrade the BIOS before you upgrade the operating system.

    ☒ **B** and **C** are incorrect because most likely the operating system and disk drive are working properly. Until you've updated the BIOS, you shouldn't suspect either of these as the source of the problem. **D** is incorrect because if you didn't have a virus before the installation, you shouldn't suspect one until you've updated the BIOS. It's a good practice to regularly scan your operating system after an upgrade, but this is less likely than a BIOS problem given the symptoms.

24. ☑ **B.** The correct reason out of the given options for preferring Windows 2000 Professional and Windows XP Professional over Windows 98 as a client operating system in a networked environment is that they have better control over system resources because they support NTFS and have better processing power. In Windows 2000 Professional and Windows XP, up to two microprocessors are supported; in Windows 98, the limit is one.

    ☒ **A** is incorrect because although Windows 2000 Professional and Windows XP have better support for multimedia and Plug and Play devices than Windows 98, this isn't the reason Windows 2000/XP Professional is a preferred client operating system. **C** is incorrect because Windows 98 and several other operating systems can also connect to Windows 2000 servers as clients. **D** is incorrect because the Windows 98, Windows 2000, and Windows XP operating systems are equally interactive and user friendly.

25. ☑ **B.** Before you start changing the computer configuration by editing the Registry, you should back up the existing Registry. This is helpful if you accidentally make a change that further damages the system configuration. A backup copy of the Registry can be used to restore the original configuration.

    ☒ **A** is incorrect because this will make no difference. **C** is incorrect because this is possible only when you're in a network environment. Because it's not specified in the question whether the computer is a stand-alone or a network computer, this isn't the best answer. **D** is incorrect because if you make the Registry Read Only, you'll not be able to make any changes to it.

26. ☑ **C.** The IRQ is assigned to the SCSI adapter and not to any device attached to the SCSI chain. Usually when you install the SCSI driver, the program will assign an IRQ to the SCSI adapter.

    ☒ **A, B,** and **D** are incorrect answers because all these are essential to make the SCSI hard disk work. You must set the SCSI ID on the hard disk or at least check to make sure it's correct. You should install the SCSI driver and run the SCSI utility to partition the hard disk. The hard disk can't be used until you partition it using the SCSI utility.

27. ☑ **B.** The Recovery Console in Windows 2000 offers advanced users a unique tool to repair the system startup and other problems. The Recovery Console either is installed on the hard disk or can be run using the Windows 2000 setup CD-ROM. This console has advanced command line features that enable you to fix complex problems in the system.

    ☒ **A** is incorrect because the Registry in Windows 2000 (and Windows 9*x*) is computer specific, so the Registry of one computer wouldn't work in another. **C** is incorrect because the emergency repair disk is usually the first option used to fix startup problems, not the *last* option, as stated in the question. **D** is incorrect because it's not a good idea to remove standard computer hardware to resolve a startup problem.

28. ☑ **C.** The HIMEM.SYS file is critical for booting the Windows 98 operating system, and if this file is missing from the \Windows folder, the system will produce the "HIMEM.SYS not loaded" error and fail to boot. As a result, you'll be able to run the operating system only in real mode (MS-DOS mode).

    ☒ **A** is incorrect because this file is used for legacy devices and isn't required by Windows 98. **B** is incorrect for the same reason. **D** is incorrect because this file isn't critical for booting Windows 98. All configurations given in these files reside in the System Registry in Windows 9*x* systems. The values given in the Registry override the values specified in these files.

29. ☑ **C.** Windows 2000 Professional and Windows 2000 Server operating systems contain a copy of the InoculateIT Anti-virus AVBoot anti-virus utility. This utility is located in the \VALUEADD\3RDPARTY\ CA_ANTIV folder on the Windows 2000 setup CD-ROM. The AVBoot antivirus utility is a command line tool that can scan computer memory and all hard disks, and can even remove viruses in the master boot record. But you should remember that this utility should be updated regularly with the latest virus signature files from the original vendor. To make a bootable disk for Windows 2000 that automatically starts the AVBoot command line tool, run the MAKEDISK.BAT file from the \VALUEADD\3RDPARTY\ CA_ANTIV folder.

☒ **A, B,** and **D** are incorrect because none of these utilities is included with the Windows 2000 operating system. The only antivirus utility that's bundled with the operating system is AVBoot.

30. ☑ **B** and **C.** The NT Loader (NTLDR) file is used by the Windows NT, Windows 2000, and Windows XP operating systems. This file is used to locate and load the operating system from the hard disk. When the computer dual boots between Windows NT or Windows 2000 and another operating system, the NTLDR program displays a menu of operating system options listed in the BOOT.INI file. The presence of the NTLDR file indicates that the computer is running Windows NT or Windows 2000 or is dual booting between one of these two operating systems and another operating system, such as Windows 9*x*.

☒ **A** and **D** are incorrect answers because neither Windows 95 nor Windows 3.11 uses the NTLDR file.

31. ☑ **D.** Right-click Network Neighborhood, and select Map Network Drive. The answer options try to confuse connecting to shares on other computers and sharing your files or printers. Note that you want only to connect to shared folders on *other* computers. This means you need to map a network drive on your computer. No other action is necessary.

☒   **A** is incorrect because enabling file and print sharing isn't necessary. This is required when you want to share the resources on your computer. **B** is incorrect for the same reason. **C** is also incorrect because you don't need to enable File and Printer Sharing to connect to shared resources on other computers. You can use either the My Computer or the Network Neighborhood icon on the desktop to map a network drive. Map Network Drive in the Tools menu in Windows Explorer can also be used to connect to a network share.

32.   ☑   **A.** The easiest way to hide important files is to set their attributes as Hidden using the File properties sheet. By default, Windows doesn't show system and hidden files when someone opens Windows Explorer.

☒   **B** is incorrect because it's neither easy nor the best answer to copy the files to floppy disks. The floppy disks may not have the capacity to store your files, and it's not advisable to use this solution. **C** is incorrect because it'll make things worse. Setting this option not only displays the files but also displays the attributes of a selected file on the left side. **D** is incorrect because it's not possible to set file permissions on a Windows 98 computer.

33.   ☑   **B.** http://website is an incorrect Uniform Resource Locator (URL). The given address is missing the root domain type, such as .com, .net, or .org. A complete URL should specify the type of root domain. If you specify a domain name without a domain suffix, the connection won't be established.

☒   **A, C,** and **D** are valid URLs and can be used to connect to the web site www.website.com. **A** is correct because it's not necessary to type "http://" with the web site address. **C** is correct because this specifies a complete URL. **D** is correct because it points to a second-level domain named WEB1 in the website.com domain.

34.   ☑   **C.** This command can't be used to map a network drive because there's no such command as MAP DRIVE. The valid command to map a shared drive is this:
NET USE F: \\COMPUTERNAME\SHARENAME

☒   **A** is incorrect because you can use this method to connect to a shared drive on the network. **B** is an incorrect answer because this is also a correct method to map a shared network drive. **D** is incorrect because you can map a network drive using this method. In all three cases, you're prompted with a dialog box where you can specify a drive letter and the path of the shared network drive. You can also choose to reconnect the drive every time your computer restarts.

35.   ☑   **B.** URL stands for "Uniform Resource Locator." The URL specifies how the domain names are formatted when accessing the World Wide Web (WWW). To access a web site, you must know the correct URL of the site.

☒   **A** is incorrect because UDP stands for "User Datagram Protocol." UDP is a transport protocol in the TCP/IP suite of protocols and is mainly used for faster file transfers. **C** is incorrect because UNC stands for "Universal Naming Convention." A UNC path is required to connect to shared resources on the network. **D** is incorrect because a host name on the Internet is known as the fully qualified domain name (FQDN). The FQDN is a part of the URL.

36.   ☑   **A.** The best defense against disasters is to regularly back up your data and store the tapes offsite, preferably out of town. In case you're performing incremental backups to save the cost of tapes, your schedule should include performing a full system backup on a regular basis.

☒   **B** is incorrect because it's not a defense against disasters. This might save backup time, but it's not helpful because a disaster situation will most likely affect both servers. **C** is incorrect because this isn't an adequate defense against disasters. **D** is incorrect because a UPS will allow your computer to stay running during a power failure, but it doesn't prevent data loss.

37.   ☑   **D.** You won't be able to share monitors between systems. Monitors are the only nonsharable devices in a computer network.

☒   **A, B,** and **C** are incorrect. Disk drives, folders, and the printer connected to your computer are the only resources you can share. When networking is fully configured, you can share any of these resources with your colleagues in the office. You'll be able to use files and folders on other computers, and other users will likewise be able to share these resources. These users will also be able to print to the printer connected to your computer when it's shared.

38.   ☑   **A.** This switch performs a check on your current system and creates a compatibility report. When used with the /CHECKUPGRADEONLY switch, the WINNT32.EXE setup command can't be used to perform setup. It creates a detailed compatibility report you can use to analyze the effects of upgrading the current operating system.

☒ **B** is incorrect because this switch is used to prepare additional hard disks for installation of Windows 2000. This option copies the Windows 2000 installation files to multiple hard disks and makes them active. These disks can then be installed on different computers, and you can run the installation independently. **C** is incorrect because this is an invalid switch. **D** is incorrect because this switch is used to copy a specified folder within the Windows folder, which isn't deleted after the setup is over.

39. ☑ **C.** The minimum requirements for installation of Windows 2000 Professional include a 133 MHz processor (166 MHz recommended), 32MB of RAM (64MB recommended), and 650MB of hard disk space (2GB recommended). The hard disk in the computer in question has only 560MB of free space. This is insufficient for installing Windows 2000 Professional.

    ☒ **A, B,** and **D** are incorrect answers because these components meet the minimum requirements for installation of the Windows 2000 Professional operating system.

40. ☑ **D.** The conversion of a disk or a partition from FAT to NTFS is a one-way process and can't be reversed without losing data. You need to delete the partition on drive D:, re-create a new partition, and format it using the FAT32 file system. But be aware that you'll lose all your data, including the operating system, because Windows 2000 is installed on drive D:.

    ☒ **A** is incorrect because there's no such utility available in Windows 2000 Disk Management. **B** is incorrect because the CONVERT command allows only /FS:NTFS as a switch; /FS:FAT32 is invalid. **C** is incorrect because this will cause loss of all data on the disk, including the currently installed Windows 2000 operating system.

41. ☑ **D.** An internal modem being listed as an Unknown Device in Device Manager can be caused by any of the listed problems. An incorrect driver, a missing device driver, or a resource conflict will all cause the internal modem to be listed as an Unknown Device.

    ☒ **A, B,** and **C** are incorrect answers because none of them can be identified as the sole reason for the internal modem to be listed as an Unknown Device in Device Manager. Even if a device driver has been installed, it might not be compatible with the operating system. Assuming that the device driver were compatible, it might have been corrupted. Supposing a compatible device driver were installed and that it hasn't been corrupted, there could still be a resource conflict with another device in the computer.

42. ☑ **D.** A secure web site will prompt you for logon credentials. FTP servers are configured to prompt the user to supply a username and password before being allowed access to the contents on the server or a particular directory on the server. FTP servers are mainly used to facilitate users in uploading and downloading files to and from the Internet, respectively. Secure web sites always prompt the user for a username and password to verify the authenticity of the user. Examples of such web sites are online stores and other web sites that deal with online financial transactions, such as the web sites of banks, credit unions, and so on.

    ☒ **A** and **C** are incorrect answers because neither HTTP nor WWW servers on the Internet are configured to prompt the user to supply a username and password. A majority of Web sites on the Internet are either HTTP or WWW sites. **B** is incorrect because an anonymous account on an FTP site won't prompt you for a login ID.

43. ☑ **D.** Windows 98 will boot normally. The Windows 98 boot process does check the files specified in SYSTEM.INI during system startup, but any missing or corrupt files don't prevent the operating system from loading. In the given situation, the operating system will probably generate an error during the boot process but will continue to load normally.

    ☒ **A** is incorrect because a missing file specified in SYSTEM.INI for a legacy device won't stop the operating system from loading. **B** is incorrect for the same reason. **C** is incorrect because no error relating to the operating system will be reported.

44. ☑ **C.** DSL stands for "digital subscriber line." This line provides downloads at the rate of 8.448 Mbps, whereas the uplink is limited to 2.7 Mbps. The DSL is an ideal choice when your work involves downloading files from Internet sites.

    ☒ **A** is incorrect because ISDN is required when you need higher bandwidth for both uplink and downlink. The Integrated Services Digital Network (ISDN) Basic Rate Interface (BRI) provides channels of 64 Kbps each, totaling up to 128 Kbps of speed. **B** is incorrect because the Public Switched Telephone

Network (PSTN) provides a maximum speed of 56 Kbps. **D** is incorrect because the plain old telephone system (POTS) is another name for PSTN, which has a speed limitation of 56 Kbps.

45. ☑ **B.** Safe mode is the best mode to start a Windows XP computer when you aren't sure which component is preventing the system from booting successfully. Windows XP loads only basic and necessary drivers in this mode. You can then check Device Manager to locate the actual component that's causing the problem.

☒ **A** is incorrect. This mode won't work because it'll attempt to load the faulty components. **C** is incorrect because this mode is used if you aren't able to find the problem in Safe mode. You should try the Safe mode first. **D** is incorrect because this mode wouldn't help you debug a problem such as this and is primarily used to connect your system to another computer for advanced debugging purposes by specially trained professionals.

46. ☑ **C.** The Domain Name System (DNS) is responsible for translating the domain name to its corresponding IP address. The name of the server is technically known as a "fully qualified domain name" (FQDN) or "host name," and the process of locating the IP address of the domain is called "name resolution." A hierarchy of DNS servers on the Internet accomplishes this name resolution process.

☒ **A** is incorrect because the purpose of the Dynamic Host Configuration Protocol (DHCP) is to assign IP address configurations to its clients. A DHCP server may assign the name of the DNS server to a DHCP client, but it doesn't resolve domain names to IP addresses. **B** is incorrect because the WINS service exists only in Windows networks and is used to resolve NetBIOS names, popularly known as "computer names," to their respective IP addresses. WINS servers keep a database of IP addresses and corresponding computer names, and when queried by WINS clients, they supply the IP address of the specified computer name. **D** is incorrect because the Internet service provider (ISP) doesn't resolve host names to IP addresses on the Internet. An ISP does have one or more DNS servers for host name resolution.

47. ☑ **C.** The Advanced tab in Internet Options found in Internet Explorer 4 and higher allows you to configure your web browser by giving you several options. If you're getting a warning message from a particular web site, you should check the Advanced tab in Internet Options. You'll find that the Secure

Sockets Layer (SSL) under Security isn't checked. Click the SSL 2.0 and SSL 3.0 check boxes to solve the problem.

☒ **A** is incorrect because this tab is used to configure security zones and security levels for a particular security zone. **B** is incorrect because this tab is used to configure ratings and install security certificates. **D** is incorrect because this tab is used to configure the programs that Windows starts automatically for a particular Internet service.

48. ☑ **A.** Disabling Simple File Sharing with NTFS will provide you the maximum security configuration in this situation. You can establish individual file protections on shared directories by disabling Simple File Sharing. This is the default sharing method for Windows XP Home Edition, and it can't be disabled.

☒ **B** is incorrect because Windows XP running on a FAT32 system will only be able to use the Simple File Sharing model. FAT32 doesn't provide the security capabilities of NTFS and isn't recommended in environments where security is a concern. **C** is incorrect because both operating systems can establish shares, but they're not flexible in configuration unless Simple File Sharing is disabled. **D** is incorrect because logon accounts are helpful, but unless they're coupled with other network security options, they won't improve security across the network.

49. ☑ **B.** This statement is incorrect because the subnet mask must be specified when configuring the IP address of a computer. The subnet mask address isn't unique to the computer but is common to all the computers in all segments of the network.

☒ **A** is incorrect because the statement is true. You should remember that the IP address and the subnet mask address are two essential entries and that the IP address is unique to the computer. All computers in this network segment share the same subnet mask. **C** is incorrect because this statement is also true. When you have a multiple segment network, you should specify the address of the default gateway. This address is used to send network packets to other (or remote) network segments. **D** is a correct statement. These are optional entries and are required only if your network is large and is dependent on DNS and WINS servers for translating host names and NetBIOS names to their respective IP addresses.

50. ☑ **A.** This is normal behavior for a Windows XP installation. Windows XP performs a dynamic update that requires a connection to the Internet. In early versions of Windows XP it could take several hours for a dial-up connection to complete the download. Newer versions of Windows XP have incorporated most of the earlier updates onto the installation media.

☒ **B** is incorrect because if the modem had malfunctioned, you'd most likely receive an error during the connection phase. **C** is incorrect because although you want to disable antivirus software, you'd normally receive an error during the update process if the antivirus software was interfering with the update. **D** is incorrect because this is normal behavior for Windows XP.

Glossary

A TO *Z*

AC Adapter   A type of power supply that converts AC power to voltages needed for the PC system. AC adapters are usually used in portable PC systems.

Access Methods   Also known as "network access," these are the methods by which a device communicates on a network. Network access provides a standard that all devices that wish to communicate on a network must abide by in order to eliminate communication conflicts.

Active Matrix Display   Based on thin-film transistor (TFT) technology. Instead of having two rows of transistors, active matrix displays have a transistor at every pixel, which enables much quicker display changes than passive matrix displays and produces display quality comparable to a CRT.

Adapter Card   Refers to any PC that is added to the motherboard to enhance functionality or expansion. Monitor cards and network cards are examples of adapter cards.

AGP   Accelerated graphics port. A monitor interface designed for high-performance graphics processing.

AMR   Audio Modem Riser. A card that allows for connection of multimedia and communications to a PC. AMR technology utilizes excess capacity in the CPU to emulate hardware devices.

ANSI.SYS   A DOS system file that is loaded by CONFIG.SYS if required. This file loads an extended character set for use by DOS and DOS applications that includes basic drawing and color capabilities. Normally used for drawing and filling different boxes for menu systems, it is seldom used today. By default, it carries no attributes and is not required for OS startup.

Antenna   Radiates and receives radio frequency signals. Usually used with wireless technology.

AppleTalk   The network protocol used by Apple Computers for inexpensive networking.

ARCHIVE Attribute   Set automatically when a file is created or modified and automatically removed by backup software when the file is backed up.

AT Advanced Technology. A type of motherboard used in older PC systems; also refers to a class of processors based on the Intel 80286 architecture.

ATA Advanced Technology Attachment. The specification used for the IDE connection.

ATAPI Advanced Technology Attachment Packet Interface. The interface standard for connecting CD-ROMs, tape drives, and optical disks to a computer system.

ATTRIB.EXE A command-line utility that can change the attributes of a file or group of files.

ATX A type of motherboard most commonly used in modern PC systems.

AUTOEXEC.BAT A user-editable system file that contains commands to modify the PC environment (PATH, COMSPEC, other SET commands) and to execute applications. It can create a menu system, prompt for user input, or call other batch files to maintain a modular structure. By default, it carries no attributes, and is not required for OS startup.

Basic Input-Output System See BIOS.

Bidirectional Print Mode Most common in some of the newer and more advanced printers, bidirectional print mode means that the printer is able to talk back to the computer, enabling, for example, the printer to send the user exact error messages that are displayed on the workstation. It also helps the spooler to avoid print spooler stalls.

BIOS Basic input-output system. A standard set of instructions or programs that handle boot operations. When an application needs to perform an I/O operation on a computer, the operating system makes the request to the system BIOS, which in turn translates the request into the appropriate instruction set used by the hardware device.

BOOT.INI The startup file that allows for selection of the operating system to be booted in Windows NT 4 through Windows XP.

Brownout Momentary lapses in power supply. Brownouts can cause problems with computer components that are not designed to withstand these events.

Bus   The actual pathway that transmits electronic signals from one computer device to another.

Bus Topology   In a local area network, a topology with each device on the network connected to a central cable, or bus. Most common with coaxial cabling.

Cable   A network connection that uses existing cable television connections for data transmission. See DSL.

Cache Memory   Stores frequently used instructions and data so that they can be accessed quickly by the computer.

Carrier Sense Multiple Access with Collision Detection   See CSMA/CD.

Case   The box that houses the system unit, adapter cards, and devices and which usually provides mounting locations for all internal devices in the system.

CD   Compact disc. Stores data or audio files; a read-only device.

CD-RW   Compact disc-rewritable. A type of compact disc that allows information to be written or burned onto it using a CD-RW drive.

Central Processing Unit   See CPU.

Centronics   A standard originally developed for connecting printers to computer systems whose connections allow for up to 36 wires to be used for communications.

Chip Creep   A phenomenon where a computer chip becomes loose within its socket.

Cleaning Blade   The rubber blade inside a laser printer that extends the length of the photosensitive drum. It removes excess toner after the print process has completed and deposits it into a reservoir for reuse.

CMOS   Complementary metal-oxide semiconductor. An integrated circuit composed of a metal oxide that is located directly on the system board. The CMOS, which is similar to RAM in that data can be written to the chip, enables a computer to store essential operating parameters after the computer has been turned off, enabling a faster system boot.

CNR   Communications Network Riser. A type of connection used for communications purposes. CNR uses excess processor capabilities to emulate hardware on the system board.

Coaxial Cable   A high-bandwidth network cable that consists of a central wire surrounded by a screen of fine wires.

COMMAND.COM   A DOS system file that is automatically executed in the root directory at startup. This file contains the internal command set and error messages. By default, it carries no attributes, but it is required for OS startup.

Complementary Metal-Oxide Semiconductor   See CMOS.

CONFIG.SYS   A user-editable system file that provides the ability to install device drivers used in DOS. Windows 9x does not require any specific settings to be made in CONFIG.SYS.

Cooperative Multitasking   As opposed to preemptive multitasking, cooperative multitasking forces applications to voluntarily relinquish control of the CPU. When an application relinquishes control of the CPU, Windows then decides which application will execute next. The most common way for an application to relinquish control is by asking Windows if any messages are available.

CPU   Central processing unit. The operations center of a computer. Its job is to provide the devices attached to the computer with directives that retrieve, display, manipulate, and store information.

CSMA/CD   Carrier Sense Multiple Access with Collision Detection. Most common on Ethernet networks, a network communication protocol that operates in much the same way that humans communicate. With CSMA/CD, a device listens to the network for a pause in communication and attempts to transmit data onto the network during the pause. The device then detects if any other devices have transmitted onto the network at the same time. If they have, the device waits an unspecified random amount of time and retransmits its data.

DB-9   A type of connector that uses nine wires for connections. Most commonly used for serial port connections.

DB-25   A type of connector that uses 25 wires for connection. Most commonly used for parallel communications or older serial communications.

DDR   Double Data Rate. A type of memory technology used to effectively double the data rate of SDRAM memory.

Digital Versatile Disc   See DVD.

Defragmentation   A process that reorganizes fragmented files in a proper, contiguous fashion. This is done by moving several of them to an unused portion of the drive, erasing the previous locations in contiguous clusters, then rewriting the files back in proper sequence. Performed periodically, defragmentation is probably the single best operation a user can perform to maintain a high-performance system.

Device Driver   Programs that translate necessary information between the operating system and the specific peripheral device for which they are configured, such as a printer.

Dial-Up Access   Access provided to the Internet, a LAN, or even another computer by using a phone line and a modem.

Dial-Up Networking   The type of network in which a modem connects two or more workstations.

DIMM   Dual in-line memory module. Similar to a SIMM, a DIMM is a small plug-in circuit board that contains the memory chips you need to add certain increments of RAM to your computer. Because the memory chips run along both sides of the chip, DIMM chips can hold twice as much memory as SIMM chips.

DIP Switch   Dual in-line package switch. Very tiny boxes with switches embedded in them. Each switch can set a value of 0 or 1 and provides user-accessible configuration settings for computers and peripheral devices.

Direct Memory Access   See DMA.

Dirty Current   Noise present on a power line caused by electromagnetic interference (EMI) that can stray or leak from the current into nearby components. EMI that leaks from power current creates a magnetic field that can damage computer components.

Display Device   A device that provides a visual output to the user, typically the CRT or monitor.

DMA   Direct memory access. A facility by which a peripheral can communicate directly with RAM, without intervention by the CPU.

DNS   Domain Name System. The Internet-based system that resolves symbolic names, also called host names, to IP addresses (which are a series of numbers) that the computer is able to understand.

Docking Station   A port that allows users to add desktop-like capabilities, such as a mouse, monitor, or keyboard, to their portable computer. The components and the portable are all plugged into the docking station, rather than the portable connecting to each individual component. Docking stations frequently allow for additional expansion capabilities for disk and other peripherals.

Domain Name System   See DNS.

DOS   Disk Operating System is the earliest operating system used on PC computer systems.

DOS Mode   Commonly called DOS Compatibility Mode. Allows execution of some older MS-DOS applications that are not capable of running in Windows 9x. Applications that require MS-DOS mode are usually blocked from operation within Windows 95.

Download   The process of transferring a file or files from one computer to another. Unlike uploading, the transfer is always initiated by the computer that will be receiving the file(s).

Downtime   The time wasted as a result of a malfunctioning computer or network.

DRAM   Dynamic random access memory. These chips use smaller capacitors, rather than unwieldy transistors and switches, that represent 0s and 1s as an electronic charge. This allows more information to be stored on a single chip, but it also means that the chips need a constant refresh and hence more power.

DSL   Digital subscriber line. A network communications method that uses existing telephone lines for network connections.

Dual In-Line Memory Module   See DIMM.

Dual In-Line Package Switch   See DIP Switch.

DVD   Digital versatile disc. A type of disc storage similar to a CD that allows for high-density storage of information. DVDs are used for video and large volumes of text/graphics materials.

DVD-RW   DVD-rewritable. A type of DVD that allows information to be written onto it using a DVD-RW burner.

Dynamic RAM   See DRAM.

EBKAC   Error Between Keyboard and Chair. As the name implies, an error that is not technical, but rather occurs on the part of the end user. Common EBKACs include power cords being unplugged, having no paper in the printer, and power switches being turned off.

ECC   Error-Correcting Code. A type of memory that uses a special code to verify accuracy of data in the memory chip.

ECP   Extended Capabilities Port. A parallel printer interface designed to speed up data transfer rates by bypassing the processor and writing the data directly to memory.

EDO RAM   Extended data out RAM. A type of DRAM chip designed for processor access speeds of approximately 10 to 15 percent above fast-page mode memory.

EIDE   Enhanced Integrated Drive Electronics. An upgraded version of IDE that allows for more devices, higher speed, and improved performance of storage devices. Usually the standard disk interface on PC systems.

EISA   Extended Industry Standard Architecture. An industry standard bus architecture that allows for peripherals to utilize the 32-bit data bus that is available with 386 and 486 processors.

Electrophotographic Printing Process   See EP Process.

EMM386.EXE   A DOS system file that, along with HIMEM.SYS, controls memory management. It is not required for system startup in pre-Windows 95 machines. Basically, this is an expanded memory emulator that performs two major functions: it enables and controls EMS if desired and enables the use of upper memory as system memory.

EMS   Expanded Memory Specification. A standard that allows programs that recognize it to work with more than 640KB of RAM.

Enhanced Parallel Port   See EPP.

EP Process   Electrophotographic printing process. The six-step process that a laser printer goes through to put an image on a page: cleaning, charging, writing, developing, transferring, and fusing.

EPP   Enhanced Parallel Port. An expansion bus that offers an extended control code set. With EPP mode, data travels both from the computer to the printer and vice versa.

Error Between Keyboard and Chair   See EBKAC.

Exit Roller   One of four types of printer rollers, exit rollers aid in the transfer and control of the paper as it leaves the printer. Depending on the printer type, they direct the paper to a tray where it can be collated, sorted, or even stapled.

Expanded Memory Specification   See EMS.

Extended Capabilities Port   See ECP.

Extended Data Out RAM   See EDO RAM.

Extended Industry Standard Architecture   See EISA.

eXtended Memory Specification   See XMS.

Fan   A cooling device that blows air over computer circuitry.

FDD   Floppy disk drive. A type of disk device used for reading and writing to floppy disks.

FDISK.EXE   A DOS-based utility program that partitions a hard disk in preparation for installing an operating system.

Feed Roller   One of the four types of printer rollers. Also known as a paper pickup roller, the feed roller, when activated, rotates against the top page in the paper tray and rolls it into the printer. The feed roller works together with a special rubber pad to prevent more than one sheet from being fed into the printer at a time.

Fiber-Optic Cable   Extremely high-speed network cable that consists of glass fibers that carry light signals instead of electrical signals. Useful for transmission over long distances because it is much less susceptible to environmental difficulties, such as electronic and magnetic interference, than other network cables.

File System   The process or method that an operating system uses to manage files and data on the storage devices.

File Transfer Protocol   See FTP.

FireWire   See IEEE 1394.

Firmware   The software or programs and hardware that are written into read-only memory (ROM) for the computer to operate.

Flash Memory   A faster version of ROM that, while still basically developed as ROM, can be addressed and loaded thousands of times.

Floppy Disk Drive   See FDD.

Fragmentation   Files that are written in noncontiguous clusters scattered all over the disk. This occurs because DOS writes files to the hard disk by breaking the file into cluster-sized pieces and then stores each piece in the next available cluster. See Defragmentation.

FTP   File Transfer Protocol. Much older than HTTP, this protocol downloads files from an FTP server to a client computer. FTP is much faster than HTTP.

Fully Qualified Path   A fully qualified path is the entire path of a file, from the root of the file system to the file being referenced.

Fusing Rollers   One of four types of laser printer rollers, fusing rollers comprise the final stage of the electrophotographic printing (EP) process, bonding the toner particles to the page to prevent smearing. The roller on the toner side of the page has a nonstick surface that is heated to a high temperature to permanently bond the toner to the paper.

Ghosted Image   Occurs when a portion of an image previously printed to a page is printed again, but not as dark. One cause of this is if the erasure lamp of the laser printer fails to operate correctly and doesn't completely erase the previous image from the EP drum. Another cause can be the cleaning blade not adequately scraping away the residual toner.

Handshaking   The process by which two connecting modems agree on the method of communication to be used.

Hard Disk Drive   See HDD.

HDD   Hard disk drive. A mass storage device that allows for rapid random access of data in a computer system.

Heat Sink   A device that is typically attached to an electronic component to remove heat from the component. Used extensively with microprocessors, a heat sink may also include a cooling fan to assist in the cooling process.

Hidden Attribute   Keeps a file from being displayed when a DIR command is issued.

HIMEM.SYS   A DOS system file that, along with EMM386.EXE, controls memory management. It is not required for system startup in pre-Windows 95 machines.

HTML   Hypertext Markup Language. Derived from the Standard General Markup Language (SGML), the markup language that dictates the layout and design of a web page.

HTTP   Hypertext Transfer Protocol. The TCP/IP-based protocol that is most commonly used for client/server communications on the World Wide Web.

Hub   Common connection points for devices in a network that contain multiple ports and commonly connect segments of a LAN.

Hypertext Markup Language   See HTML.

Hypertext Transfer Protocol   See HTTP.

IDE   Integrated Drive Electronics. A standard for connecting hard drives to a computer.

IEEE 1394   A high-speed interface that connects video and other devices to a computer system. Also known as FireWire.

Impact Printer   As the name suggests, these printers require impact with an ink ribbon to print characters and images. An example of an impact printer is a daisy wheel.

Industry Standard Architecture   See ISA.

Infrared   See IR.

Input Device   Takes data from a user and converts it into electrical signals used by your computer. Examples of devices that provide input are keyboards, mice, trackballs, pointing devices, digitized tablets, and touch screens.

Internet Service Provider   See ISP.

Internetwork Packet Exchange/Sequenced Packet Exchange
See IPX/SPX.

Interrupt Request   See IRQ.

IO.SYS   A DOS system file that defines basic input/output routines for the processor. By default, it carries the hidden, system, and read-only attributes and is required for OS startup.

IPX/SPX   Internetwork Packet Exchange/Sequenced Packet Exchange. A very fast and highly established network protocol most commonly used with Novell NetWare.

IR   Infrared. A portion of the nonvisible light spectrum used extensively for communications. Both transmitter and receiver must be in visual proximity of each other for IR to work.

IRQ   Interrupt request. The physical lines over which system components such as modems or printers communicate directly with the CPU when the device is ready to send or receive data.

ISA   Industry Standard Architecture. An industry standard bus architecture that allows for peripherals to utilize the 16-bit data bus that is available with 286 and 386 processors.

ISDN   Integrated Services Digital Network. A network technology that used existing copper cable for high-speed data networking. ISDN has been largely replaced by DSL and cable applications.

ISP   Internet service provider. A company that provides people with access to the Internet, usually for a fee. Conversely, a company that gives their employees Internet access through a private bank of modems is usually not considered an ISP. ISPs typically charge customers for the use of their connection to the Internet.

Jumper   Like DIP switches, jumpers accomplish configuration manually. Jumpers are made of two separate components: a row of metal pins on the hardware and a small plastic cap that has a metal insert inside of it. The two parts together form a circuit that sets the configuration. Jumpers can set only one value for a feature at a time, as opposed to DIP switches, which can handle multiple configurations.

Keyboard   An input device that accepts user input by depressing keys.

LAN   Local area network. A network made up of two or more computers in a limited geographic area (within about a two-mile radius) linked by high-performance cables that allows users to exchange information, share peripheral devices, or access a common server.

LCD Panel   Liquid crystal display panel. A type of display or monitor that is very thin and lightweight. Used extensively in portable systems and thin screen monitors.

Liquid Cooling   A process or method where a special cooling liquid is passed through a device to remove heat from it. Liquid cooling is very common in large-scale computer systems where heat sinks and fans are not adequate for cooling.

Legacy Device   A device that is considered obsolete or out-of-date and does not utilize the newest capabilities and technologies available to PC users. Manufacturers recommend that legacy devices be replaced by newer devices.

Local Area Network   See LAN.

Material Safety Data Sheets   See MSDS.

MEM.EXE   A simple command-line utility that, using various command switches, can display various reports of memory usage.

MEMMAKER.EXE   A Microsoft utility that automatically determines the best possible configuration and load sequence for a given set of applications and drivers used. Before using MEMMAKER, the PC should be configured for normal operation (for example, the mouse driver, network operation, sound support, and so forth), including any items that are loaded from the AUTOEXEC.BAT and CONFIG.SYS files.

Memory   The internal storage areas in the computer. Memory is either considered volatile, such as RAM, which loses its contents when the power is turned off, or nonvolatile, such ROM, PROM, or EPROM, which retains its contents during power off states.

Memory Address   Receives commands from the processor that are destined for any device attached to a computer. Each device must have a unique memory address in order for it to function.

Memory Bank   The physical slot that memory goes into.

Memory Effect   When a nickel cadmium (NiCad) battery is recharged before it is fully discharged, the battery loses the ability to fully recharge again; this is the memory effect.

MicroDIMM   A type of DIMM used in subnotebooks and computers that are too small for SoDIMM.

Microprocessor   See CPU.

Modem   Modulator/demodulator. A device that connects the computer system to an analog connection, most typically the phone network, for communication.

Motherboard   The main circuit card of a PC system. The motherboard contains all of the critical circuitry necessary for the computer to operate. The motherboard also contains all of the expansion slots, connections, and circuitry for the system to function properly. Also known as the system board.

Mouse   A device that controls the cursor or pointer by movement on a flat surface. A mouse is typically used as an alternative or augmentation to a keyboard on modern computer systems.

MSD   Microsoft Diagnostics. A DOS-based utility that provides a great deal of information about the system. It is most useful in determining what the system has installed in it, such as memory and hard drives.

MSD.EXE   A Microsoft Diagnostics program that roots out almost every conceivable item about your system that you'd ever want to know (and then some!) and displays it in a menu-driven format for you to browse.

MSDOS.SYS   A DOS system file that defines system file locations. By default, it carries the hidden, system, and read-only attributes and is required for OS startup.

MSDS   Material Safety Data Sheets. White pages that contain information on any substance that is deemed hazardous, most notably cleaning solvents. The purpose of MSDS is to inform employees about the dangers inherent in hazardous materials and the proper use of these items to prevent potential injuries from occurring.

Multiboot Configuration   A system that has been configured to allow a user to select one of multiple installed operating systems at boot time.

Multimeter   A device that measures current, resistance, or voltage to determine whether certain computer components are functioning correctly.

NetBEUI   NetBIOS Extended User Interface. An extremely fast network transport protocol that is most common on smaller networks.

NetBIOS Extended User Interface   See NetBEUI.

Network Interface Card   See NIC.

Network Topology   The arrangement of cable links in a local area network. There are three principal network topologies: bus, ring, and star.

NIC   Network interface card. Connects a PC to a network cable.

Noise Filter   A special filter in a UPS that reduces the amount of noise present in electrical current and eliminates magnetic fields caused by noise, thus providing some protection to the components that utilize the current or are nearby.

Nonimpact Printer   Printers that do not use an ink ribbon and therefore do not require direct contact with the paper for printing. An example of a nonimpact printer is a laser printer.

Normal Mode   The mode in which Windows 9x is started by default, which provides full functionality of the Windows 9x Explorer.

NTLDR   A file that helps Windows NT through Windows XP boot. When first run, it displays the Windows NT startup menu.

Null Modem Cable   A special cable that has the send and receive lines reversed on the connector and enables you to connect two computers directly without using a modem.

Operating System   See OS.

Operator Error   Occurs when the customer inadvertently makes a configuration change.

OS   Operating system. A set of computer instruction codes, usually compiled into executable files, whose purpose is to define input and output devices and connections and provide instructions for the computer's central processor unit (CPU) to operate on to retrieve and display data.

Output Device   A device that takes electronic signals from a computer and converts them into a format that the user can use. Examples of output devices include monitors and printers.

Overlays   Library files that include additional commands and functions. Most developers choose to modularize their applications by creating overlays rather than put all available functions into a single huge executable file.

Page Description Language   See PDL.

Parallel Port   One of two types of communication ports on a motherboard (the other is the serial port), the parallel port connects a peripheral device (most commonly a printer for this type of port) to the computer. A parallel port allows transmission of data over eight conductors at one time. The processor socket is the physical socket that attaches the processor to the motherboard.

Parallel Processing   The ability to execute instructions simultaneously and independently from each other. The Intel 586 (Pentium) chip combined two 486DX chips into one, called the dual independent bus architecture, which made this possible.

Parity   An error-checking mechanism that enables the device to recognize single-bit errors.

Partition   A section of the storage area on a computer's hard disk. A hard disk must be partitioned before an operating system can be installed.

Passive Matrix Display   Most common on portable systems, the passive matrix display is made from a grid of horizontal and vertical wires. At the end of each wire is a transistor. In order to light a pixel at (X, Y), a signal is sent to the X and Y transistors. These transistors then send voltage down the wire, which turns on the LCD at the intersection of the two wires.

PC Card   A bus first created to expand the memory capabilities in small, hand-held computers and now used mostly with laptop computers. These provide a convenient way to interchange PCMCIA-compatible devices, which are only slightly larger than credit cards. Before the name was changed to PC Card these cards were referred to as PCMCIA cards.

PCI   Peripheral Component Interconnect. A bus that was designed in response to the Pentium-class processor's utilization of a 64-bit bus. PCI buses are designed to be processor-independent.

PCMCIA   See Personal Computer Memory Card International Association.

PDA   Personal Digital Assistant. A small handheld device that stores information such as telephone numbers and appointments. The two most popular PDA systems are based on the Palm OS or Windows CE.

PDL   Page description language. A language that laser printers use to send and receive print job instructions one page at a time, rather than one dot at a time, as with other types of printers.

Peripheral Component Interconnect   See PCI.

Personal Computer Memory Card International Association
International standards organization concerned with promoting interchangeability of computer cards for mobile computers. PCMCIA promotes a commonly accepted standard called PC Card. See PC Card.

Photosensitive Drum   The core of the electrophotographic process inside the laser printer. This light-sensitive drum is affected by the cleaning, charging, writing, and transferring processes in the six-step laser printing process.

PIO   Programmed Input/Output. Data transfer that occurs through the CPU. PIO speeds are very high and utilize processor resources to be accomplished.

Plug and Play   A software interface that offers automatic driver installation as soon as hardware or software is "plugged in," or installed. Microsoft first offered PnP support on the PC with Windows 95.

Pointing Stick   A small pencil-eraser-size piece of rubber in the center of the keyboard, one of the three most common types of pointing devices on portable systems. The on-screen pointer is controlled by pushing the pointing stick in the desired direction.

Point-to-Point Protocol   See PPP.

POLEDIT.EXE   This Windows 9*x* System Policy feature builds a Registry template that is later used during logon to set common-denominator defaults for all network users, and add certain restrictions on a global basis if deemed necessary.

POP   Post Office Protocol. A common protocol by which an Internet server lets you receive e-mail and download it from the server to your own machine.

Port   An interface that allows connection to a computer system. Common ports include disk connectors, serial, parallel, and USB ports. A port may be either internal or external depending on the configuration of the system.

Port Replicator   A type of device that contains expansion ports such as serial, parallel, and USB connections for a portable PC. Usually does not contain additional storage expansion capabilities. See also Docking Station.

POST   Power-on self test. A self-test performed by the computer that occurs during boot time and diagnoses system-related problems.

Post Office Protocol   See POP.

Power-On Self Test   See POST.

Power Spike   A sudden, huge increase in power that lasts for a split second. Power spikes can fry computer components.

Power Supply   The component of the computer system that provides power for all components on the motherboard and devices that are internal to the system case.

PPP   Point-to-Point Protocol. A serial communications protocol that connects two computers over a phone line via a modem. SLIP is the alternate protocol that is acceptable to most browsers, but it's not as common as PPP.

Preemptive Multitasking   As opposed to cooperative multitasking, preemptive multitasking passes control from one program to another automatically through the Windows process scheduler.

Primary Corona Wire   A highly negatively charged wire inside a laser printer that is responsible for electrically erasing the photosensitive drum, preparing it to be written with a new image in the writing stage of the laser print process.

Processor   See CPU.

Processor Socket   The physical socket that attaches the processor to the motherboard.

Protocol   A set of communication standards between two computers on a network. Common protocols include TCP/IP, NetBEUI, and IPX/SPX.

PS2   Early computer standard introduced by IBM as an update to the AT class computer systems. Now most commonly used when referring to connector types for keyboards and mice.

PS2/Mini-DIN   Connects keyboards and mice to computer systems.

RAID   Redundant array of inexpensive disks. A disk system that utilizes multiple disks to provide enhanced performance and fault tolerance. Used extensively in servers and higher-end PC systems.

Rambus   Rambus is the developer of memory interface technologies that include RDRAM. Systems that use Rambus technology are frequently referred to as Rambus systems.

Read-Only Attribute   Prevents a user or application from inadvertently deleting or changing a file.

Refresh   The automatic process of constantly updating memory chips to ensure that their signals are correct. The refresh rate is the frequency by which chips are refreshed, usually about every 60 to 70 thousandths of a second.

Registration Roller   One of four types of laser printer rollers, the registration roller synchronizes the paper movement with the writing process inside the EP cartridge. Registration rollers do not advance the paper until the EP cartridge is ready to process the next line of the image.

Registry   A complex database used by all Windows operating systems since Windows 95 and NT 4. Contains application settings and hardware configuration information.

Removable Storage   A type of storage device that can be removed from a computer and used in other computers. Removable storage is also extensively used for system backup operations.

RIMM　Rambus Inline Memory Module. A copyright name for memory similar to DIMM.

Riser Card　A type of expansion card that allows connection to external connections. The most common riser cards are used for audio and networking connections.

RJ-11　A type of UTP cable used extensively for telecommunications connections.

RJ-45　A type of UTP cable used extensively for networking connections.

Roller　A device located inside a printer to aid in the movement of paper through the printer. There are four types of rollers: feed, registration, fuser, and exit.

Safe Mode　A diagnostic mode of Windows that starts the operating system with minimal drivers. This special mode allows you to change an incorrect setting, which will in most cases allow you to return an abnormally functioning system to its correct operation.

Satellite Connection　A type of connection that uses orbiting satellites for network communications.

SCSI　Small Computer System Interface. A parallel interface for connecting peripherals such as storage devices to the computer system. SCSI is very fast and efficient when compared to other serial and parallel interfaces. SCSI devices are frequently used in high-volume server and graphics-intensive environments.

SDRAM　Synchronous dynamic RAM. A type of RAM that can run at much higher clock speeds than conventional RAM. SDRAM can operate in burst mode for high-speed transfers of data.

Serial Port　One of two types of communication ports on a motherboard (the other is the parallel port), the serial port connects to a serial line that leads to a computer peripheral. Used most commonly with modems and mice. The serial port transmits data sequentially, bit by bit over a single conductor.

SIMD　Single instruction multiple data. Processor architecture introduced with the Pentium III. SIMD allows a single instruction to operate on multiple pieces of data when an application is performing a repetitive loop. This is used extensively with graphics-oriented applications.

SIMM   Single in-line memory module. A small plug-in circuit board that contains memory chips that you need to add certain increments of RAM to your computer. The chips are positioned along one side of the board.

Simple Mail Transfer Protocol   See SMTP.

Single In-Line Memory Module   See SIMM.

Single Instruction Multiple Data   See SIMD.

Slack   The space left between the end of a file and the end of the cluster in which the file resides.

SLIP   Serial Line Internet Protocol. A protocol that manages telecommunications between a client and a server over a phone line. PPP is the alternate (and more common) protocol that is acceptable to most browsers.

Small Computer System Interface   See SCSI.

SMTP   Simple Mail Transfer Protocol. The underlying protocol for Internet-based e-mail.

Socket Services   A layer of BIOS-level software that isolates PC Card software from the computer hardware and detects the insertion or removal of PC Cards.

SoDIMM   Small Outline DIMM. A type of DIMM typically used in notebook computers.

Solenoid   A resistive coil in dot-matrix and daisy wheel printers. When the solenoid is energized, the pin is forced away from the print head and impacts the printer ribbon and ultimately the paper, thus impressing the image on the page.

Sound Card   A type of expansion card that provide multimedia capabilities to a computer system. A sound card will typically have both audio input and output capabilities.

SRAM   Static RAM. Unlike DRAM, SRAM retains its value as long as power is supplied; it is not constantly refreshed. However, SRAM requires a periodic update and tends to use excessive amounts of power when it does so.

Star Topology   In a local area network, a topology with each device on the network connected to a central processor, usually a hub. Most common with twisted-pair cabling.

Static RAM   See SRAM.

Storage Device   Any device that permanently stores large quantities of information. Disk drives, CD-ROM drives, and floppy drives are examples of storage devices.

STP   Shielded twisted pair. A type of twisted-pair wiring that includes an electrical shield to reduce interference.

Stylus   Shaped like a pen, a stylus selects menu options and the like on a monitor screen or draws line art on a graphics tablet.

Sync Frequency   A setting that monitors use to control the refresh rate, which is the rate at which the display device is repainted. If this setting is incorrect, you get symptoms such as a "dead" monitor, lines running through the display, a flickering screen, and a reduced or enlarged image.

System Attribute   The System attribute is usually set by DOS or Windows and cannot be modified using standard DOS or Windows commands, including the ATTRIB command or File Manager.

System Board   See Motherboard.

SYSTEM.DAT   The Registry file that contains hardware or computer specific settings.

SYSTEM.INI   A Windows system file that configures Windows to address specific hardware devices and their associated settings. Errors in this file can and do cause Windows to fail to start or crash unexpectedly.

Tape Drive   A type of mass storage device that uses magnetic tape to record and play back data.

TCP/IP   Transmission Control Protocol/Internet Protocol. The suite of protocols upon which the Internet is based. It refers to the communications standards for data transmission over the Internet, although TCP/IP can also be used on private networks without Internet connectivity. TCP/IP is the most common protocol suite in use today.

Time Slicing   The process of the CPU dividing time up between applications for preemptive multitasking.

Token Passing   A network communications protocol in which a token is passed from device to device around a virtual (and frequently physical) ring on a network. Whenever a device receives the token, it is then allowed to transmit onto the network.

Token Ring   A LAN specification that was developed by IBM in the 1980s for PC-based networks and classified by the IEEE (Institute of Electrical and Electronics Engineers) as 802.5. It specifies a star topology physically and a ring topology logically. It runs at either 4 Mbps or 16 Mbps, but all nodes on the ring must run at the same speed.

Toner   Finely divided particles of plastic resin and organic compounds bonded to iron particles. Toner is naturally negatively charged, which aids in attracting it to the written areas of the photosensitive drum during the transfer step of the laser printing process.

Touch Pad   A stationary pointing device commonly used on laptop computers in place of a mouse or trackball. They are pads that have either thin wires running through them, or specialized surfaces that can sense the pressure of your finger on them. You slide your finger across the touch pad to control the pointer or cursor on the screen.

Touch Screen   A type of display device that includes a touch-sensitive face to accept input from the user.

Trackball   A device most commonly used in older portable computers in place of a mouse. Trackballs are built the same way as an optomechanical mouse, except upside-down with the ball on top.

Transfer Corona   A roller inside a laser printer that contains a positively charged wire designed to pull the toner off of the photosensitive drum and place it on the page.

Transistor   A device that processes information in the form of electronic signals and is the most fundamental component of electronic circuits. A CPU chip, for example, contains thousands to millions of transistors. The more transistors a CPU has, the faster it can process data.

Transmission Control Protocol/Internet Protocol   See TCP/IP.

Twisted Pair By far the most common type of network cable, twisted pair consists of two insulated wires wrapped around each other to help avoid interference from other wires.

Ultra-DMA A disk drive data protocol that allows for high-speed data transfer between the disk drive and the motherboard.

Uninterruptible Power Supply See UPS.

Universal Serial Bus See USB.

Upload The process of transferring files from one computer to another. Unlike downloading, uploading is always initiated from the computer that is sending the files.

UPS Uninterruptible power supply. A device designed to protect your computer and its components from possible injury from the problems that are inherent in today's existing power supply structure.

USB Universal serial bus. A type of connection used in modern computer systems to connect multiple devices to a computer system. USB eliminates the need for individual adapters for each device.

USER.DAT The Registry file that stores user-specific information.

UTP Unshielded twisted pair. A type of twisted-pair wiring used for network and communications. UTP does not provide any external electrical shielding. See also STP.

VESA Local Bus See VL-Bus.

Video Card A type of expansion card that provide connection between the CPU and the display adapter or monitor.

Virtual Memory Virtual memory is memory that the processor has been "tricked" into using as if it were actual physical memory.

Virus Any program that is written with the intent of doing harm to a computer. Viruses have the ability to replicate themselves by attaching themselves to programs or documents. They range in activity from extreme data loss to an annoying message that pops up every few minutes.

VL-Bus   Originally created to address performance issues, the VESA (Video Electronics Standards Association) Local Bus (VL-Bus) was meant to enable earlier bus designs to handle a maximum clock speed equivalent to that of processors.

VRAM   Video RAM. A type of high-speed RAM used for video applications.

WAN   Wide area network. A network with two or more computers linked by long-distance communication lines that traverse distances greater than those supported by LANs (or greater than about two miles).

Wide Area Network   See WAN.

WIN.COM   The executable file that is responsible for starting up Windows.

WIN.INI   A dynamic Windows system file that contains configuration information for Windows applications. Errors made in this file seldom have global implications to Windows's operation, but they can cripple specific applications or features. Printing is also controlled by settings in this file.

Windows Accelerator Card RAM   See WRAM

WINFILE.INI   The configuration file in pre-Windows 95 systems that stores the names of the directories that the file manager displays when starting.

Wireless   A type of communications technology that uses either radio frequency or infrared to communicate information between systems.

Wireless Access Point   A type of connection point in a building or area that allows for wireless-equipped computer systems to connect to a network.

WRAM   Window random access memory. WRAM utilizes memory that resides on the video card to perform Windows-specific functions, and therefore speeds up the OS.

XMS   eXtended Memory Specification. A set of standards that allows applications to access extended memory.

Zoomed Video   See ZV.

ZV   A direct data connection between a PC Card and host system that allows a PC Card to write video data directly to the video controller.

Sound Off!

Visit us at **www.osborne.com/bookregistration** and let us know what you thought of this book. While you're online you'll have the opportunity to register for newsletters and special offers from McGraw-Hill/Osborne.

We want to hear from you!

Sneak Peek

Visit us today at **www.betabooks.com** and see what's coming from McGraw-Hill/Osborne tomorrow!

Based on the successful software paradigm, Bet@Books™ allows computing professionals to view partial and sometimes complete text versions of selected titles online. Bet@Books™ viewing is free, invites comments and feedback, and allows you to "test drive" books in progress on the subjects that interest you the most.

OSBORNE DELIVERS RESULTS!

OSBORNE
www.osborne.com

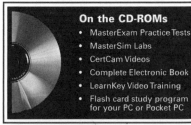

INTERNATIONAL CONTACT INFORMATION

AUSTRALIA
McGraw-Hill Book Company
Australia Pty. Ltd.
TEL +61-2-9900-1800
FAX +61-2-9878-8881
http://www.mcgraw-hill.com.au
books-it_sydney@mcgraw-hill.com

CANADA
McGraw-Hill Ryerson Ltd.
TEL +905-430-5000
FAX +905-430-5020
http://www.mcgraw-hill.ca

**GREECE, MIDDLE EAST, & AFRICA
(Excluding South Africa)**
McGraw-Hill Hellas
TEL +30-210-6560-990
TEL +30-210-6560-993
TEL +30-210-6560-994
FAX +30-210-6545-525

MEXICO (Also serving Latin America)
McGraw-Hill Interamericana Editores
S.A. de C.V.
TEL +525-1500-5108
FAX +525-117-1589
http://www.mcgraw-hill.com.mx
carlos_ruiz@mcgraw-hill.com

SINGAPORE (Serving Asia)
McGraw-Hill Book Company
TEL +65-6863-1580
FAX +65-6862-3354
http://www.mcgraw-hill.com.sg
mghasia@mcgraw-hill.com

SOUTH AFRICA
McGraw-Hill South Africa
TEL +27-11-622-7512
FAX +27-11-622-9045
robyn_swanepoel@mcgraw-hill.com

SPAIN
McGraw-Hill/
Interamericana de España, S.A.U.
TEL +34-91-180-3000
FAX +34-91-372-8513
http://www.mcgraw-hill.es
professional@mcgraw-hill.es

**UNITED KINGDOM, NORTHERN,
EASTERN, & CENTRAL EUROPE**
McGraw-Hill Education Europe
TEL +44-1-628-502500
FAX +44-1-628-770224
http://www.mcgraw-hill.co.uk
emea_queries@mcgraw-hill.com

ALL OTHER INQUIRIES Contact:
McGraw-Hill/Osborne
TEL +1-510-420-7700
FAX +1-510-420-7703
http://www.osborne.com
omg_international@mcgraw-hill.com